THE COOPERSTOWN CHRONICLES

THE COOPERSTOWN CHRONICLES

Baseball's Colorful Characters, Unusual Lives, and Strange Demises

Frank Russo

ROWMAN & LITTLEFIELD
Lanham • Boulder • New York • London

Published by Rowman & Littlefield
A wholly owned subsidiary of The Rowman & Littlefield Publishing Group,
Inc.
4501 Forbes Boulevard, Suite 200, Lanham, Maryland 20706
www.rowman.com

16 Carlisle Street, London W1D 3BT, United Kingdom

British Library Cataloguing in Publication Information Available

Library of Congress Cataloging-in-Publication Data

Russo, Frank, 1959–
The Cooperstown chronicles : baseball's colorful characters, unusual lives, and strange demises /
Frank Russo.
pages cm
Includes bibliographical references and index.
ISBN 978-1-4422-3639-4 (cloth : alk. paper) — ISBN 978-1-4422-3640-0 (ebook)
1. Baseball players—United States—Social life and customs. 2. Baseball players—United States—
Death. 3. Baseball players—United States—Biography. 4. Baseball—United States—History. I.
Title.
GV865.A1R863 2015
796.3570922—dc23 [B]
2014019500

Printed in the United States of America

This book is dedicated to the various players, managers, coaches, and umpires who have graced major league ballparks since the inception of the professional game in 1871. This volume is also dedicated to my wonderful mother Rose, who was born but a scant few miles from Yankee Stadium, and my late father Frank Sr. (1921–1971), whose love of the New York Yankees was handed down to me, for which I am forever grateful. In addition, this book is dedicated to "My Pal"—my wife Joanne—for her constant encouragement, which was vital during the writing of this book.

CONTENTS

FOREWORD

Frank Russo, one of the pioneers in the activity that has become known as baseball necrology, has outdone himself. The coauthor of *Bury My Heart at Cooperstown* and creator and webmaster of thedeadballera.com, he has now written *The Cooperstown Chronicles: Baseball's Colorful Characters, Unusual Lives, and Strange Demises*.

This is a book of short biographical profiles on a number of baseball personalities. The subjects range from the early days of the National League (even the short-lived National Association is mentioned) to the current decade. Little-known players like Terry Enyart, who pitched only one and two-thirds innings in the majors, and superstars like Mike Flanagan, who had an 18-year major league career and continued working in baseball administration and broadcasting, are included.

So many baseball player biographers cover only a player's major league career and list, ad nauseum, at bats, hits, batting average, innings pitched, earned run average, etc. Not Frank. He realizes there is more to baseball than just numbers. He addresses players' careers in the minor leagues, which so many ignore, and also delves into their personal lives, personalities, and interaction with societal issues of the day.

Today's game of baseball, like the world around it, has become money-driven, technology-driven, and dominated by political correctness. Many of the players in this book competed for the fun of the game long before speed-monitoring devices, pitch counts, and sabermetrics. They were a rowdy, fun-loving group of guys who had a talent for playing baseball, enjoyed what they did, and didn't worry what they said or to whom they said it. This is obvious from Frank's description of the lives of his subjects. He also dispels some of the myths perpetrated by the press and revisionist historians.

Prepare to be entertained!

Bill Lee, "The Baseball Undertaker"
Foley, Alabama

ACKNOWLEDGMENTS

Many people helped me when it came to researching the various ballplayers included in this book. My undying gratitude goes to my wife, Joanne DiGiovanni Russo, for help with the editing of this book; Bill Lee, "The Baseball Undertaker"; Dr. Fred Worth, professor of mathematics, Henderson State University, and "grave hunter" extraordinaire; Dr. Stephen Boren, assistant professor of emergency medicine at the University of Illinois, Chicago; Tim Copeland; Connie Nisinger; Bill Carle, head of SABR's biographical committee; and Bill "Diz" Deane.

Thanks also to Jim Tipton, Russ Dodge, and A. J. Marik of findagrave.com; Ty Cobb historian Wesley Fricks; New York Yankees historian Marty Appel, the most positive person in the world; Brandi "Miss Congeniality" Davison-Edralin (Brandi, you're a fine girl); my long-lost sister/buddy, Lisa Koster, physician assistant certified; Robin Axel, licensed clinical social worker; Kristian T. Peterson; Mike "Hi Ho" Silva, freelance radio host, blogger, and writer and proprietor of MikeSilvaMedia.com; Sergeant Kenneth "Gunny" Dawson, USMC, retired; Sharlene Caruso, Tim Wiles, Fred Berowski, and Claudette Burke of the Baseball Hall of Fame; and Tony Siegel, senior advisor of baseball operations, San Francisco Giants.

Special thanks go out to the various cemetery employees and office personnel who helped with the grave locations for the players listed in this book.

INTRODUCTION

Anyone who knows me will tell you that Major League Baseball has always been an obsession, in particular the lives of the players. Since the summer of 1968, when I researched my first player, the great Eddie Plank, I have been fascinated with the lives of the players who "laced 'em up."

For several years it seemed like every time I've had a discussion with a fellow baseball fan or researcher, I would always be asked, "When is your next book coming out?" Well, it is finally here! I give you, for your reading pleasure, *The Cooperstown Chronicles: Baseball's Colorful Characters, Unusual Lives, and Strange Demises*. Writing this book was a true labor of love. I can't begin to tell you how many hundreds of hours I spent in my office (usually at night), working on this project. The most frustrating part of the process, of course, was deciding which players to include and which ones to leave out. After all, Major League Baseball has been around for more than 140 years if you include the National Association of 1871–1875 (which I do). Thousands of men have played in the majors, each with their own special, interesting story to tell. My goal from the beginning has always been to write a book that is both informative and educational, and sometimes even funny. My sincere hope is that you will find the players included in *The Coopers-town Chronicles* to be as interesting as I find them to be.

I

BAD TO THE BONE

Baseball has long had its share of tough guys and bad asses sprinkled throughout its long, rich history. In the early days of the game, it was common for teams to cheat and take advantage of every situation on the field by breaking the rules. Infamous teams like the Cleveland Spiders and old Baltimore Orioles drew huge crowds that came to see the "hooliganism" on the field. Some players, like Ty Cobb and Enos Slaughter, played the game hard and clean but wound up gaining unfair reputations for being dirty and racist players without any facts to support the claims. Others, like Cap Anson and Ben Chapman, as well as catchers Boss Schmidt and Clint Courtney, were considered the toughest hombres to ever lace up a pair of spikes, and they deserved the negative publicity. One of the things that makes the game of baseball so great is that it truly takes all kinds of personalities. The following are but a few of the close-knit fraternity of players who were truly "bad to the bone."

THE OLD ORIOLES

The original Baltimore Orioles were charter members of the American Association when it was founded in 1882. In its 10 years in the American Association, the club usually floundered in the league's basement, never finishing better than third.

The Orioles actually dropped out of the American Association in 1890, after a dispute with league management. They played in the minor Atlantic Association for half a season and then rejoined the American Association when the Brooklyn Gladiators folded in late August. With the American Association going out of business after the '91 season, the Orioles were absorbed by the National League. Their first season in 1892 was a complete disaster—they finished dead last under Bald Billy Barnie.

Ned Hanlon was hired to manage the club near the end of that season, and eventually, under his leadership, the Orioles became one of the preeminent baseball clubs of the 1890s. Known as the "nastiest baseball team of all time," they never failed to break the rules and would try everything short of murder to win games. When they played the Cleveland Spiders, another team known for roughhouse tactics, all hell would break loose. The Orioles were more than the thugs and dirty, low-life sods often portrayed by the press.

Hanlon had at his disposal some of the great players of the era, including future Hall of Famers John McGraw, Hughie Jennings, Wilbert Robinson, Dan Brouthers, and Wee Willie Keeler. In addition, he had a host of talented complementary players, including Dirty Jack Doyle, Steve Brodie, Heinie Reitz, and Boileryard Clarke, to name a few. Hanlon also had a succession of solid starting pitchers toe the rubber for him during this time, including Matt Kilroy, Joe Corbett, Arlie Pond, Sadie McMahon, Jerry Nops, Doc McJames, Jim Hughes, Al Maul, and Bill Hoffer. But it was the starting nine who got the most attention from both press and fans.

Oriole players were well known for running their mouths and using an assortment of swear words that might have made comedian Lenny Bruce blush. Of course, the focal (and vocal) point of the franchise was McGraw, who despite being cordial and polite off the field, glowed with an intensity and focus on the field never before seen in the game. The Oriole teams led by McGraw were known for their "old Oriole spirit," which impelled men to ignore injuries and keep on playing. McGraw, of course, personified this attitude. Under Hanlon, the Orioles specialized in the practice of what was termed "inside baseball," which used relays and cutoffs, the hit-and-run, bunts, the stolen base, and the "Baltimore chop," where a hitter would intentionally pound a baseball into the notoriously hard ground around the home-plate area at Oriole Park to run out a base hit.

During their period of success, the Orioles played in four straight Temple Cup World Series from 1894 to 1897, winning two of them. They, along with the two other premier teams of the period—the Boston Beaneaters and the Cleveland Spiders—made the rest of the National League look like also-rans.

Before the 1899 season, Hanlon left the Orioles to manage the Brooklyn Superbas. Baltimore owner Harry Von der Horst, who was part of the group that owned the Superbas (Hanlon was also in this group), engineered a deal where several of the Orioles' best players were transferred to Brooklyn. The move proved to be a fantastic one for Brooklyn, as they went on to win the 1899 pennant. The depleted Orioles finished fourth.

After the '99 season, rumors circulated that the franchise would be dropped from the league. Oriole fans hoped that something could be done to save the franchise, but the odds were against it. With hearty approval from Von der Horst, the Orioles were officially dropped from the league during the National League's winter meetings, along with Cleveland, Louisville, and Washington. Although the National League Orioles died an untimely death, they left behind a lasting legacy of winning, excitement, and controversial baseball that will forever be a part of the proud heritage of the Monumental City.

THE CLEVELAND SPIDERS

The team that was to become known as the Cleveland Spiders was originally a member of the American Association, joining the National League in 1889, where it remained until its ouster at the end of the 1899 season. Frank DeHaas Robison, a tycoon who made his money in the horse-drawn trolley business, was the prominent owner of the team, along with his brother Stanley. Originally known as the "Forest Citys," after 1889, the team came to be known as the Spiders, allegedly because of the skinny and spidery build of most of the players. A park was built by Robison at E. 39th and Payne Avenue, alongside the trolley lines he owned.

Oliver "Patsy" Tebeau was hired as manager in 1891. Tebeau was an advocate of "rowdy baseball," the same style that would be incorporated by the Baltimore Orioles. Tebeau, of "French extraction," harassed umpires and opposing players, implored his team to use such "bully tactics" as blocking and holding runners, and ordered his pitchers to flip batters. He was quoted as saying that a "milk and water, goody-goody player, can't ever wear a Cleveland uniform."

In 1891, Robison replaced the original ballpark with a new one at Lexington and East 66th, known as League Park. It became home for Cleveland baseball teams until Municipal Stadium opened on the Lakefront in the 1930s. By 1892, the Spiders, now a contender, were, along with the Baltimore Orioles, the only two teams to make money in the National League that year.

The Spiders were loaded with talented players like Cy Young, Jesse "The Crab" Burkett, Nig Cuppy, John Clarkson, and Charles "Chief" Zimmer. In 1892, the last year of the 50-foot pitching distance, Cleveland finished a strong second, behind the Boston Beaneaters. In 1895 and 1896, the Spiders again finished second, behind the Baltimore Orioles. Each time they wound up playing the Orioles for the Temple Cup, a trophy symbolic of the National League championship.

In '95 the Spiders won the whole shabang. This series would go down as one of the dirtiest in baseball history. As the Spiders went a perfect 3–0 at home during the series, the Orioles were subjected to a mortar barrage of vegetables and other unsavory missiles by the Cleveland fans. After the three wins in Cleveland, the Spiders headed to Baltimore, where they lost under a hail of eggs and rocks in retaliation for the way Oriole players were treated in Cleveland. The series came to an end when the Spiders won a fourth and final game, ending with the Cleveland players being chased from the field by an angry mob of fans.

The next year, the Spiders lost the Temple Cup to the Orioles in four games. Throughout the next two years, fan attendance, although still good by standards of the times, was not up to snuff in the eyes of the Robison brothers. Rumors circulated that the team would be moved to another town. In 1898, Robison purchased another National League team, St. Louis. It was the era of syndicate baseball, where an owner could own more than one team. As so-called punishment for the Cleveland fans' failure to keep up attendance figures, he moved his best

Spiders players, including Cy Young, to the St. Louis team for the start of the 1899 season.

The Spiders were horrible. Attendance was so bad that games were played in other cities, and the club was called the Wanderers by the Cleveland press. Inept play by Spider players caused fans to refer to them as the "Misfits." They finished the season with a 20–134 record and a .129 winning percentage, the worst in baseball history, dwarfing even the '62 Mets.

National League ball in Cleveland ended when the team was dropped from the league in 1900. Although the 1899 team comes to mind nowadays when the Cleveland Spiders name is evoked, the Spiders should be remembered as a talented, no-nonsense team who played the game as tough and hard as the Baltimore Orioles—the team that always comes to mind when rough, rowdy baseball in the 1890s is thought of.

CAP ANSON (1852–1922)

He was a tremendous leader, but an overt racist. Adrian Constantine "Cap" Anson was the first man to draw the color line in the sand against blacks in baseball, on the diamond and in the dugout as player/manager of the Chicago White Stockings. In 1883, Anson refused to play in an exhibition game at Toledo of the American Association because Toledo had a black catcher, Moses Fleetwood Walker, on its roster. Anson eventually backed down when threatened with forfeiture of the gate. Pandering to prejudice again in 1887, he helped ban black pitcher George Stovey when John M. Ward attempted to sign him for the New York Giants. A secret gentleman's agreement, lasting until 1947, was struck in both leagues amongst the owners that banned black players.

Throughout the years, Anson's White Stocking teams were packed with a plethora of drunks and rowdies, including King Kelly, Ned Williamson, Silver Flint, Larry Corcoran, George Gore, and Billy Sunday. The liquid libations and overindulgences of his troops eventually got under his skin so badly that he asked Chicago owner Al Spalding to hire detectives to follow them around during their late-night activities.

Despite his bigotry, Anson was, without question, the greatest and arguably most consistent player of the 19th century. He twice hit .400

or better and wound up with a lifetime average of .339. The first player to reach 3,000 hits, Anson led the Stockings to a total of 15 first division finishes and five National League championships. In 20 years of managing, he had only three losing seasons.

So beloved was Anson by Chicago fans that when he left the team, they were renamed the "Orphans" because they felt as if they had just lost a father. Nicknamed "Pop," one can only wonder what his endearing influence on the game would have been if he was as tolerant as he was talented.

Voted into the Hall of Fame in 1939, Anson died of a cerebral hemorrhage at the age of 70 on April 14, 1922, and he was buried at the Oak Woods Cemetery in Chicago in Section E, Division 4, Lot 10 on April 17. After his death, there was a huge display of affection for him in the national media, as everyone from Judge Landis to club owners, executives, former players, and luminaries extolled his virtues, integrity, and sportsmanship. Interestingly, the press neglected to mention his involvement as one of the ringleaders in helping to shape Major League Baseball's ban on black players.

BOSS SCHMIDT (1880–1932)

Charles "Boss" Schmidt might have been the epitome of the early 20th-century baseball player—the type of individual who would ignore pain and go out and do his job when called upon no matter the circumstances, and who would rub dirt or tobacco juice into a spike wound and keep on playing. While he has been all but forgotten, Schmidt gained a reputation during his brief six-year career in the majors as the toughest player, pound for pound, that the national game had to offer.

A brawler of the first magnitude, he was always ready to come to the defense of a teammate in a pinch. As Hughie Jennings, his manager on the Tigers, put it, "He was simply without fear."

His nickname "Boss" supposedly came from his take-charge attitude on the baseball diamond. Some newspaper accounts, however, have credited him with getting his nickname from his time working in the coal mines, while others reported that he received his moniker from his time spent as a prizefighter, since he became "The Boss" every time he stepped inside the ring.

Born in London, Arkansas, on September 12, 1880, Schmidt began working in the harsh, dark conditions of the local coal mines at an early age. This arduous work helped him build an incredibly strong physique, toughening him to the point that it seemed he was almost oblivious to pain. As a young teenager, Charlie became known for his pugilistic skills and wrestling abilities, as he was more than willing to scrap with anyone who would oblige him, often for money. So confident was he of his boxing skills that he briefly became a prizefighter, successfully competing in local bouts throughout the county and state. Although he could have made boxing his vocation, it was clearly baseball that was his first love and the thing he concentrated on most.

Schmidt's first professional assignment was with the Little Rock Travelers of the Southern Association in 1901. The 5-foot, 11-inch, 200-pound switch-hitting catcher immediately impressed manager Duke Finn by displaying good judgment and hard, heady play at his position. He also attained a reputation as a "hard ass" on the field for his willingness to block the plate from marauding intruders, in spite of the fact that he didn't wear shin guards.

It was also at this early stage in his career that people began to take notice of the hard, grotesque-looking shapes that were his hands. Covered with calluses and scar tissue from years of abuse in the coal mines (his boxing career didn't help the problem either), his knuckles and joints had become gnarled and disfigured to the extent that they looked as if they had been taken from the Grim Reaper himself. As painful as his "paws" looked, Schmidt never looked at them as handicaps, instead using them as weapons when the occasion arose. In the days of hard-bitten, inside baseball, players often slid spikes high with ill intent, especially on plays at the plate. With ball in hand, Schmidt would often use what he called his "right mitt" to either punch an opponent or knock him away from the plate.

After five seasons in the minors, his contract was purchased by the Detroit Tigers from the Minneapolis Millers of the American Association shortly before the 1906 season. As a 25-year-old rookie, Schmidt went to spring training to join a Bengals roster where the average age was 27.4 years. Included in this group was 19-year-old Ty Cobb, beginning his first full season with the club, and Wahoo Sam Crawford, a hard-hitting Nebraskan considered to be one of the game's great power hitters. Schmidt appeared in 67 games that season, as he split time with

Fred Payne and Jack Warner behind the plate. While he batted a disappointing .218, manager Bill Armour constantly reminded him that his main focus as a catcher was to handle the pitching staff and play good defense. Schmidt quickly established a good rapport with a veteran staff that included George Mullin, Wild Bill Donovan, Ed Siever, Ed Killian, and Red Donahue.

A tough, hard-nosed character on the field, off the field Schmidt was the exact opposite. Known for having an affable disposition, he could be rather shy, especially when photographers were around. He was so self-conscious about his hands that he almost always put his arms behind his back when he posed for a picture. One of the things Schmidt loved to do was impress people, especially members of the opposite sex, by driving nails into wood floors using nothing more than his knuckles. Teammate Wild Bill Donovan noted that, "It was one of the most impressive feats I have ever witnessed." Schmidt also loved to show off his adroit wrestling skills. He would often challenge teammates and players from other teams to wrestling matches, usually for money. During his time as a member of the Tigers, none of his fellow players could recall him losing a wrestling match. Interestingly, Schmidt's most famous grappling bout occurred not against a man, but a grown bear. One day when he and several of his teammates visited a local carnival, they happened upon its most popular attraction, a wrestling bear. Ever confident, Schmidt eagerly took the challenge from the carnival vendor and stepped into the cage. In just a few quick moves, Schmidt had the bear pinned.

Schmidt also got along with his teammates—except for Ty Cobb, whose brashness and confidence in his abilities often rubbed people the wrong way. Schmidt was originally part of the anti-Cobb faction of the Tigers led by outfielder Matty McIntyre, a Connecticut-born Yankee who grew up on Park Avenue in the Port Richmond section of Staten Island. McIntyre was extremely jealous of Cobb's talents, and in the days before guaranteed contracts, he became paranoid that he would lose his job to him. Thus, he went out of his way to make the young Georgian's life as miserable as possible. Although Schmidt never admitted it, Ty eventually came to the conclusion that he was the one who destroyed his cherished homemade ash bats.

Schmidt's two most famous scraps were, of course, against the Georgia Peach. During the last 100 years, so much misinformation and so many lies and myths (you can blame sources like Wikipedia for much of this) have been mixed with reality that the truth has become muddied. Round one of Cobb versus Schmidt occurred on March 16, 1907, at Warren Park in Augusta, Georgia. On this particular afternoon, the Tigers had just walked onto the field to start another round of spring training workouts. Cobb was met by a familiar figure, that of the park's black groundskeeper, a gentleman named "Bungy." The two men, who had known one another since Ty's playing days with the Augusta Tourists, had what can be best described as an "extremely cordial" relationship, with Cobb usually taking great delight in Bungy's admiration for him. This day, however, would prove to be very different.

As Bungy, obviously tipsy, slue-footed his way over to Cobb with an open hand of friendship, he gleefully called out, "Hello you Georgia Peach." Not wanting to deal with the old man in his inebriated state, Cobb tried to shoo him away, telling him that he was preparing for his workouts. When Bungy persisted, Cobb's temper got the best of him as he began chasing him back toward the clubhouse. Suddenly, and out of nowhere, Ty was confronted by a precipitously large, buxom woman, who began yelling at him. It was Bungy's wife coming to the defense of her husband. "Go way white man! We ain't done nothin' to you!" Thus began a verbal exchange between the two that could be heard throughout the stadium.

Out of nowhere, "like the Cavalry coming to the rescue," Schmidt and several other Tiger players rushed in. Whether Schmidt was goaded into getting involved by other Tiger players remains a mystery. What is certain is that he became involved and told Cobb in no uncertain terms that he was being overly zealous in his verbal treatment of the woman. Schmidt yelled at Cobb, "Whoever does a thing like that is a coward," to which Ty replied, "I don't see how it interests you." The two men then exchanged blows, as Ty yelled out, "I'll get you, one way or another." Standing his ground as he always did, Schmidt reportedly cursed under his breath.

It should be duly noted that one of baseball's great urban myths had Cobb "choking" Bungy's wife that day. It is a myth that has been debunked by Cobb historian Wesley Fricks, whose hard-core research on the incident refutes all claims that Ty laid his hands on the woman.

"Cobb–Schmidt I" received considerable play in the press, even though it was nothing more than a minor dustup and preamble to what would happen shortly thereafter, as both combatants were eager to once again get at one another's throats. As newspapers of the time played up the rematch, Schmidt smartly decided to wait until the team left Cobb's home state before he agreed to another fight.

"Cobb–Schmidt II" was held at a ballpark in Meridian, Mississippi, on one of the Tigers' off days. By all accounts, Schmidt put his prize-fighting skills to good use as he shredded Cobb to pieces, knocking him down several times in a scene reminiscent of the fight in *Cool Hand Luke* in which George Kennedy beats the hell out of Paul Newman. Refusing to stay on the ground, Ty faced continued abuse by Schmidt's "hands of granite." After what seemed like an eternity, the brawl was finally stopped when teammates intervened. To Schmidt's credit, not once during the skirmish did he think about hitting Cobb when he was on the ground, something that Cobb was appreciative of and would never forget. "He fought the fight clean and on the square," Cobb would remark years later. "A lot of men would've hit me when I was down, but Charlie didn't, he stood there and waited for me to get up."

After the fight was stopped, Schmidt helped to revive Cobb, who was in a semiconscious state. Because of the way Cobb fearlessly fought that day, and because of the way Schmidt helped to revive him after the fight, the two former adversaries would become lifelong friends. They became so close that even members of the anti-Cobb faction would hold their tongues and refrain from making disparaging remarks about Cobb when Schmidt was in their presence.

Known more for his bat than his defense, Schmidt's best year at the plate was 1908, when he batted .265. His bête noire was definitely throwing out runners. For whatever reason (many people point to his gnarled hands, which made it difficult to grip the ball), he had a hard time throwing to second base. A member of three consecutive American League pennant-winning Detroit teams from 1907 to 1909, Schmidt batted just .159, with 5 RBI in 14 World Series games. Defensively, his stats in the Fall Classic are even worse, as he set records for futility that will likely never be broken. Aside from the fact that he is the only player to make the last out in two World Series, in 1907 and 1908, he also allowed an astounding 35 stolen bases in 13 World Series games. The 1910 season would see Oscar Stanage catch the majority of games for the Tigers, with 84 games to Schmidt's 66. When Detroit manager Hughie Jennings announced during spring training of 1911 that

Schmidt would be relegated to full-time backup, the writing was on the wall.

At this point in their careers, Stanage was clearly the better player defensively, in terms of hitting and, more importantly, health. Schmidt was worn down from abusing his body throughout the years. In the eyes of Detroit management, he had outlived his usefulness, and it was time to move on. After the 1911 season, Schmidt was waived by the Tigers and apparently done as a ballplayer at the ripe old age of 31.

Schmidt spent all of 1912 working in the coal mines and playing local ball to keep his baseball skills sharp. He was determined to get back into the pro game. "I'll take playing baseball any day of the week over working in the mines," he proclaimed to a writer when asked about his intentions for the 1913 campaign. His wish to once again play the game he loved so dearly came true when he signed on with the Double-A Providence Grays of the International League. Reports about him being done as a player were quickly squashed, as he appeared in 132 games that season, batting a lusty .342. After the season, Schmidt told his old friend Ty Cobb that he hadn't felt better physically in years. Schmidt would continue on in the minors as player, coach, and manager until 1927, when he retired to his home in Arkansas.

Grave of Boss Schmidt. Courtesy of Bill Lee.

Schmidt spent his last years in relative comfort. He would occasionally get together with Cobb to talk about the "good old days, when players hustled and didn't loaf." Sadly, the former catcher died of an intestinal obstruction at his doctor's home in Altus, Arkansas, at the age of 52, on November 14, 1932. He was laid to rest in St. Mary's Catholic Cemetery in Altus four days later. News of his old friend's demise brought Cobb to tears as he affectionately remembered, "In all my years in baseball, I don't think I ever saw anyone tougher than my old friend Charlie Schmidt. I will always remember him fondly."

But the story of Boss Schmidt doesn't end with his passing. Flash forward to 1969, when the Tigers, now the defending world champions, were informed that one of their well-known players of a half-century before had been lying in an unmarked grave for the past 37 years. Immediately, and without hesitation, the Detroit organization paid for a new headstone to be placed at Schmidt's grave at St. Mary's Cemetery. The simple, flathead stone is engraved with his name and birth and death dates, along with the following fitting inscription: "A DETROIT TIGER 1906–1911." As one member of the Tigers' front office so aptly put it, "Boss Schmidt can now finally rest in peace."

HAL CHASE (1883–1947)

If not for his unsavory reputation, which he garnered during his 15-year major league career, Harold Homer Chase might very well be in the National Baseball Hall of Fame. There have been many words used to describe the man who sportswriters dubbed "Prince Hal," but the one that almost always comes to mind today is *corrupt*.

Born in Los Gatos, California, on February 13, 1883, it was said that as a lad growing up in Northern California, Chase was fairly easygoing and laid back. As his skills on the ball field improved however, so did his sense of self-worth. By the time he reached his late teens, Chase was certain that he could play the game and play it well. As with most players of his era, playing baseball was a monetary issue. Chase wanted to be properly compensated for his play, and if owners were not willing to fully open up their coffers to give proper dispensation, then there were certainly other ways to make up for the lack of income.

Chase had already played five years of minor league ball when he signed with New York's American League entry, the Highlanders, before the start of the 1905 season. His charismatic style of playing, both on the field and in the batter's box, gained him legions of fans. With Babe Ruth naming him as his all-time first baseman, many old-timers also considered him to be the best fielding first baseman ever. His fielding style was a cross between Don Mattingly and Keith Hernandez. Chase was extremely adroit at fielding bunts, routinely intercepting them on the third-base side of the pitcher's mound. Once described as having a corkscrew brain, he began to look for ways to make extra cash almost from the time he joined New York. In the days when baseball players were ruled by the reserve clause and clubs kept salaries as low as possible, there was good money to be made by either betting on games or taking bribes to throw them. It was especially easy for the talented Chase to help his team lose. A bad throw here, a misplayed grounder there. It was all in a day's work.

As great as he was, he still led American League first basemen in errors year after year. The holder of the American League mark for career errors by a first sacker, with 285, it's a wonder his contemporaries did not sniff out problems sooner, especially since they thought he was so talented. Known as a modest fellow and good teammate when he first got to New York, Chase eventually transformed into a selfish prima donna who cared more about his personal stats than the good of the team. Chase was truly a lover of Gotham's nightlife, with its gambling establishments, nightclubs, saloons, and, of course, brothels. In 1910, manager George Stallings accused Chase of throwing games. Chase beat the charge and demanded that the New York owners relieve Stallings and hire him as manager. In his only full year as New York skipper, he took the Highlanders from second place (88–63) to sixth (76–76).

When Frank Chance took the helm, he eventually had Chase traded to the White Sox in 1913. His lackadaisical play became so blatant that fans and players alike would shout out, "What's the odds?" when he appeared before ball games. Chase spent time in the Federal League, going there for a bigger contract. When the Federal League folded, he was signed by the Cincinnati Reds. In 1916, his first year back from the Federal League, he batted a career-high .339. When rumors circulated that Reds manager Buck Herzog was about to be let go, many in the press thought Chase was the heir apparent. Unfortunately for "Prince Hal," it was Christy Mathewson who would get the job as Reds skipper.

In August 1918, Matty had Chase suspended for offering bribes to teammates and opposing players to throw games, most notably, Giant pitcher Pol Perritt. After the season, Chase was called to the offices of National League president John Heydler, where three Cincinnati players—Greasy Neale, Jimmy Ring, and Mike Regan—testified that Chase attempted to bribe them to help throw games. Chase, who maintained his innocence, lucked out because his main accuser, Mathewson, was serving in France with the U.S. Army's Chemical Warfare Unit. Chase's other accuser, Perritt, did not show up to testify, and Giant manager John McGraw, who did testify, could not confirm that Perritt ever received offers of a bribe. Heydler **had no recourse but to allow Chase to walk.**

McGraw, in need of a first baseman, almost immediately stepped in and offered him a contract, but when Chase showed up to spring training, he found that his accuser and former friend, Mathewson, was now a coach with the team. As the season started, it appeared that Little Napoleon's gamble paid off. Chase was winning games and playing flawlessly in the field. By August, however, things had gone south, and in a hurry. Chase found a partner in crime with Giant third baseman Heinie Zimmerman. The two began bribing other players, not only on the Giants, but also on other teams. It was supposedly Mathewson who brought the duo's dirty deeds to McGraw's attention, although there was little on the field or in the clubhouse that McGraw didn't know about. When McGraw finally got wind of the shenanigans, he benched Chase with a "wrist injury" and suspended Zimmerman. It would be the last time that either would play in the major leagues.

Chase's name came up again in the press in 1920, when he was implicated in the Black Sox Scandal. Reports surfaced that he was one of the go-betweens between the Sox players and the gamblers. According to Giant pitcher Rube Benton, Chase made $40,000 betting on the 1919 series, but his allegations were never proven. Despite the fact that baseball commissioner Judge Landis never officially expelled him, Chase was blacklisted by organized baseball. He did manage to find work in the game playing with semipro teams in California, Texas, and Arizona. In 1926, he was involved in an auto accident that severed his Achilles tendons. He continued to play semipro baseball intermittently well into the early 1930s. His years of hard partying and late nights eventually reduced him to a shadow of what he once was on the field.

Like many former ballplayers, Chase didn't have a lot to fall back on after his career was over. He had a hard time adjusting to life outside the game. He supposedly worked as a self-employed gold prospector in California's Sierra Nevada Mountains, but nothing much came of the venture. Having a hard time maintaining steady employment, he was forced to work hard-to-find odd jobs. During the last decade of his life, Chase spiraled into a deep chasm of alcoholic misery. Around 1940, he moved to Williams, California, where he was allowed to live in a small cabin located on a ranch owned by his sister Jessie and her husband, Frank Topham. Broke, with little means of self-support, he had to rely on the good graces of his sister for the essentials of living. Near the end of his life, Chase showed remorse for what he had done to tarnish the game but always maintained that he had never bet against his own team.

In January 1947, Chase entered Colusa Memorial Hospital, suffering from a variety of ailments. He died there on the morning of May 18, as a result of acute cardiac failure due to chronic nephritis, myocarditis, and general arteriosclerosis. He was 64 years of age. Chase was interred at Oak Hill Memorial Park in San Jose, California, in Section S, Block 39, Lot 3, Grave 5.

TY COBB (1886–1961)

"Let he who is without sin cast the first stone." That line from John 8:7 could easily have been used as the epitaph on the tomb of Tyrus Raymond Cobb. When his name is mentioned today, all sorts of emotions and images come to mind for the average fan, not knowing the true story of who Cobb was both as a player and a human being. While many fans judge Cobb solely by his wonderful career and the countless records that he set, the majority are inclined to view him through the eyes of the anti-Cobb media, which has grown precipitously since his death in 1961. That, in itself, is a great crime.

There is no denying that Cobb ranks as one of baseball's greatest players, if not the game's fiercest competitor. His records speak for themselves. A lifetime .367 hitter, he hit .300 or better each year from

Ty Cobb, Detroit Tigers, 1913. Courtesy of the Library of Congress.

1906 to 1928, and won the American League batting championship each year from 1907 to 1915 and 1917 to 1919. He accumulated 4,191 hits, 12 batting titles, three .400 seasons, and 897 career stolen bases, including a then-record 96 steals in 1915. And unlike Pete Rose, he never bet on baseball. Since his death, revisionist historians and members of the "Fourth Estate" have done everything in their power to marginalize and discredit him, making him appear to be nothing more than a "mental patient in spikes," as one blogger wrote.

Cobb grew up in the post–Civil War South, where institutionalized racism was a given and accepted practice. Many people point to the time period that Cobb grew up in, using a "guilty by association" argument to explain his views on race. If anything, Cobb's makeup, both as a young man and a player, had more to do with the death of his father in 1905, shortly before he was called up to the Tigers.

Around midnight on August 8, 1905, Ty's mother (Amanda Chitwood Cobb) fatally shot her husband (Ty's father), William Herschel Cobb, on the balcony of the family residence. The elder Cobb, who had long suspected his wife of infidelity, was apparently trying to catch her in the act. As he attempted to open a bedroom window, he was hit by two shots from a pistol at close range. One shot ripped open his stomach, the other hitting him in the head. The scene was later described by a policeman as a "sickening, bloody mess."

Arrested and charged with involuntary manslaughter, Amanda Cobb was found not guilty by an all-male jury the following March. Despite the rumors of his mother's infidelity and sexual trysts, Ty stayed true and steadfast by her side during the trial. One interesting aspect that revisionist historians have also overlooked when assessing Cobb is the fact that he was just 18 years old when his father was killed. In today's modern world, he would have been a prime candidate to receive some sort of mental health or grief counseling, along with medication to help him cope, but in the early 1900s, there were no such things available. This left him with the impossible task of having to deal with his emotions and feelings alone. With no real support system or mental health facilities, short of a sanitarium, it was almost a given that he would have "emotional issues" going forward. As for his aggressive play, Cobb always attributed it to his late father, saying, "I did it for my father. He never got to see me play . . . but I knew he was watching me, and I never let him down."

Another aspect of Cobb's life that is almost always ignored is the fact that in his second year with the Tigers, 1906, he was unmercifully hazed by a group of Tiger players, led by outfielder Matty McIntyre, a Staten Island-raised "Yankee" who was both jealous of Ty's talents and paranoid about keeping his own job. McIntyre, along with Ed Seiver, Ed Killian, George Mullin, and a few other players, became part of what was later known as the anti-Cobb faction. When people look at the raw cruelty Ty was subjected to, they can better understand why he had to harden himself the way he did. From having his prized homemade ash bats destroyed to having his cleats nailed to the clubhouse floor, Cobb also underwent the humiliation of having his clothes soaked in water and tied up in knots, coupled with constant verbal abuse. This went beyond simple hazing and would never be tolerated in today's media-driven world of 24-hour news cycles.

In 1906, however, the kind of cruelty that was heaped upon Cobb was an accepted practice. Things became so bad during his first full season that he had to take several weeks off (July 18, 1906 to September 3, 1906) to rest and rehabilitate. Even after he rejoined the Tigers, he retained the practice of sleeping with a pistol under his pillow. Ty had trust issues with his teammates, and why wouldn't he? The two he got along with best early on were pitcher Wild Bill Donovan and infielder Germany Schaefer, both loquacious types who gave young Ty the bene-fit of the doubt when he first joined the team. Maybe if McIntyre and his cohorts had known the full extent of what Ty was going through emotionally, they would have backed off. As it was, he was under a tremendous amount of pressure after becoming the sole breadwinner of the family. With his widowed mother Amanda, younger brother John Paul, and sister Florence depending on him and his baseball salary for their existence, there was no way he was ever going to back down, especially against bullies like McIntyre. As he told his old friend Grant-land Rice years later, "Except for Donovan and Schaef, they were all out to get me, the whole lot of them. I was a young player, and I fought back and they didn't like that."

One only has to point to the writing of Al Stump as to why Ty's career and character have taken such a beating throughout the past six decades. A nationally known writer, Stump was hired by Doubleday to ghostwrite Ty's autobiography, *My Life in Baseball: The True Record*. The collaboration produced what many consider one of the great base-ball books of all-time. Released in August 1961, to great acclaim and solid sales, *My Life in Baseball* is the kind of literary work that most authors would have been gloriously satisfied just being a part of, but not Stump, who had other plans.

Unbeknownst to Cobb, Stump had been secretly writing down notes, quotes, and stories that, according to Ty's wishes, were never to be made known to the general public. Of course, this didn't stop Stump from stabbing Ty in the back in a way that would have made Mao Zedong proud. Stump waited for Cobb to pass away before he went about getting a venue to showcase his work. This he found in *True* magazine. Entitled "Ty Cobb's Wild 10-Month Fight to Live," it is a three-part article whose first installment was published in December 1961, right around Ty's 75th birthday. Stump's reasoning for writing the article was that he felt that *My Life in Baseball* was nothing more than a canard and a whitewash. Interestingly, when the article came out, many of Cobb's former teammates, along with opposing players, came to his defense, as they attacked Stump for his viciousness and callous portrayal. Incredibly, the article won Stump the Associated Press award for the best sports story of 1962.

Stump's literary assassination of Cobb's character didn't end there. In 1994, a follow-up work by Stump entitled *Cobb: A Biography* was published. This hit piece continues to perpetuate a negative myth from which Ty's reputation has never truly recovered. The incident where he beat an invalid man, Claude Lueker, at Hilltop Park in 1912, is a perfect example of this. What is rarely mentioned is that Lueker, a Tammany Hall lackey and two-bit punk, was allowed to verbally abuse Ty for several innings prior to Cobb's attack on him, and that he had a history of harassing Cobb when he was in town. On the day of the "infamous" attack, May 15, 1912, Cobb had done everything he could to diffuse the situation, even going as far as not returning to the dugout between innings and asking for help from the police and gendarmes at Hilltop Park, pleas that fell on deaf ears. Not only did the crowd cheer wildly for Ty that day as he beat the hell out of Lueker, but American League president Ban Johnson, who happened to be at the game, received hundreds of affidavits from fans sitting close enough to Lueker to confirm the verbal abuse he was hurling at Cobb—just another fact that historians have often overlooked.

The lies and mistruths that have been told about Cobb during the decades since his death could easily fill a file at the National Baseball Hall of Fame. Some of the myths include that Cobb killed a man in Detroit in 1912, and left the body in an alley. Actually, while Ty and his wife were accosted by three men who attempted to rob them, Cobb fought them off and suffered only a minor scratch from the knife of one of the assailants.

Another myth is that Cobb was the most hated man in all of baseball and had no friends. Cobb most certainly was not the most hated man in baseball. While he certainly had his detractors, he also had legions of fans. He may have had problems with members of the "anti-Cobb faction" early in his career, but he got along well with many of his teammates. Ty's friends on the Tigers included Davy Jones, Bobby Veach, Harry Heilmann, Germany Schaefer, Ray Hayworth, George Burns, Wild Bill Donovan, Boss Schmidt, and Bob Fothergill, to name just a few. The list of opposing players who he was friends with reads like a who's who of baseball greats. Few people know that two of his best friends in the game were none other than Christy Mathewson and Walter Johnson. Cobb admired "Big Six" and visited him when he got the chance. He even went out of his way to serve with him in the Chemical Warfare Unit (also known as the Gas and Flame Division) during World War I. When Mathewson died in 1925, it was said that Cobb broke down in tears. Cobb and "The Big Train" remained good friends until Johnson's death from a brain tumor in 1946. In fact, Ty would often visit the Johnson household and bring presents for the children. Ty was also there for Walter when his oldest daughter passed away from influenza in 1921, as well as when his wife Hazel passed away at the age of 36 in 1930. When he visited, Ty was always the essence of the southern gentleman.

Cobb was also great friends with Ted Williams, Joe DiMaggio, Rogers Hornsby, George Sisler, Casey Stengel, Mickey Cochrane (a hard loser like himself), Ray Schalk, Nap Rucker, Tris Speaker, Smoky Joe Wood, Eddie Collins, Frank "Home Run" Baker, and Shoeless Joe Jackson. He even buried the hatchet with Babe Ruth after the Bambino married a friend and fellow Georgian, the beautiful Claire Merritt Hodgson. The two, who had a venomous rivalry, became friends after Cobb's retirement in 1928.

Some of the famous nonbaseball personalities who he was good friends with included J. G. Taylor Spink, comedian Joe E. Brown, and General Douglas MacArthur. After watching the movie *Cobb* or the documentary *Baseball*, you would think he was a cross between Hitler, Attila the Hun, and the Anti-Christ himself. According to Cobb historian Wesley Fricks, who knows more about Cobb and his family than probably any researcher, "Ty Cobb's family was kind to blacks, and Ty's father (Herschel) fought for black education in the Georgia State Senate 60 years before desegregation. Many, many kind things were done for blacks by the Cobb family." Cobb himself was extremely kind to blacks and even brought the Tigers' batboy, Lil Rastus, home to live with him. And the story where Cobb supposedly "choked" the wife of a groundskeeper named "Bungy" was a complete fabrication as well. So why do people continue to use the word *racist* when discussing Ty, even now, more than 50 years after his death? Again, one only has to look at such sources as the Stump books, Ken Burns's *Baseball*, and, of course, redundant websites like Wikipedia to realize that it might take decades before Cobb's reputation is wiped clean. Ty was a huge fan of both Jackie Robinson and Willie Mays, as well as Hank Aaron and Roy Campanella, among others.

Another lie that was propagated by Stump was that Cobb was estranged from his family. The scene in the movie *Cobb* where Ty visits his daughter Shirley and she draws the shades, not wanting to speak to her father, is completely bogus. When Ty's sister Florence became crippled with arthritis in the early 1940s, it was her big brother who took care of her and paid her medical bills. When Florence passed away on June 9, 1944, in Sarasota, Florida, at the age of 51, it was Ty who paid Cunningham and Weatherly Funeral Home for the wake and funeral.

What has become one of the biggest lies told about Cobb is that because he was so disliked and had no friends, only three former major league players showed up for his funeral. Because Ty's family didn't trust the media, they decided the services should be as private an affair as possible, going so far as asking newspapers to print respectful requests that people outside the family not attend the services. It was out of this respect that the majority of well-wishing players, including Ted Williams and Joe DiMaggio, sent written notices of respect, a fact that Stump omits from his book. Even Babe Ruth's widow Claire, who had known Ty for more than 40 years, sent a note of condolence. In addition, the majority of his close friends in baseball had already passed away, including Tris Speaker, Christy Mathewson, and Walter Johnson. The only three former major leaguers who were allowed to come to both the wake and funeral were Ray Schalk, Mickey Cochrane, and Nap Rucker. Cochrane went to the funeral despite being ill with lymphoma, and he would die some eleven months after his friend, in June 1962. Never let the truth get in the way of a good story.

Aside from being a great ballplayer, Cobb was quite shrewd with money, becoming baseball's first millionaire. He bought stock in Coca-Cola, General Electric, Gillette, Bethlehem Steel, and General Motors, amongst others, to amass great wealth. Cobb would often give financial advice to other players, and he also gave advice when it came to contract negotiations and money to players who were down and out. How many people know that he told none other than Lou Gehrig that he was being underpaid by the Yankees, and that Ed Barrow and company were taking financial advantage of him? Despite his greatness as a player, his records, and the truth about who he really was, the sad reality is that Ty Cobb's legacy will most certainly continue to be defined by his detractors.

In the fall of 1959, Cobb was diagnosed with prostate cancer. After getting a second opinion from doctors whom he trusted, his prostate was removed in the hopes that it would prolong his life, a procedure that is still used today in extreme cases of the insidious disease. As he always did, Ty would battle on, hoping for a miracle that unfortunately never came. There were few options for him other than the cobalt treatments that he would undergo and the various medications that helped to kill the pain.

On June 5, 1961, a little more than a month and a half after he saw his last major league game in person, Cobb checked himself into Emory University Hospital in Atlanta for the final time. By now, the cancer, which had metastasized and spread to his spine and brain, was racking him with pain. He also suffered from Type 1 diabetes, Bright's disease (kidney disease), and high blood pressure. In typical Cobb fashion, Ty kept a loaded Lugar and $1 million in negotiable securities in a brown paper bag on the table next to his bed. On the afternoon of Monday, July 17, 1961, at approximately 1:15 in the afternoon, Tyrus Raymond Cobb passed away in his sleep. By his side when he died was his first wife Charlie, his only surviving son, Jimmy, and his two daughters, Shirley and Beverly. He was 74 years old. He was laid to rest several days later at Rose Hill Cemetery in Royston, Georgia, in the Cobb family mausoleum (which he had personally constructed) in a crypt located across from his sister Florence, beloved father Herschel, and mother Amanda.

CHICK GANDIL (1888–1970)

The story of Arnold "Chick" Gandil is the story of two players. The first story was that of a highly talented player who was considered to be one of the best first basemen in the game. The second is that of a player who was the go-between for the gamblers and players involved in fixing the 1919 World Series. Gandil was born January 19, 1888, in St. Paul, Minnesota, to Christian and Louise Bechel Gandil, both Swiss immigrants. An only child, he and his parents moved to Berkeley, California. It was in this Northern California town, situated across the bay from San Francisco, that he grew up learning and loving the game of baseball.

At the age of 16 or 17, Gandil left school to play ball in towns situated near the badlands of the Arizona–Mexico border. He supplemented his income by boxing in the local heavyweight division, picking up $150 a fight, and also working as a boilermaker, skills he would use to become a plumber later in life. The first teams he played for were semipro and outlaw teams who played outside the rules of organized baseball. In 1908, the same year he broke into organized baseball, Gandil married a pretty Irish American girl named Laurel Fay Kelly. He played part of the 1910 season with the White Sox and was then sold to Washington, where he remained until 1916.

Gandil made the acquaintance of Sport Sullivan, a sports gambler and bookie. Sullivan had rich, powerful friends, and his friendships with ballplayers like Gandil were crucial elements in his plan to fix the World Series.

Gandil rejoined the White Sox in 1917, as the regular first baseman, but like many on the team, he was a malcontent and had a bad temper and selfish personality. Vastly underpaid by cheapskate Charles Comiskey, Gandil was considered the ringleader of the 1919 World Series fix. He and seven other players made a deal with Sullivan to drop the series.

In the 1919 Fall Classic, Gandil batted .233, committing one error but playing lethargically in the field. Sitting out the 1920 campaign over a salary dispute, he was banned from baseball the following year by Commissioner Landis, becoming one of the infamous "Eight Men Out." Gandil was rarely heard from after his career was over, and except for a September 1956 *Sports Illustrated* interview in which he tells his version of the scandal, he lived in relative anonymity.

Gandil, who worked as a self-employed plumber after his baseball career ended, died from heart disease at Convalescent Hospital in Calistoga, California, on December 13, 1970. His cremated remains were buried at St. Helena Cemetery, in St. Helena, California. Interestingly, Gandil's ashes were not buried until March 15, 1971, two days after the death of his wife Laurel, who passed away on March 13. The couple, who was married for 62 years, is buried in the Gandil plot located in Lot 34, Block 20 Extension.

CLINT COURTNEY (1927–1975)

You would be hard pressed to find a nickname that better fit a ballplayer than the one that was hung on Clinton Dawson Courtney. Given the moniker "Scrap Iron," he was a tough, hard-nosed catcher whose on-field personality and playing style seemed better suited for the gridiron than the baseball diamond. Born in the northwestern Louisiana town of Hall Summit in impoverished conditions, his family later moved to Arkansas, where his father found work in the oil fields. Even as a youngster, Courtney showed an aggressive attitude when it came to playing sports. Whether it was basketball, where he was known to throw an elbow or two, or playing on the sandlots, Clint never gave way to anyone, friend or foe.

After graduating from Standard–Umstead High School in Smackover, Arkansas, Courtney found work with his father in the Smackover Oil Fields and then took a job as a welder in a shipyard in Orange, Texas. Drafted by the U.S. Army in 1944, he served in Korea, the Philippines, and Japan, playing for several service teams in the process. Shortly after his discharge in 1947, he was signed by New York Yankees scout and former player Atley "Swampy" Donald, a fellow Louisianan. It was during his minor league career that the squat, left-handed hitting Courtney began wearing glasses, although the exact time is unknown. According to Jimmy Cannon, Courtney's glasses, which were shatterproof, made him look "more like a librarian than a baseball player, though nothing is farther from the truth."

During his time in the minor leagues, Courtney solidified his reputation as a "hard ass player" and brawler, while also becoming known for dirty play. It was in 1947 that Courtney met his match in terms of intensity in the form of one Alfred Manuel "Billy" Martin. Martin played the game as if it was a war. During the 1947 campaign, the two men would start one of the more colorful player rivalries of the modern era. "Billy the Kid's" dislike for Courtney was born while the latter was playing for the Phoenix Senators of the Arizona-Texas League. In a game against the Bisbee Yankees, Courtney purposely spiked Senators player/manager Arky Biggs in a play at second base, setting off a minor brawl. From that point onward, Martin's hatred of Courtney grew to such an extent that he always went out of his way to take him out whenever he got the chance.

After four seasons in the minors, it appeared that Courtney was ready to stick with the parent club. Invited to spring training in 1951, he did well enough to make the Opening Day roster, although he was sent to Kansas City after a few games without making a single appearance. Disappointed with his demotion, he continued to play the same style of aggressive baseball that made him successful. He was also involved in several "incidents" that season that caught the eye of Yankees management. In a game against the Milwaukee Brewers, he did his best impersonation of "Concrete Charlie" Bednarik when he knocked out the front teeth of future Braves second baseman Johnny Logan with an elbow slide. Later in the season, he got into a fight with St. Paul Saints first baseman Danny Ozark. Finally, on September 3, in a game against the Brewers at Milwaukee and shortly before his call-up to New York, he spat, not once, but twice, in the face of umpire John Fette and, adding insult to injury, hit him with a bat. Courtney, who was tossed from the game, was fined $100 and given an indefinite suspension by American Association president Bruce Dudley. The incident with Fette and the suspension didn't stop the Yankees from bringing him up at the end of the month.

Courtney finally made his big-league debut on September 29, 1951, in the second game of a doubleheader at Yankee Stadium against Boston, going 0-for-2 and getting hit by a pitch thrown by Red Sox pitcher Mickey McDermott. Despite his inauspicious debut, Clint felt that he deserved a shot to contend for the starting catcher's position, held by Yogi Berra. "I'm as good as any catcher out there," he was quoted as saying after the season. "Give me a chance and I'll show 'em."

It came as no surprise to anyone in the Yankee organization when he was traded to the Browns that November in a swap for pitcher Jim McDonald. Yankee president and general manager George Weiss was not exactly a fan of the squatty catcher and had been keeping track of his on-field incidents. Coming to the conclusion that he was not worth the trouble, Weiss gladly sent him packing when St. Louis manager Rogers Hornsby, who had managed Courtney in the minors when he was with Beaumont, requested a trade. Weiss also didn't hesitate to trade him because he already had an agitator in Billy Martin. Even though Clint would have been a marked improvement over the two other backup receivers, Ralph Houk and Charlie Silvera, Weiss had made up his mind.

Gil McDougald once said,

> Besides the fact that we already had Yogi as our catcher, who had
> won the MVP that season, I think one of the main reasons why they
> traded Courtney was because Billy really disliked him. Everyone
> knew that Billy was Casey's boy, so if one of the two had to go, it was
> going to be Clint . . . but could you imagine the two of them together
> on the same team? They would have killed each other. Personally, I
> think Clint was too hardheaded. I played with him in the minors, and
> he would often do the exact opposite of what the manager told him
> to do. I don't think that would've gone over very well with Casey.

Courtney received the nickname "Scrap Iron" near the end of spring
training in 1952, after he fell during a footrace with sportswriter Milton
Richman at a railway yard, after which he looked like a candidate for a
M.A.S.H Unit. Despite the fact he was battered and cut up, he still
played in the next day's exhibition game. Teammate Duane Pillette and
Browns announcer Buddy Blattner are both credited with coming up
with the moniker.

In retrospect, Courtney's trade to St. Louis was the best thing that
could have happened to his career. As the Browns' starting catcher, he
had a fine season, batting .286, with 5 homers and 50 RBI in 116
games—good enough that *Sporting News* named him the American
League Rookie of the Year. Of course, his season was not without controversy. On July 12, in a game against the Yankees at Sportsman's Park,
Courtney was involved in an altercation with former nemesis Billy Martin after Courtney spiked him in the top of the second inning. The
Yankee enforcer waited to exact his revenge. Martin said, "Courtney
was coming down to second. Instead of tagging him, I wound up and hit
him right between the eyes with the ball."

Said Phil Rizzuto,

> Billy told me at the start of the inning that if Courtney got anywhere
> near him he was going to get him but good, and boy did he. Holy
> Cow, he hit him square in the face, bull's eye . . . knocked his cap
> clean off, broke his glasses. As Billy started walking away, Courtney
> followed him and tried to throw a punch. Billy was ready and turned
> around and punched him in the face, and kept on punching him. He
> probably got a half-dozen punches in before Courtney could throw
> one.

When the fight ended, Courtney was ejected by umpire Bill Summers, who himself had been flattened by a punch. As for Billy, he was allowed to stay in the game because Summers felt that not only had he been defending himself, but that his retaliation for Courtney's spiking was within the bounds of baseball etiquette. Courtney was fined and suspended for three days; adding insult to injury was the fact that the Yankees won the game, 5–4, in extra innings.

In 1954, Courtney became one of the original Orioles when the Browns moved to Baltimore, and he hit the first home run in Memorial Stadium history. He appeared in 122 games that season, batting .270, with 4 homers and 37 RBI. In November 1954, the Orioles acquired catcher Hal Smith and catcher/first baseman Gus Triandos as part of a multiplayer deal with the Yankees. This left Courtney as the odd man out, and he was dealt to the White Sox that December. Relegated to backup duty on the South Side, he appeared in 19 games before being traded to the Senators on June 7, 1955, as part of a three-for-one deal, with Chicago receiving outfielder Jim Busby in return.

Courtney spent five seasons in the nation's capital, appearing in a career-high 34 games in 1958. Traded back to the Orioles on April 3, 1960, he was once again relegated to backup duty, and even though he appeared in just 63 games, while batting a career-low .227, life remained interesting, as he soon found himself the personal catcher for future Hall of Famer Hoyt Wilhelm. Armed with an oversized catcher's mitt that was referred to as "Big Bertha," Courtney handled Wilhelm beautifully, although he maintained that he could never have done it without the help of his gargantuan mitt.

As his career wound down, Scrap began to think about the future. Since he already had managerial experience at the minor league level (he made his managerial debut in 1949, at the age of 22, with the Guaymas Ostioneros of the Mexican Winter League), coaching/managing seemed like a natural fit. Since his time in the minors, he had always had it in the back of his mind that he would like to manage again. Because of his on-field leadership skills and qualities as a catcher, and since he was a true student of the game, Scrap seemed almost destined to become a manager. He had often looked at other members of the catching fraternity who had gone on to become big-league skippers and thought why not him. This, of course, would eventually become Courtney's goal. Because of his country-boy persona, there were many in baseball who looked at him as nothing more than a country bumpkin. Nothing could have been further from the truth.

On January 24, 1961, Courtney was again traded, this time to the Athletics as part of a multiplayer deal. The A's returned him to Baltimore the next season after just one appearance on April 14. Scrap would appear in 22 games in his third go-around with the Orioles, making his final big-league appearance on July 1, 1961. It was during this time that he began a new journey, one that would help him realize his dream of managing again.

After his release from Baltimore, and as a favor to O's skipper Paul Richards, Courtney went to the minors to play for the team's Triple-A club, the Rochester Red Wings, who were in dire need of catching help. Following Richards to the recently formed Houston Colt .45s the next year, he would spend the next three seasons playing for several different minor league franchises. In 1965, Courtney made it back to the majors when he was promoted to work as the bull pen coach for the newly named Astros. When Richards and his staff were let go by Houston following the 1965 season, Clint followed Richards to Atlanta, where he was director of the Braves' farm system. Working as a minor league catching instructor, Courtney helped develop several future major league backstops, including Jerry Grote.

Scrap officially began his (American) minor league managerial career when he took the reins of the American Association Shreveport

Grave of Clint Courtney. Courtesy of Bill Lee.

Braves. The next season, he piloted Class AA Savannah of the Southern League. Everywhere he managed he had success. In 1973, Courtney replaced Bobby Hofman as manager of Triple-A Richmond. It was there that Courtney really made a name for himself, so much so that in 1974, he was mentioned as a successor to Eddie Mathews as Braves manager. When the job went to Clyde King instead, Courtney continued his stewardship of Richmond, knowing that it was just a matter of time until he secured a job at the major league level.

Unfortunately for Courtney, his time had almost run out. On June 16, 1975, he was playing Ping-Pong with one of his players during a road trip in Rochester, New York, when he was stricken with a fatal heart attack at the age of 48. Clint Courtney was buried at Mount Zion Cemetery in Hall Summit, Louisiana, in Plot N. His wife Dorothy and five children survived him.

BEN CHAPMAN (1908–1993)

During an era of baseball when players policed themselves and beanballs and spikes carried high were still the norm, Ben Chapman was amongst the toughest of the tough that the game had to offer. Like fellow southerner Ty Cobb, he played the game with reckless abandon and a win-at-all-costs attitude. Unfortunately for Chapman, his baseball career will forever be defined by his bench jockeying/race baiting of Jackie Robinson while he was manager of the Philadelphia Phillies.

He was given the nicknames the "Alabama Flash" and the "Tennessee Tactician" by sportswriters. To his teammates, however, he was known simply as Ben, Benny, or his preferred nickname, "Chappy." William Benjamin Chapman was born on Christmas Day 1908, in Nashville, Tennessee. While attending Phillips High School in Birmingham, Alabama, he was scouted and signed by the New York Yankees. After two seasons in the minors, where he played both third and shortstop, Chapman made the Yankees as an infielder in 1930. He had a fine rookie season at the plate, batting .316, with 10 homers and 81 RBI, but his erratic play in the infield necessitated a move to the outfield the following season. It was there that he flourished, and he eventually became known for his speed, quickness, and great defensive instincts. Yanks manager Joe McCarthy became so confident in his young outfielder's abilities that he often had him switch positions with Babe Ruth so that Chappy regularly played the "sun field," thus allowing an aging Babe to play in more visually hospitable conditions. This did not always sit well with Chappy, who often ragged on the Bambino about his eroding skills.

Chapman's play soon gained him a reputation for being a tough, no-nonsense player. Becoming the team's unofficial enforcer and chief instigator, he was always ready to come to the aid of a teammate in a pinch, even if it was someone whom he had a less-than-stellar relationship with, for example, Ruth. Unswervingly loyal to his team, Ben was often used by McCarthy to settle scores with other clubs. Well-liked by his teammates for the most part, Chappy had great affection and respect for several of his Yankee teammates, in particular, Lou Gehrig.

Interestingly, in his autobiography, former major league catcher Birdie Tebbetts talks about a brief conversation he had with Gehrig in May 1938, when the "Iron Horse" supposedly offered to buy him the "best suit he'd ever own" if he managed to land two good punches on Chapman. Gehrig's "offer" was supposedly made after Tebbetts and Chapman (now playing for the Red Sox) had gotten into a fight at Fenway Park a few days earlier. After a hard slide into home, Tebbetts took exception, and the two began slugging it out. Both players were ejected by umpire Joe Rue. Tebbetts's assertions were apparently nothing more than an old ballplayer embellishing a story, as Chapman and Gehrig continued to have a good relationship well after Chappy's departure to the Senators.

Other than Tebbetts's story, there is no recorded evidence that Chapman and Gehrig had any ill feelings toward one another. Chappy remembered Lou as the "kind of teammate and man I admired," adding,

> He went out there every day and never complained. He just went about doing his business. What a terrific guy he was. He would always greet you with a smile and open hand! I remember when he started getting sick. I remember him telling me how he just didn't feel right. No one knew at that point how sick he really was. When he died, I just broke down. It's still hard to talk about him to this day without getting emotional. God how I loved that man. Everyone did.

Perhaps the greatest example of Chapman's tenacity as a player occurred during a game at Griffith Stadium on April 25, 1933. Chapman was involved in a fourth-inning play at second base with Senators second baseman Buddy Myer that escalated into a bench-clearing brawl that would eventually see several hundred fans and dozens of District of Columbia police join in the fray. The aftermath of this donnybrook-turned-riot would see Chapman, Myer, and Senators pitcher Earl Whitehill (whom Chappy had knocked out while trying to get back to the Yankees' clubhouse) fined and suspended by American League president William Harridge. Afterward, both teams accused one another in the newspapers of "dirty pool." Washington players accused Chappy of targeting the Mississippi-born Myer because he was Jewish (he was actually half Jewish) and making anti-Semitic comments during the skirmish. It was a charge that both Chappy and McCarthy firmly denied, with McCarthy stating that Chapman had been playing the game as hard as he always had. Furthermore, McCarthy went out of his way to mention that Myer had intentionally tried spiking Gehrig on several occasions, and he also referenced a beaning at the hands of Whitehill two days earlier that had briefly knocked the Iron Horse unconscious. In retrospect, the Chapman-Myer brawl was simply a case of the players policing themselves.

As far as the charges of anti-Semitism are concerned, it should be noted that Chappy was known as an equal opportunity agitator, taking every opportunity to get under an opponent's skin. If that meant calling someone like Hank Greenberg a kike or Joe DiMaggio a dago or wop, then so be it. No one was off limits. As Bill Dickey once remarked, "Chappy would get on his own mother if it meant getting an edge on the field."

One long-standing urban legend charges that Chapman taunted Jewish fans at Yankee Stadium with Nazi salutes and anti-Semitic epithets. Yet, there has never been any hard documentation of Chapman ever using a Nazi salute.

Chapman played for New York until June 14, 1936, when he was traded to, of all teams, the Senators, for reserve outfielder Jake Powell. The move coincided with the team debuting their new center fielder, a young lad from San Francisco named Joseph Paul DiMaggio. Chapman would go on to play for seven teams during his big-league career. A four-time American League All-Star, he appeared in 1,707 games in 15 seasons, with a lifetime .302 batting average, 1,958 hits, and 977 RBI. Other notable accomplishments included leading the Junior Circuit in stolen bases from 1931 to 1933, as well as 1937, with a career total of 287, and scoring 100 or more runs six times. He also collected the first-ever hit in an All-Star Game in 1933. To top it off, Chapman had a brief second career as a pitcher in the mid-1940s, accruing an 8–6 record, with a 4.26 ERA in 21 games for the Brooklyn Dodgers. When analyzed on the basis of pure stats, one can come to the conclusion that Chapman had a solid career in baseball. Of course, his stats as a player don't tell the entire story.

Chapman's tenure as the Phillies' manager in the mid-1940s, specifically 1947 to 1948, is marked by his racial taunting and bench jockeying of Jackie Robinson. While many historians question how Chapman got a job as a major league manager in the first place, his hiring was simply a combination of being in the right place at the right time and being part of baseball's "Good 'Ole Boy Network," as he was hired by former teammate and friend Herb Pennock, who was running the Phillies at the time. It also didn't hurt that he already had experience managing at the minor league level, since he piloted the Richmond Colts of the Piedmont League in 1942 and 1944 (he was suspended from baseball for one year in 1943 for assaulting an umpire). Both Pennock and Phillies owner Bob Carpenter felt that a move to a more intense, driven personality was needed for the club, and Chappy fit the bill perfectly.

Under his leadership, the team showed some improvement, although they still finished dead last, with a horrendous record of 46–108, by far the worst in baseball. The next season, Chappy guided his troops to a 69–85 record, good enough for fifth place in the National League and a 23-game improvement over the previous campaign. Chapman kept his temper pretty much intact, as he was tossed from games only four times in 1946, two of those instances coming in contests against Brooklyn. None of Chapman's ejections were for unusual behavior, and certainly not a portent of things to come when Robinson made his debut a year later. Interestingly, of Chapman's 21 career ejections, both as player and manager, he was only tossed once for bench jockeying. That lone incident occurred at League Park in Cleveland in June 1936, in a game against the Indians. In 1947, it was not Chapman, but one of his coaches, Benny Culp, who was tossed for bench jockeying in a game against the Giants in August.

It retrospect, given when and where he was born and raised, it should come as no shock that Chapman would target Robinson. In fact, many in the press expected it. Even before the season started, columnist Bob Considine expressed concern that several "hotheads" were preparing to do their best to stop Rickey's "Great Experiment," as many called it. While he wasn't alone in his feelings, Chapman has been rightfully singled out for the sheer viciousness and vituperative nature of his verbal assaults.

The worst of it came on April 22, 1947, the first time that the Phillies and Dodgers met with Robinson in the lineup. The game, played at Ebbets Field, was a Tuesday afternoon affair and the first of a three-game set. Just 6,790 of the "Flatbush Faithful" were in attendance that day, and by all accounts, there was nothing showing in the Phillies' pregame demeanor to indicate that the game would be different from any other that the two teams would play against one another.

Robbie was scheduled to bat second in the bottom of the first. As he stood in the on-deck circle, he could hear the verbal assault begin in earnest. The situation went from bad to worse as his name was announced over the public address system. As he dug in, waiting for the first pitch from Dutch Leonard, almost everyone in the ballpark could now hear the filth coming from the visitor's dugout. Even at this early point of the game, only the most ardent apologist could conclude that what was going on was nothing more than standard bench jockeying. In his 1972 aubiography, Robinson describes his feelings about what happened that day, saying,

> I have to admit that this day, of all the unpleasant days in my life, brought me nearer to cracking up than I ever had been. Perhaps I should have become inured to this kind of garbage, but I was in New York City and unprepared to face the kind of barbarism from a northern team that I had come to associate with the Deep South. . . . For one wild and rage-crazed minute I thought, "To hell with Mr. Rickey's 'noble experiment.' It's clear it won't succeed." Then, as I thought of Mr. Rickey—how his family and friends had begged him not to fight for me and my people—I thought of all his predictions, which had come true. Mr. Rickey had come to a crossroads and made a lonely decision. I was at a crossroads. I would make mine. I would stay.

Fittingly, Robinson scored the winning run in the eighth inning when he singled, then attempted to steal second base. Catcher Andy Seminick made an ill-advised throw that sailed into center field, which allowed Robbie to reach third base. Moments later, he gleefully scored the winning run when Gene Hemanski singled him in. Final score, Dodgers 1, Phillies 0. It was a small moment of retribution for Robinson, but it wouldn't last for long.

The next day, the Phillies were up to their old tricks as they continued with their verbal attacks. Robinson's teammate Eddie Stanky came to his defense, challenging the Phillies to a brawl. When Chapman obliged, Stanky went ballistic. Cooler heads prevailed when players from both sides intervened. The next day, Chapman stayed at the hotel, excusing himself from the game because he was feeling under the weather. Sadly, for Robinson, the three games against the Phillies were just the beginning of an ordeal that would last several seasons.

Chapman always maintained that the verbal abuse directed at Robinson was solely for the purpose of getting him off his game, and that even though he was against integration, it was nothing personal. One would be hard-pressed to find any excuse for Chapman's vile behavior, yet there were many people in organized baseball who gave him a pass. One such entity was the *Sporting News*, which firmly believed that Chapman's bench jockeying should neither have been singled out nor curtailed. Such executives and owners as Connie Mack; Tom Yawkey; Herb Pennock; Red Sox general manager Eddie Collins; Giant owner Horace Stoneham; and Yankee owners Larry MacPhail, Dan Topping, and Del Webb remained silent on the matter.

League and team officials eventually arranged for a photo-op handshake between Robinson and Chapman, with the two adversaries holding a bat rather than shaking hands. By 1948, attitudes had changed somewhat toward Robinson and integration. Larry Doby was starting his second campaign with the Indians after making his debut a few weeks after Robinson's. In addition, several high-profile black players were making their entry into the leagues, including the legendary Satchel Paige. The tide was finally turning against the Old Guard. Chapman also felt that by 1948, the league was protecting Robinson, and that league offices had sent down word that anyone who threw at him would get his manager fired. Whether that edict was handed down to all teams or just the Phillies was never made clear, but Chapman felt that the league was taking away one of his pitchers' primary weapons, the "brushback" pitch. Despite the unwritten rule, Chapman told his pitchers in no uncertain terms, "I don't care what color his skin is, if you need to knock him down, do so."

Chapman's tenure as Phillies skipper came to an end when he was given his pink slip on July 16, 1948. Phillies president Bob Carpenter turned control of the club over to Eddie Sawyer, who had managed much of the team's young talent in the minors. He was also the complete opposite of Chapman in terms of personality. Sawyer, of course, would go on to fame in 1950 as manager of the famous "Whiz Kids."

Contrary to popular belief, Chapman was not run out of the game after his firing as many have suggested. After taking the rest of the 1948 season off, he went back to managing at the minor league level before taking a coaching position with the Reds in 1952. Although he would have other coaching offers, he decided to walk away from Major League Baseball because he didn't like where the game was headed, with players making too much money and the league having too much power. After one more season managing in the minors, he left professional baseball for good to concentrate on a career in insurance, where he became highly successful.

With the release of the movie *42* in the spring of 2013, there has been renewed interest in Ben Chapman, both the player and person. Many revisionist historians, in particular those whose political views

Grave of Ben Chapman. Courtesy of Bill Lee.

lean far left, have come to the conclusion that Chapman was nothing more than a clueless, dimwitted, ignorant, redneck racist. Of course, nothing could be further from the truth. Ironically, it was not until he became a born-again Christian that Chappy found the error of his ways. As he grew older, he took great pride and found solace in the fact that he was able to change his views toward blacks and minorities. Those who had a chance to get to know him during this period of his life pretty much all agree that he was truly a changed man.

In a 1994 article in *Sporting News* (published after his death), Chapman states,

> A man learns about things and mellows as he grows older. I think maybe I've mellowed. Maybe I went too far in those days, when I thought it was okay to try to throw guys off-balance and upset them with jockeying. I'm sorry for many of the things I said. I guess the world changes, and maybe I've changed, too.

These seem like the words and reflections of a man who had grown to see the folly of his ways, as he had evolved into a far different man than the one who had led the charge against Robinson. This was the Ben Chapman the majority of baseball fans never got to read about and, for many, never had the chance to come to accept.

Ben Chapman spent his remaining years living in Hoover, Alabama, where he continued to follow the Yankees and would occasionally work as a guest instructor at places like Samford University and local area high schools. He passed away from a heart attack at his home in Hoover on July 7, 1993, at the age of 84, and is interred at Birmingham's Elmwood Cemetery in Block 34, Lot 418.

ENOS SLAUGHTER (1916–2002)

Enos Slaughter was a tough, hard-nosed, no-nonsense ballplayer who played most of his career with the St. Louis Cardinals. He was signed in 1935 by Cardinal scout Billy Southworth, who would later manage the Cards. Slaughter started out with the Class D farm team in Martinsville, Virginia. Coming up in 1938, he played the game with abandon and nonstop hustle. He became a regular in the Cards' outfield in 1939. Slaughter was the first player noted for running to first base when issued a base on balls. This trademark started in the minor leagues, where he adopted his energetic playing style.

In 1936, in Columbus, Georgia, Slaughter's manager, Eddie Dyer, caught him walking off the field and confronted him. He said, "Son, if you're tired, I'll get somebody else." In a 1994 interview with the Associated Press, Slaughter recalled, "From that day on, I ran from spot to spot."

Slaughter is best remembered for his "Mad Dash" from first base that scored the winning run for the Cardinals against the Boston Red Sox in the eighth inning of Game 7 of the 1946 World Series. With the score tied, 3–3, Slaughter opened the bottom of the eighth with a single. Two outs later, he was still on first base. With Harry Walker at bat, Slaughter took off for second on what he later said was nothing more than an attempted steal. Walker hit the ball over short and into center field. With Slaughter steaming around second, Leon Culberson fielded the ball. Third base coach Mike Gonzalez tried to stop Slaughter as Culberson relayed the ball to Johnny Pesky, but Slaughter ran right past Gonzalez. Pesky held the ball for an instant and then hurried his throw to catcher Roy Partee. Slaughter slid past the tag for the deciding run. "On that particular play, he outran that ball the last 10 yards," Stan Musial said. "He just outran it. It was an exciting play and won the Series for us." The Mad Dash is commemorated outside Busch Stadium in St. Louis by a bronze statue depicting Slaughter sliding home.

Slaughter was not without controversy during his career. He was accused of being one of the leaders in the racist taunting of Jackie Robinson, who broke Major League Baseball's color line in 1947. There were allegations that Slaughter had tried to lead the Cardinals in a strike against Robinson, but St. Louis sportswriter Bob Broeg sets the record straight in his autobiography. Broeg writes,

> It's a canard that the Cardinals were going to strike. I was there, and it never happened. I quote [National League president] Ford Frick in my autobiography as saying the Cardinals were more fair to Robinson than any other team. That was because of Dyer, who told his players, "If you get Robinson mad, he'll beat you all by himself."

Slaughter always denied that he had anything against the Dodger star. "There's been a hell of a lot of stuff written on that because I was a Southern boy," he said in a 1994 interview. "It's just a lot of baloney."

The famous spiking of Robinson happened during a close play at first base in August 1947. Robinson later insisted it was intentional. Papers at the time never reported the spiking incident as intentional. According to Broeg, "Nobody knows if Enos deliberately spiked him or not. That's just the way Enos played. The previous year, he put Eddie Stanky in the hospital twice." Slaughter also spiked Bill Rigney later that season at the Polo Grounds. "I spiked a lot of guys that I hadn't intended to because they had their foot blocking the base paths," Slaughter writes in his autobiography. "The color of Robinson's skin was the farthest thing from my mind while I was trying to beat out a low throw to first base." The so-called "problems" with Robinson reportedly kept Slaughter out of the Hall of Fame for years.

It should be noted that Giant outfielder Monte Irvin, another of baseball's first black stars, was a friend of Slaughter and a member of the committee that elected him to the Hall of Fame. Slaughter was also a hero and mentor of sorts to many black Cardinal players who came along years after his retirement, for instance, Lou Brock. Slaughter served three years in the Pacific Theater during World War II, helping to organize baseball teams and leagues on Tinian and Saipan. The games drew crowds of 20,000 or more and were instrumental in helping build moral amongst the troops.

Traded to the Yankees in 1954, Slaughter became a part-time player and devastating pinch hitter. He also spent some time with the Kansas City A's and Milwaukee Braves. He was a 10-time All-Star, playing on five pennant winners and four world championship teams. He coached the Duke University Blue Devils baseball team from 1971 to 1977. He also supported the Person County Museum of History, Piedmont Community College, and the Duke Children's Classic. In nineteen major league seasons, Slaughter accrued a lifetime batting average of .300, with 2,383 hits, 169 homers, and 1,304 RBI in 2,380 games. He also stole 71 bases and scored 1,018 runs. He was elected to the National Baseball Hall of Fame in 1985.

Enos Slaughter passed away at Duke University Medical Center on August 12, 2002, at the age of 86. He died two weeks after undergoing colon surgery to repair perforated stomach ulcers. At the time of his passing, he was also suffering from non-Hodgkin's lymphoma, which he had been diagnosed with earlier in the spring and for which he had started a regimen of chemotherapy and radiation treatment in late May.

Married and divorced five times, Slaughter was survived by his four daughters: Gaye (a nurse at Duke University Hospital), Patricia, Rhonda, and Sharon. He was interred at the Allensville United Methodist Church Cemetery in Allensville, North Carolina.

2

BEER DRINKERS AND HELL-RAISERS

Alcohol. It's as much a part of baseball tradition as hotdogs, peanuts, and crackerjacks. Since the beginning of the pro game, players have consumed huge quantities of it, sometimes at alarming rates. Some players, like Hall of Famers Mickey Welch and Casey Stengel, were able to control their imbibing. Others, for instance, Rabbit Maranville, realized that both their career and life were at a crossroads because of it. Then there were such players as Terry Larkin and King Kelly, who seemed destined for a crash and burn due to the overindulgence of alcohol, whether it be beer or whiskey. Many people, including former ballplayers Bill Sunday and Ryne Duran, brought attention to the effects of alcohol on players, while also railing against its sale at ballparks. Alcohol is a touchy subject for Major League Baseball, as beer sponsors help drive commercial revenue, both at the ballpark and on radio and television. It will literally be a cold day in hell before Major League Baseball and alcoholic beverages part ways.

TERRY LARKIN (1856–1894)

Right-handed pitcher Terry Larkin seemed destined for stardom after his first three seasons in the major leagues. Unfortunately for the Brooklyn native, arm injuries, combined with alcohol and mental health issues, derailed not only his career, but his life, at the young age of 38.

Born Frank S. Larkin in Brooklyn, New York, in 1856, he gained notoriety as a teenager for his rough-and-tumble, hard-nosed style of play. Larkin was known by the first name "Terry" by the majority of his friends, although he was almost always mentioned in the press by his birth name. Larkin's career was short, as he pitched for five teams during a six-season career. He made his major league debut on May 20, 1875, for the New York Mutuals in a 7–4 loss to the Boston Red Stockings at the Union Grounds in Brooklyn. Larkin pitched a decent game, as he gave up 9 hits in 9 innings of work, while giving up just 3 earned runs. The game, which lasted all of two hours and five minutes, was won by Joe Borden.

After his lone appearance, Larkin went back to play with the Atlantic Club. He got his big break the next season when he signed to play with the Hartfords of Brooklyn, posting a 29–25 record, with a 2.14 ERA and 501 innings pitched. In 1878, he was signed by Al Spalding to replace George Bradley for the Chicago White Stockings. Larkin didn't disappoint; he started and completed 56 of the team's 60 games that season, going 29–26, with a 2.24 ERA and 506 innings pitched. Despite arm problems that plagued him the next season, he again threw more than 500 innings, while going 31–23, with an ERA of 2.44. He hoped a period of rest would revive his pitching arm.

Signing with the Troy Trojans in 1880, Larkin appeared in just five games before getting his release. Despondent about both his release and arm problems, he took to drinking even more than usual and could almost always be found in one of Brooklyn's local saloons, where he would spend his evenings hoisting beers and doing shots of whiskey. It was also about this time that he apparently began carrying a pocket pistol. While the reasons for this move remain unclear, many of his former teammates felt that he was becoming more aggressive and, at times, extremely depressed. He began blaming his arm injury on former managers, particularly Cap Anson, for overworking him. Despite his personal struggles, Larkin eventually found work as a second baseman in the minors in the Eastern Championship Association and League Alliance in 1881 and 1882; however, playing in the minors didn't help with his drinking problem or mood swings.

On April 24, 1883, in a drunken fit of rage, Larkin shot his wife Kate (Catherine) in the cheek after she complained about his drunkenness. He then outdid himself by shooting and wounding police officer Timothy Phelan, who responded to the disturbance. Holding off police with his revolver, he attempted to commit suicide by slashing his own throat with a straight razor. Arrested and taken to St. Catherine's Hospital, he again tried to kill himself by running headlong into a steam register. The *Brooklyn Daily Eagle* reported that as he was being restrained, he yelled out to a policeman, "For God sake, hit me in the head and put an end to my suffering." Despite the sheer violence of the attack, Larkin got off lucky, as Kate, in a typical example of battered wife syndrome, refused to press charges, even citing doctors who told her that he was not responsible for his actions because of his state of mind. Larkin's excuse for the shootings was that he had been suffering from malaria and had turned to liquor to help with his suffering, since the medication he was taking for his malady was doing him no good.

Back on the street and unable to play ball due to the severity of his wounds, the ace took the remainder of the year off, but this didn't prevent him from self-medicating, as he continued consuming his magic elixir of beer and whiskey. Even before he was completely healed, Larkin began seeking employment for the following baseball season. His search for work would not prevent him from once again getting himself mixed up with the police.

On February 18, 1884, he was arrested once more, this time for threatening to shoot his father. Yet again, his stay in jail was brief. After his release from the clink he signed on to play second base for the Richmond Virginias of the Eastern League. He finally got another shot to play in the majors when Richmond joined the American Association as a mid-season replacement for the disbanded Washington Nationals. Considering what he had put himself through, his play with the newly named Virginians wasn't that bad, at least in the field, where he was second on the team in fielding, with a .907 percentage. At the plate, Larkin was pretty terrible, batting a paltry .201 in 40 games. Richmond would wind up being his final stop in the majors.

The next season, Larkin played with Norfolk of the Eastern League, after which he briefly played semipro ball with local teams in the greater Brooklyn area. In January 1886, Larkin was arrested again, this time after challenging James McEnery, who employed him as a bartender, to a duel with pistols. Again he got off lightly. No matter how hard he tried, he could never seem to get his act together. The odds were stacked against him due to his alcoholism. Combined with his apparent mental health issues, Larkin was in an impossible situation.

For almost 120 years, it was believed by baseball historians that Larkin took his own life by slitting his throat, but the true facts of his demise are quite different and, in a way, much sadder, as the last years of his life saw him living in utter despair and poverty. The *Brooklyn Daily Eagle* reported in its June 20, 1894, edition that the former pitcher and infielder, now homeless and friendless, had been found, suffering from alcoholism, on First Avenue in Brooklyn by a policeman from the Fifth Precinct. Removed to the Eastern District Hospital, he passed on September 16 due to chronic nephritis and marasmus, which is a severe protein-energy malnutrition characterized by energy deficiency. One could make the case that, in the end, Terry Larkin did commit suicide, by way of the bottle, slowly and insidiously. He was buried two days later at Calvary Cemetery in Woodside, Queens, in Section 12, Range 22, Plot C, Grave 1.

KING KELLY (1857–1894)

Kelly, who played every position, was one of the greatest players of his era and baseball's first superstar. He started his career with the Reds in 1878, and soon was given the title "King of Baseball," becoming the number-one idol of the nation. Joining Cap Anson's Chicago team in 1880, he helped lead a group of hard-drinking, fast-living men to five National League titles.

A man who loved the limelight, Kelly could be found most every night on the town, enjoying what Chicago had to offer. A strikingly handsome man, his baseball celebrity only amplified his touch with the ladies. He could have his pick of almost any woman he wanted, and usually did. He didn't have to frequent whorehouses like some players, because the ladies came to him, a real accomplishment during those conservative Victorian times of the 1880s. An impeccable dresser, he wore silk shirts and spats, and was once named one of the best dressed men in the United States.

In an era when games were played during the day and schedules were only about 120 games a season, there was plenty of time for someone like Kelly to carouse and night crawl. Cap Anson once sent out a detective to tail Kelly, and the investigator came back with a report that he had seen "Old Kel" drinking lemonade at 3:00 a.m. When confronted, Kelly angrily replied, "It was straight whiskey! I never drank lemonade at that hour in my life!"

Lost in the mystique of his legend is the fact the King Kelly was one hell of a ballplayer. He hit .300 or better eight times, leading the National League in hitting with a .354 average in 1884, and .388 in 1886. He also led the league three times each in doubles and runs scored, and once scored six runs in one game. Kelly was also a daring base runner, stealing at least 50 bases for four successive years, once stealing six bases in a game. His baserunning feats led to a popular song in 1889 entitled "Slide, Kelly, Slide."

One interesting tale about Kelly goes like this: In a game in Chicago one terribly hot summer day in the mid-1880s, Kelly was playing right field. Tired and hot, he brought a mug of beer with him to the outfield. He decided to take a few sips as White Stocking pitcher Larry Corcoran heaved a fastball right down the middle of the plate. The hitter, whose name has been lost to time, swung and sent a screaming shot to right. Without missing a step, Kelly, mug in hand, ran and made a one-handed catch and, according to some witnesses, never spilled a drop of the precious liquid.

Anson sold Kelly to the Braves in 1887, for a record $10,000 in one of the biggest deals in baseball's early history. Chicago fans were so upset they boycotted their team, except when Boston played there. Jumping to the Boston Players' League Club in 1890 as player-manager, his team captured the league's pennant. He hung around the game for a few more years but was pretty much through as a player, winding up his career with the Giants for a spate of games in 1893.

After his major league career was over, Kelly managed in the minors for a while, but as always, his love of the nightlife made his stint in the bushes a short one. Kelly went back to work doing what he did best, being "King Kelly." He opened a saloon in New York that actually made decent money for a while, but the establishment eventually folded because Kelly was more interested in being a customer than an owner. Never known as a man who held onto his money, he was generous to a fault with his friends.

In late 1894, Kelly was invited to go to Boston to appear at the Palace Theatre. Hopping a steamer from New York, he caught a cold.

The cold eventually turned into pneumonia, which took his life on November 8. He was only 36 years old.

If one thing can be said about Mike "King" Kelly, he definitely enjoyed life and thoroughly loved the game of baseball. While one can never condone his bad habits, he was one of the most colorful and interesting characters in the history of the national game. King Kelly is buried in Mount Hope Cemetery in Boston on Walnut Avenue, Lot 1650, Grave 21.

ED MCKEAN (1864–1919)

Largely forgotten by most modern baseball historians, Edwin John McKean was a member of one of the rowdiest teams of all time, the 1890s Cleveland Spiders. The son of Martin and Margaret McKean, both Irish immigrants, he was born in Grafton, Ohio, on June 6, 1864. McKean began his career in 1884, with the Youngstown, Ohio, entry of the Iron and Oil Association, which was comprised of teams from Pennsylvania and Ohio. In 1885, he played with the Nashville Sounds of the Southern League and, in 1886, split time between the Rochester Maroons and Providence Grays of the International League. Signing a contract with the Cleveland Blues of the American Association for 1887, he almost immediately became the team's starting shortstop. Moving with the team when he joined the National League for 1889, McKean didn't miss a beat, as he batted .318 for the newly named Spiders. McKean would go on to bat .300 or better five times during his eleven seasons in the National League, including a career-high .357 in 1894.

Defensively, "Mack," as he was known to his teammates, was never noted for having great range, and his throwing arm was never the greatest. Thickly set, he also had the tendency to put on weight during both the regular season and off-season. Despite his defensive shortcomings, McKean was an essential component of a Cleveland club that became one of the powerhouse teams in the National League in the 1890s.

Although the Spiders, like their main rivals of the time, the Baltimore Orioles, were known for roughhouse tactics on the field, McKean was an exception to the rule, as he was known for clean but hard play. His best years were from 1893 to 1896, when he batted over .300 and drove in more than 100 runs each year. In 1895 and 1896, the Spiders participated in the Temple Cup Series, the equivalent of the modern-day World Series. Cleveland won their only championship in 1895, by which time, despite his error totals, McKean was considered one of the premier shortstops in the National League. His stay in Cleveland would end in a rather strange fashion in the spring of 1899.

The owners of the Spiders, who also owned the St. Louis Browns, decided that it was more financially lucrative to have a winning team in St. Louis. Thus, they began assigning the best Cleveland players to the St. Louis roster. McKean became one of the "Cleveland casualties" when his contract was sent to the newly renamed Perfectos on March 29, 1899. In St. Louis, he was eventually supplanted at shortstop by future Hall of Famer Bobby Wallace. In what proved to be his final big-league campaign, McKean batted a career-low .260 in just 67 games in 1899. Given his release by St. Louis management at the end of the season, he would never return to the majors. After being out of baseball for two seasons, McKean returned to play pro ball as player-manager of the Rochester Bronchos of the Eastern League in 1902. He retired from baseball for good after the 1908 season.

During the course of McKean's major league career, he accrued a lifetime .302 average, with 66 homers, 1,124 RBI, and 323 stolen bases in 1,654 games. After his baseball career, Mack delved into several business ventures, including wrestling, boxing, and horse racing. Like many of his Spider teammates, he was known for being a two-fisted drinker during his playing days, so it was no surprise when he opened an inn in Cleveland where he was not only the proprietor, but also a bartender. Of course, being a bartender for his own establishment brought its own set of problems, and his drinking, already a problem for many years, escalated.

McKean's alcoholism eventually led to severe physical problems, most notably gastric ulcers. It was this malady that led to his demise on the evening of August 16, 1919, at his home, which was located at 2615 Jay Avenue. Mack, who was just 55 years old, was survived by his wife Belle, three sons, Edward, Robert, and Martin, and a daughter, Marie. He was buried in Calvary Catholic Cemetery in Cleveland in Section 8, Lot 648 on August 19.

BOB SPADE (1877–1924)

Right-handed pitcher Bob Spade was a hard-partying power drinker who played the majority of his four-season career with the team that he grew up rooting for, the Cincinnati Reds. The son of Calvin and Louise Spade, he was born in Akron, Ohio, on January 4, 1877. Growing up, Bob was known to friends as "Ace," in reference to the ace of spades. His first stop in professional ball was in 1896, at the age of 19, with the Class C Youngstown Puddlers of the Interstate League, where he pitched and played outfield.

Spade's baseball career after the Interstate League is sketchy at best, although there is hard evidence that he played a stint of semipro ball with the Kent Base Ball Club of Kent, Ohio, and also tried to latch onto other teams in Ohio and New York. The next minor league team with available records that he toiled for was the 1905 Macon Brigands of the "Sally League" (South Atlantic League), for which he pitched to a 25–8 record. The following season, he again won 20 games, this time split between the Brigands and the Akron Rubbernecks of the Ohio-Pennsylvania League. In 1907, he went 18–12 for the famous Atlanta Crackers of the Southern Association. This brought him to the attention of the Cincinnati Reds, who selected him in the Rule 5 Draft on September 1.

Spade made his major league debut as a 30-year-old "rookie" on September 22, 1907, in the first game of a doubleheader against the Giants at Cincinnati's Palace of the Fans. He pitched a gem, hurling a complete-game shutout and defeating "Iron Man" Joe McGinnity and the Giants, 1–0. The contest, which only took one hour and thirty minutes to execute, saw Spade strike out two and walk four. The *New York Times* reported in its September 23 edition that Spade pitched "clever ball and showed nerve in several bad situations." Spade would pitch twice more that season for the Reds, both complete-game losses. He lost, 1–0, to George McQuillan and the Phillies on September 29, and 4–3 to the Pirates and Lefty Leifield on October 6, the last day of the season. While his record was only 1–2, Spade found solace in the fact that his ERA was 1.00 in 27 innings.

Because of his work in September, Spade was given a shot to crack the Reds' rotation the next spring by new manager John Ganzel. The Reds would play below expectations in 1908, as they finished with a

73–81 record, good enough for fifth place in the National League. In the midst of what would be his best major league season, Spade would see himself become part of a series of crazy transactions that left both he and fans confused and wondering.

The wild shenanigans started on July 8, when the Reds unexpectedly placed him on waivers. Two teams, the Giants and Boston Doves, put claims in on him. With both teams asserting rights to the pitcher, National League executives decided to settle the matter by way of a "drawing" that would decide the winner of the waiver claim. This "drawing," which was held on July 9, saw the Giants come out victorious. The next day, John McGraw worked out a deal where he sent Spade back to the Reds, along with $5,000, in return for Dave Brain and Jake Weimer. In the span of a little more than 48 hours, Spade had been waived to New York and traded back to Cincinnati without ever having thrown a pitch in a Giants uniform.

There is one interesting side note to Spade's trade back to Cincinnati. Pitcher Jake Weimer, one of the players involved in the deal, told Reds management in no uncertain terms that he would not report to New York unless he was given half of the $5,000 that the Reds received in the transaction. When management told him no, Weimer jumped his contract to play outlaw baseball in Chicago. Spade, who had become a fan favorite, finished the season with a 17–12 mark and a 2.74 ERA in 249.1 innings pitched.

After the season, Spade joined the Reds on a tour of Cuba, playing the outfield while appearing in six games as a pitcher. In 1909, he decided to hold out for more money. In a letter published in the *Pittsburgh Gazette* on April 9, Spade stated the following: "I am through with the Cincinnati Club. I was not treated right and will not be a member of the Reds this season unless someone else undergoes a great change of heart." While Spade eventually signed for a modest raise, his holdout wound up setting the tone for the rest of his season. The new Reds manager, Clark Griffith, looked at Spade as a troublemaker and malcontent, and used him sparingly. Spade only started in 13 games all season, going a mediocre 5–5, with a 2.85 ERA. The next season would again see Spade get himself in trouble with Reds management, although this time it would be for off-field problems.

In late May, Spade was involved in the escapades of his teammate, rookie outfielder Swat McCabe. Spade and McCabe had apparently gone out on the town together and became quite inebriated and rowdy. When McCabe was arrested for disorderly conduct, Reds president Gary Herrmann suspended Spade and fined him $200. Having enough of his poor attitude, drinking, and carousing, the Reds waived him to the St. Louis Browns on June 15. The change of scenery did him no good, and he was let go after just seven games. Spade signed on to play with the Newark Indians of the Eastern League, which was managed by Joe McGinnity. Also on the Indians was the eccentric and hard-drinking Rube Waddell, a man who could match Spade drink for drink. Newark would be Spade's last professional stop as a player, although he did manage briefly in the Blue Grass League in 1912. Also in 1912, in March, the *Providence Evening News* reported that Spade was planning to open up a baseball school in Cincinnati. Whatever became of this endeavor is anyone's guess. He later opened up what would become a highly successful saloon in Cincinnati, but it was forced to close due to Prohibition. With little means of support outside of his business, Spade turned to bootlegging to sustain himself, which he did for several years.

On December 6, 1923, Spade was arraigned in Cincinnati municipal court for possession of liquor (bootleg whiskey). Luck smiled his way for a change, for the presiding judge, the Honorable Meredith Yeatman, happened to be a huge baseball fan who remembered Spade's accomplishments with the Reds. Yeatman set a continuance of the trial for late December, after which Spade was fined a small sum.

Spade's health, which was no great shakes in the first place, continued to deteriorate at a rapid pace. Divorced and with no visible means of support, he died from atrophic cirrhosis of the liver on the night of September 7, 1924, at Seton Hospital in Cincinnati. If not for an outpouring of monetary gifts from hundreds of fans, he would have been buried in a pauper's grave. Instead, he was given a proper internment at Springfield Center Cemetery in Akron, Ohio, two days later. Bob Spade was just 47 years old.

"TURKEY MIKE" DONLIN (1878–1933)

One can only wonder what kind of ballplayer Michael Joseph Donlin would have been if he had applied himself to the game more and not had a fondness for the nightlife, and the life of an actor. As it was, he accrued a lifetime .333 average during parts of 12 major league seasons between 1899 and 1914. Most famous for being a member of John McGraw's Giant teams of the early 1900s, Donlin was one of the most colorful characters in the National League.

Born in Peoria, Illinois, on May 30, 1878, Mike's family later moved to Erie, Pennsylvania, where, as a child, he took up the rudiments of the game. Tragedy touched him early in life when, at the age of eight, both of his parents were killed in a bridge collapse. Bad luck would continue to dog him, as he contracted consumption in his early teens. Eventually moving west to California, his health took such an upswing that he was fit enough to take up athletics again. Donlin played pro ball, first with Los Angeles and then the Santa Cruz Sandcrabs, from whom the St. Louis Perfectos signed him to a contract in 1899. Originally a left-handed pitcher, he was converted to a full-time outfielder to make maximum use of his hitting prowess.

After batting .323 in 1899 and .326 in 1900, he jumped to the American League's Baltimore Orioles for the 1901 campaign. It was while playing for the Orioles that he struck up a friendship with manager John McGraw. Although the two would often be at odds during the coming years due to their different temperaments, they would remain lifelong friends. Donlin's Achilles' heel as both a person and ballplayer was his fondness for liquor. Prone to late nights of boozing and chasing women, he was a night crawler in the truest sense. His stay in the Monumental City ended in March 1902, when he was released by the Orioles after being arrested and sentenced to six months in jail after a wild drinking binge. (He reportedly propositioned two call girls and was caught urinating in public.) On May 20, while still in jail, Donlin signed a contract to play with the Cincinnati Reds.

Paroled a month early for good behavior, he joined the Reds in August, appearing in 34 games, while batting .287. His stay in the Queen City was notable for his great hitting and numerous drinking escapades. In the summer of 1904, at a time when he was batting .351, he went on a drinking rampage while the team was in St. Louis. This latest episode so outraged Reds manager Joe Kelley that he suspended his outfielder and traded him to the Giants as part of a multiplayer, three-team deal.

It was in New York, playing for his friend McGraw, that Donlin finally found his comfort zone. Always a loquacious individual who be-

Mike Donlin, 1909, White Borders Baseball Card. Courtesy of the author.

lieved in his own worth, he became a fan favorite due to his cocky personality and hitting heroics. It was also in New York that the press gave him the nickname "Turkey" (later changed to "Turkey Mike") because of his strutting walk. Remarking on his player, McGraw once chortled, "That Donlin was born on Memorial Day and has been strutting around ever since." A member of the Giant world championship team of 1905, Donlin batted .356 that season, as he continued to play hard on and off the field. One of his teammates on the 1905 squad, pitcher Hooks Wiltse, recalled that, "The combination of Donlin and a bottle was a bad mix. Trouble seemed to follow him, and the liquor never helped."

Marrying Broadway and vaudeville actress Mabel Hite in April 1906, it was thought that the union might settle him down somewhat, although it did not prevent misfortune from striking. In the seventh inning of a game played at Cincinnati on May 15, he was dealt a bad break when he injured himself sliding into second base. Newspapers published conflicting reports that Donlin had suffered a severe ankle sprain and then later a broken ankle. Either way, the resulting injury proved serious enough that he was lost to the team for several months. When he returned to play in a spate of games in August and September, newspapers noted that he did not seem like his old self and that his speed seemed diminished. For Donlin, just getting back on the field was an accomplishment in itself. After the season, he got the notion of following his wife onto the vaudeville circuit, even though he had no formal training. Contract problems arose before the start of the 1907 season, when he demanded a $600 raise. With Giant owner John T. Brush holding firm, Donlin decided to sit out the season and go full bore with his acting career.

Returning to the field in 1908, he once again proved to be the same haughty fellow remembered by the Polo Grounds faithful. The 1908 season proved to be one of his best, as he finished second in the National League with a .334 average. Donlin, who was always aware of his own self-worth, once again went to New York management asking for a pay raise. He commented on the matter to the *New York Times*, stating, "I have asked for more money for my playing in New York next year, and if I don't get it . . . I won't play." Giant secretary Fred Knowles responded, saying, "Donlin is one hard nut to crack. You offer the man a square deal, he accepts, then turns around and asks for more." Even as spring training approached, Donlin held firm on his monetary request. "They say I am to blame, but it's not the truth," he said. "I have not heard from Brush once. They know my terms, and I cannot go back from them, and besides, Mabel and I have contract obligations to fulfill. If I have to miss the season, well, then it's all off." True to his word, Donlin remained "retired" from the game for the next two seasons, although numerous reports of his reinstatement were reported at various times by the press.

Returning to the Giants in 1911, the slugger played just 12 games before being traded to the Boston Rustlers (Braves) that August. Even though he batted .312, Boston management deemed him to be a liability because of his diminished skills on the field.

Traded to the Pirates in February 1912, he was, at first, hesitant to report due to the fact that Mabel had been diagnosed with intestinal cancer the previous fall. Assured by his wife that she was not in any immediate danger, Donlin reported to the Pirates that spring, determined to show the baseball world that he still had the stuff to play the game. Even with the distraction of his wife's illness, Donlin managed to bat a respectable .313 for the campaign. When Mabel passed away in New York on October 22, at the age of 27, Donlin was devastated. "She battled to the last," was his response to a reporter. John McGraw remarked, "Mike dearly loved that girl."

Donlin's grieving was interrupted one month later by an incident befitting the television series *The Twilight Zone*. On November 22, a burly gentleman carrying a rather large package dropped by Murray's Restaurant in Manhattan to have dinner. Checking the package at the front door, he halfheartedly told the boy in charge, "Be awful careful with this. Don't drop it or it will blow up the place." The young man, thinking that the package might be a bomb, told his boss, who hurriedly took the parcel to an empty café next door. He submerged the package in a bucket of water. When police opened the package, they discovered a bronze urn containing the remains of Mabel Hite. The gentleman who checked the package in was Raymond Frye, head of the undertaking establishment that was entrusted by Donlin with his wife's remains. He was in the process of moving the ashes to a new columbarium when he stopped for dinner. Donlin, who was unamused by the incident, spent the rest of the winter grieving and getting his affairs in order. Picked up off waivers by the Phillies on Christmas Eve, he announced in late February that he would not report to spring training, instead concentrating on his vaudeville act. "I'm through," he declared to the press.

A change of heart later that summer saw him sign with Jersey City of the International League, a move that brought him to the attention of his old manager, John McGraw. McGraw named him to an all-star team that was to participate on a postseason barnstorming tour of European, African, and Asian nations. Showing good form during the tour, McGraw invited his old war horse to spring training for 1914, declaring, "That Donlin, he can hit in his sleep." Donlin appeared in just 34 games, mostly as a pinch hitter.

The 1914 season would prove to be his swan song. That October, he married actress Rita Ross, niece of Charles Ross of the comedy team of Ross and Fenton. Released that December, he attempted to catch on with the St. Louis Terriers of the Federal League, but nothing came of it. Ross supported her husband fully in his acting endeavors and even helped with financing when he invested in a semipro team based in Long Branch, New Jersey. In 1915, he appeared in his first film, the autobiographical *Right Off the Bat*. Donlin then managed the Memphis Chicks of the Southern Association in 1916, and with the entry of the United States into World War I, he was hired by the War Department to teach baseball to doughboys stationed in France.

Returning home, Donlin moved with his wife to Hollywood to be closer to the film industry. Although his film career never materialized the way he wanted it to, he appeared in more than 60 movies, in mostly untitled roles. During his time on the West Coast, he even found work as a scout for his old manager, McGraw. In 1927, Donlin was diagnosed with a condition known as "athlete's heart," which, at the time, was a common term for an enlarged heart associated with repeated strenuous exercise. Forced into semiretirement, his condition didn't stop him from continuing to carouse and party with his buddies and make the most of the Hollywood nightlife.

When Turkey Mike Donlin died in his sleep from a massive heart attack on the night of September 24, 1933, at the age of 55, he was lauded in the newspapers as one of the all-time great New York Giant players. John McGraw said that Donlin was "right up there with the best of them when it came to striking the ball." His good friend and drinking buddy John Barrymore remembered him as a "swell pal who was always good for a laugh." Although there was talk that he might be buried in California, Donlin's cremated remains were buried in Glenwood Cemetery in West Long Branch, New Jersey, in the Fenton family plot. As far as his legacy is concerned, perhaps Mike summed up his own life best when he commented on night baseball, which had recently been introduced to the minors: "Jesus! Think of taking a ballplayer's nights away from him!"

MICKEY WELCH (1859–1941)

Nicknamed "Smiling Mickey" due to his infectious smile and disposition, Mickey Welch was one of the premier pitchers of the 1880s. Born Michael Francis Walsh in Brooklyn's old Eighteenth Ward on July 4, 1859, he broke into the highest level of baseball in 1880, with the Troy Trojans, after just two seasons in the minors. His major league debut, on May 1, was an inauspicious affair, as Troy lost to Lee Richmond and the Worcester Ruby Legs, 13–1. Welch hurled to a 34–30 record during his rookie season, teaming up with Tim Keefe for a devastating one-two punch. Despite this great pitching tandem, the Trojans were a mediocre lot who were never able to finish out of the second division.

Welch made the move when the Troy franchise transitioned to New York in 1883, and started in the first game played at the Polo Grounds. He won 20 games or better seven straight years in New York, with a career high of 44 in 1885. He set the major league record for most consecutive batters struck out to begin a game on August 26, 1884, in a tilt against the Cleveland Blues. A true workhorse, he was usually good for 400 innings or more each year. Welch once attributed his durability on the mound to the fact that he didn't rely on velocity, but instead a devastating curveball and a pitch that one can only describe as a screwball.

Beginning in 1884, he had a clause inserted into his contract stipulating that he could not pitch more than every other day. Welch was quite happy playing in New York, with its saloons, restaurants, and bustling nightlife. Although he was just five feet, eight inches tall, he pitched and partied like a man twice his size. No stranger to John Barleycorn, he always enjoyed his cold grog after, and sometimes before, a game.

The Giants first-ever mascot/batboy, Fred Engle, remembered Welch as being "everyone's favorite" because of his wonderful disposition and adeptness at composing and reciting ditties. Engle's father, Nick, owned a popular restaurant called the Old Home Plate, which was a favorite of Welch and other Giant players. According to Engle, Welch knew as much about barley and hops as he did pitching. Welch, along with most of the Giants, lived at the Broadway Central Hotel, located on Broadway between 8th Avenue and 9th Avenue, easy access to some of New York's finest bars and eateries. On game day, most of the Giant players would head to the ballpark in an open horse-drawn carriage. It was during these excursions that, according to Engle, Welch would recite his poetry, much to the delight of teammates and cheering fans. His most famous dirges were, of course, dedicated to his favorite activity, drinking: "Pure elixir of malt and hops / Beats all the drugs and all the drops." He even wrote a dirge dedicated to Nick Engle's restaurant: "The Rarebit served at Nick Engle's Place / Would please the taste of any man. / A mug of ale without a question / When drunk on top would aid digestion."

Welch's habits off the field never affected his work on the field, as was noted by his manager, Jim Mutrie, who said the pitcher was a "conscientious lad whenever he stood in the box." Welch and Keefe, who, unlike his good friend, neither drank nor smoked, pitched the Giants to consecutive pennants in 1888 and 1889. Even though Welch liked to party and have a good time, he was always more grounded than the average player of his time. Engle believed that Welch had seen too many of his friends pass to the "Great Beyond" due to excess. According to Engle, Welch often recited the following popular poem: "Beneath these stones / Repose the bones / Of Alexander Prim / Who took his beer / For many a year / And then his beer took him." Welch often recited the poem when remembering a fallen teammate.

Becoming the second pitcher to win 300 games in 1890, he finished his career with a lifetime 307–210 record. Unlike many of his contemporaries, he lived to be an old man. After his retirement, he settled in Holyoke, Massachusetts, where he had played minor league ball. He later became steward of the Elks Club there. He returned to New York in 1912, to work at the Polo Grounds as a bleacher watcher, regaling fans with stories of his days as a player.

Mickey Welch, 1887, Old Judge Baseball Card. Courtesy of the Library of Congress.

While visiting a grandson in July 1941, he took ill, eventually passing away from complications from gangrene of the foot at the age of 82. His remains were sent back to New York, where he was buried at Calvary Cemetery in Woodside, Queens, in Section 4, Range 17, Plot 2, Grave 6. In 1973, Welch finally received his just due when he was elected to the National Baseball Hall of Fame by the Veterans Committee. It may have taken too long, but Mickey Welch finally took his place among baseball's all-time greats.

HACK WILSON (1900–1948)

Lewis "Hack" Wilson loved two things almost equally: a high fastball and a good time out. Once described as being "built along the lines of a beer keg, and not unfamiliar with its contents," he was, more than any other player of his time, except Babe Ruth, the epitome of the free-swinging slugger, a man who swung first and asked questions later. Born in the steel mill city of Ellwood City, Pennsylvania, Wilson was all muscle, a barrel-chested powerhouse with blacksmith arms and bulging thighs and calves on short legs that tapered to tiny feet. He had an 18-inch collar and a size five and a half shoe, sporting 200 pounds on a five-foot, six-inch frame. The prototypical slugger in the new age of the lively ball, he was also a man of extremes, a larger-than-life personality who was the perfect fit for Chicago, a 24-hour-a-day town that offered every excess imaginable.

There are two supposed reasons for Wilson's nickname. According to one explanation, it was taken from the late George Hackenschmidt, the famous old-time wrestler. Per another theory, it was due to his resemblance to Lawrence H. "Hack" Miller, a player who preceded him on the Cubs. Either way, the moniker was truly a perfect fit.

Quitting school in the sixth grade to work for a printer, Wilson later worked in a locomotive shop, shipyard, and steel mill before deciding on a career as a professional ballplayer. A catcher by trade, he signed with Martinsburg of the Blue Ridge League for 1921, but broke his leg while attempting to score in the first game of the season. After the injury healed, Wilson realized that he was unable to crouch properly behind the plate, thus necessitating his shift to the outfield the following season. Free of the stress and strain of catching, he batted a lusty

.366, with 30 homers. His play the next season with Portsmouth of the Virginia State League brought him to the attention of Giants manager John McGraw, who purchased his contract on September 6, 1923.

Making his major league debut on September 29, Hack appeared in three games for the rest of the season. The next year, he batted .295, with 10 homers and 57 RBI in 107 games. Playing alongside Ross Youngs and Irish Meusel in the outfield, Wilson's star appeared to be on the rise, although he only batted .233 in the World Series against the Senators. His struggles at the plate continued the following season, as he batted just .239 in 62 games before McGraw sent his contract to Toledo of the American Association on August 8, along with a player to be named later (Pip Koehler), for Earl Webb. Playing for the Mudhens proved to be just the tonic for the burly slugger, as he batted .343 in 55 games. His resurgence brought him to the attention of several major league clubs, including the Chicago Cubs, who eventually selected him in that October's Rule 5 Draft for a mere $5,000. Although the Giants vehemently protested the transaction to Commissioner Landis, insisting that they held an option on the young slugger, Wilson would remain property of the Cubs.

Wilson would go on to star in the Cub outfield for the next six seasons, playing under the tutelage of the great Joe McCarthy, who inserted him in the cleanup spot of what became one the most awesome lineups in the National League. At the plate, the menacing-looking Wilson was an intimidating figure who swung his bat with brute force. A two-fisted brawler who never backed down from a fight, Hack fancied himself to be such a good boxer that he pondered taking on professionals but was prevented from doing so upon edict from the commissioner. His outfield partner, Kiki Cuyler, remarked years later that, "Hack loved to have a good time, but woe to the man who got in his way when he was in a bad mood, especially if he had had a few. No one was safe from his wrath; players, newspapermen, and even fans were fair game."

A month before the 1931 season, Wilson was suspended and eventually traded for getting into a fight with a Chicago newspaperman, even though it was teammate and drinking buddy Pat Malone who had done most of the swinging. Wilson, whose partying exploits and drinking escapades became the stuff of legends, had a fondness for both beer and whiskey. A lack of discipline, coupled with a failure to stay in shape, drove Cub management crazy. McCarthy often tried to set his wayward star on the straight and narrow path to sobriety.

The most famous and hilarious of these episodes happened when McCarthy, after calling for a clubhouse meeting with his slugger, dropped a live worm into a glass of water. The worm happily swam about, with no ill effects. As Wilson intensely watched, McCarthy took another live worm and dropped it into a glass of bourbon. After a few seconds, the worm died. McCarthy asked, "What does that prove Lewis?" to which Wilson replied, "Well it just goes to prove that if you drink whiskey, you won't get worms!" McCarthy just sat there, shaking his head in amazement.

Chicago management once even considered using his teammates to keep tabs on him, but the idea was quickly scrapped when they realized that with such teammates as Kiki Cuyler, Pat Malone, Gabby Hartnett, Lynn Nelson, and Cliff Heathcote (who were all known to take a swig or two), it would be paramount to the blind leading the blind. In hindsight, it was an impossible task to keep Wilson under any sort of control, especially with easy access to Chicago's speakeasies, brothels, and nightclubs. He was able to pick and choose where and with whom he wanted to hang out and was often seen at both the park and in public in the company of celebrities (he once had his picture taken with gangster Al Capone).

A great defensive outfielder with a cannon arm, Wilson once played a part in one of the zaniest nonplays in baseball history. One afternoon, with his team trailing badly, he was standing in the outfield, half asleep, after another night of hard partying. When a pitching change was made, the angry starter heaved the ball all the way out to the right field wall, which was made of tin. The ball made a loud noise that woke up the half-dosing Wilson. Thinking that it was a base hit, he quickly retrieved the ball and threw a strike to second base. After the game, the outfielder's manager reportedly said that it was his best throw of the year.

Wilson is also remembered for two fly balls that he lost in the sun in Game 4 of the 1929 World Series against the Athletics. One of them went for a three-run, inside-the-park homer by Mule Haas. The blunders were part of a 10-run rally in the bottom of the seventh inning that propelled Philadelphia to 10–8 victory. Although he left the field in tears that day, in the end, Wilson had nothing to be ashamed off, leading all hitters with a .471 World Series average.

The next year, 1930, was a season for the ages, as he blasted a National League record 56 home runs, a feat that went unsurpassed for 70 years, and recorded the all-time record of 191 RBI, a mark that has stood the test of time. (RBI number 191 was not credited to him until 1999, when research showed that a RBI was accidentally credited by an official scorer to his teammate, Charlie Grimm.) One of the more amazing facets to that monster season was that Wilson accumulated his RBIs without the help of a grand slam.

Following his tremendous 1930 season, Hack dropped to a pedestrian .261, with 13 home runs and 61 RBI. Many blamed the poor showing on a personality clash with Cub manager Rogers Hornsby, who had replaced McCarthy during the 1930 season. Others, for example, writer Westbrook Pegler, noticed a distinct correlation between McCarthy's departure and the slugger's sudden decline. Pegler noted that, "McCarthy was Hack's biggest backer, and without him, he seemed lost." Frequent benchings and fines by Hornsby also did little to warm their already frosty relationship.

When Wilson was traded to the Cardinals in December 1931, he found himself going from one bad situation to another. When Cardinal president Branch Rickey sent him a contract for only $7,500 for the upcoming season, Hack vehemently protested, feeling that he was worth more than what the notoriously cheap "Mahatma" was prepared to pay. The slugger finally got a contract to his liking with a trade to the Brooklyn Dodgers on January 23, 1932.

The '32 season would prove to be his last decent one in a major league uniform, as he batted .297, with 23 homers and 123 RBI in just 135 games. He would appear in a mere 117 games in 1933, and only 74 in 1934, as years of excessive drinking and partying turned him into a shell of his former self. He would play in his final seven games after a September 1934 trade to the Phillies. Released after the season, he finished his career with Albany of the International League and Portland of the Pacific Coast League in 1935.

His career over, Wilson worked at various jobs, including one as an emcee at a Chicago nightclub. His last known job was as a manager of a municipal swimming pool in Baltimore. Nearing the end of his life and having faced numerous health problems and financial reverses, it became apparent that he had found the error of his ways. Appearing on the CBS radio show "We the People," a sober Wilson talked about his life and the effects of "Demon Rum" on it:

> Today there are many kids in and out of baseball who think that just because they have natural talent, they have the world by the tail. It isn't so. In life, you need many more things besides talent. Things like good advice and common sense. I'd like to say this to the youth of America. Kids, don't be afraid to take advice. . . . Learn to be considerate of others. That's the only way to live. If anyone tries to tell you different . . . you tell them the story you just heard, the story of Hack Wilson.

One week later, on November 23, 1948, Hack Wilson died from an internal hemorrhage. He was only 48 years old. Virtually penniless, his funeral expenses were paid for by contributions from friends, fans, and even National League president Ford Frick. Wilson (who was elected to the National Baseball Hall of Fame by the Veterans Committee in 1979) was laid to rest at Rosedale Cemetery in Martinsburg, West Virginia, in Section E, Lot 60.

RABBIT MARANVILLE (1891–1954)

Walter "Rabbit" Maranville was a five-foot, five-inch baseball clown with a goblin face full of laugh lines. One of the most animated players in history, his humor was antic and visible to fans. Nicknamed "Rabbit" because of his large ears and fast running style, he left a legacy of wild nights and zany stunts.

The shortstop for the 1914 "Miracle Braves," after the World Series, Maranville and several of his teammates went on tour in a vaudeville act. The act consisted of songs, anecdotes, and recreations of plays in the World Series. One night while in Lewiston, Maine, the Rabbit declared to the audience, "I will now demonstrate how I stole second base off Bullet Joe Bush in the Series." Sprinting off a mythical first base, he executed a picture-perfect slide. Unfortunately, he miscalculated the distance and wound up landing on a drum in the orchestra pit, breaking his leg.

Maranville was a photographer's dream. He would pull the bill of his cap over one ear—baseball's oldest comic gesture—and jump into the arms of his biggest teammate. He would make fun of umpires by putting on a pair of glasses and mock slow pitchers and ponderous batters in pantomime. He was an after-hours mainstay who loved to have a good time. After a few drinks to help him get the nerve, Rabbit would pull such stunts as walking hotel ledges, swallowing goldfish, and tossing firecrackers. Even when he wasn't partying, he would enjoy himself by pulling stunts.

Once when he was in New York, Maranville arranged for pitcher Jack Scott to chase him through Times Square shouting, "Stop, thief!" One another occasion, his teammates heard wild noises coming from his locked hotel room—screams, gunfire, breaking glass—with the Rabbit moaning, "Eddie, you're killing me!" It sounded like a murder in progress. When the door was finally broken down, the Rabbit and two accomplices paraded right by his shocked teammates as if nothing had happened, with the Rabbit greeting them with a "Hiya fellas!"

Another time, Maranville snuck into a movie theater where a few of his teammates were enjoying the afternoon matinee. While his buddies were enthralled by the actors on the screen, Maranville snuck up on them from behind, lit a large firecracker, and, without warning, gleefully threw it under their seats.

Lost in all his shenanigans is the fact that he was also a superior fielder, famous for his basket catch of high infield flies. He led National League shortstops in putouts each year from 1914 to 1919 (except for 1918, which he spent in the U.S. Navy), assists twice, double plays three times, and fielding average once. He was traded to Pittsburgh in 1921, for outfielders Billy Southworth and Fred Nicholson, shortstop Walter Barbare, and $15,000.

Maranville led shortstops in fielding average in 1923, eventually moving to second base when Glenn Wright took over at short in 1924. Dealt to the Cubs after the 1924 season, he continued his solid play. His late-night partying and devil-may-care antics finally began to catch up with him in Chicago.

When Maranville was named manager in July 1925, he failed miserably. He had no set rules for the team except that they couldn't go to bed before him. One can imagine how worn out the team was after just a week under his guidance. After 53 games and Chicago in eighth place, he was let go.

From that point onward, it was downhill for Maranville. The Cubs waived him to Brooklyn. The Dodgers then released him unconditionally halfway through 1926. The Cardinals finally picked him up and optioned him to Rochester of the International League. It was there that Maranville finally saw the light. "Going back to the bushes was the best thing for me!" he said in an interview years later. "I knew that that was one place I didn't want to finish my career in. Either I had to lay off the booze and get serious with the game or it would be the end of me."

Rabbit's change of attitude started on May 24, 1927, the day he took a pledge to lay off the sauce. Branch Rickey spoke of him later in the season, exclaiming, "Walter is a changed man . . . it is apparent that he has seen the light . . . his change in attitude is remarkable." He was brought back up to the Cardinals, where he played nine games at the end of the '27 campaign. Rewarded with a contract for 1928, he helped the Cards during their pennant-winning efforts. Sold back to the Braves in 1929, he continued his steady play, never playing fewer than 142 games a season during the next six years.

During a spring training game against the Yankees in 1934, the 42-year-old Maranville was on the front end of a double steal of home when he snapped the tibia and fibula in his left leg. Sitting out the season, he tried a comeback in 1935, but he just wasn't his old self. He retired as a player and turned to coaching in the minors, where he had some success. Rabbit was even a player-manager one year, batting .323 in 123 games for Elmira of the New York-Penn League in 1936. After several more stints as a minor league manager, he left the game to work for youth baseball programs in Detroit and Rochester, New York, before finally settling in Queens as director of sandlot baseball programs for the *New York Journal-American*. Maranville loved working with kids and getting the opportunity to tell stories about his baseball career and "make the boys laugh!" He was always quick to point out the error in his judgment and never encouraged the same vices that had almost ruined him. There was a drive by many writers to have him elected to the Hall of Fame, but he would never live to see Cooperstown.

In the early morning hours of Wednesday, January 6, 1954, Rabbit Maranville died of a heart attack at his home at 55–25 31st Avenue in Woodside, Queens. He was only 62 years old. He was laid to rest a few days later in St. Michael's Cemetery in Springfield, Massachusetts, in the Holy Family Section B, Lot 206, Grave 5. He made it to the Hall of Fame posthumously later that year.

FABIAN KOWALIK (1908–1954)

The son of Peter and Mary Lorenz Kowalik, Fabian Lorenz Kowalik was born in the sleepy town of Falls City, Texas, on April 14, 1908. Falls City, which is located about 40 miles southeast of San Antonio, was the perfect setting to learn the game of baseball. Fabian's father was the owner of the highly successful Kowalik Lumber Company. Fabian's paternal grandparents, John and Agnes, had emigrated from the part of East Prussia that is in present-day Poland. In an interview with the Associated Press, Kowalik talked of his days growing up in Falls City, commenting, "There was always a game being played on the sandlots when I was growing up, always a league you could join, even as a youngster. We would play all day and all night if we could, and we did."

Breaking in with the Coleman Bob Cats of the Class D West Texas League in 1929, Kowalik pitched to a 7–2 record in 12 games. After spending the 1930 season with the Topeka Senators, he joined the San Antonio Indians of the Western League for the 1931 campaign, where he would spend the majority of the next three seasons. Making his major league debut for the Chicago White Sox as a late season call-up on September 2, 1932, he appeared in two games, going 0–1. In September 1934, 17,000 fans jammed Buffalo's War Memorial Stadium to celebrate "Fabian Kowalik Night." Kowalik would not disappoint, as he notched his 15th win of the season.

Selected by the Cubs on October 2, 1934, in the Rule 5 Draft, Kowalik had come highly recommended by Buffalo manager Ray Schalk, who looked at him as a tough, rugged competitor who was willing to do anything to help his team. Kowalik made his return to the majors the next season, appearing in 20 games for the pennant-bound Cubbies, going 2–2, with a 4.42 ERA. Kowalik was ecstatic when he was selected by manager Charlie Grimm to be on the World Series roster. The Cubs, who had won 100 games in the regular season, were a talented, rough-and-tumble lot, with such notables as Gabby Hartnett, Chuck Klein, Billy Herman, Billy Jurges, Stan Hack, Lon Warneke, and Charlie Root. Their opponents in the Fall Classic were the Detroit Tigers, looking for their first world championship. Talented in their own right, they were led by manager/catcher Mickey Cochrane and a host of heavy hitters headed by Hank Greenberg and Charlie Gehringer.

With the type of "lumbermen" that Detroit had on its roster, Grimm knew that the bull pen would most likely need an extra arm, hence the reasoning for adding Kowalik to the playoff lineup. Grimm's logic came into play in the first inning of Game 2, when starter Charlie Root gave up four runs on four base hits. Grimm called upon reliever Roy Henshaw to put out the fire, and for almost four innings he did just that. When the Detroit bats erupted again in the fourth inning, Grimm tasked Kowalik with setting things straight. Despite the score, Kowalik shined in his lone World Series appearance, hurling 4.1 innings while giving up just one earned run. He also banged out a seventh-inning single to third base and later scored. Kowalik's solid performance was unfortunately marred by an inside pitch he threw to Hank Greenberg in the seventh inning that broke the big slugger's wrist. Chicago would go on to lose the game, 8–3, and the World Series, four games to three.

After the season, with both his personal and professional future looking bright, Kowalik decided to take the plunge and marry girlfriend Hilma Goetz on February 3, 1936. He fully expected to be part of the Cubs bull pen in 1936, but things did not go according to plan. Coming to spring training out of shape, he was never able to get himself back on track. After going 0–2 in just six games, the World Series ace found himself traded to the Phillies, along with Chuck Klein, on May 21, with Chicago receiving Ethan Allen and pitcher Curt Davis in return. The move to Philly did not improve his fortunes on the mound, as he pitched to a 1–5 record and bloated 5.38 ERA in just 22 games.

While never considered an overpowering pitcher, Kowalik saw his usually reliable breaking pitches get smacked around with regularity. Worse yet, he seemed to act lethargic and depressed at times. Phillies manager Jimmy Wilson actually flirted with the idea of turning Kowalik into a full-time outfielder, but the move never happened. As September rolled around, Philadelphia management had had enough. Placed on waivers, Kowalik was picked up by the Boston Bees on September 6. Beantown would be his final stop in the majors. (Ironically, his only appearances for Boston were as an outfielder.) Kowalik's final major league outing came in the second game of a doubleheader on September 27 against his old team, the Phillies. Replacing Hal Lee in left field, Kowalik smacked a RBI single in the 4–3 loss.

Released after the season, Kowalik eventually signed on with his old club, the Buffalo Bisons, which was still managed by Ray Schalk. Fabian would experience a revitalization of sorts, as he pitched to records of 10–10 and 15–13 in 1937 and 1938, respectively. In January 1939, Bison manager Steve O'Neill told the Associated Press that he was pinning his pennant hopes on Kowalik and 38-year-old Ken Ash, but bad luck once again intervened, as injuries limited the pitcher to a 6–8 record in just 30 games. Sold to the Fort Worth Cats of the Texas League in December 1939, the 1940 season would prove to be his swan song as a professional player. Still plagued by arm injuries, Kowalik gave up 11 hits and 5 walks in just 5 innings of work. Knowing that the writing was on the wall, he retired after realizing that he had not fulfilled the promise that his natural talent should have allotted him.

Grave of Fabian Kowalik. Courtesy of Dr. Fred Worth.

Classified 4F, Kowalik eventually opened up a highly successful wholesale beer distributorship, although baseball was never far from his mind. In 1950, he came out of retirement to briefly manage the Robstown Rebels of the Rio Grande Valley League but drew his release when the team folded on May 13. In 1953, he attempted a comeback with the San Angelo Colts of the Longhorn League but failed to make the club.

With his beer distributorship flourishing, Kowalik should have had a long, productive, and happy life spent with wife Hilma, but alas, it was not to be. Kowalik, who long had a heavy thirst for the "suds," literally drank the profits from his business, dying from cirrhosis of the liver at Karnes County Hospital at 5:30 a.m. on August 14, 1954, at the age of 46. He was buried two days later in Holy Trinity Catholic Church Cemetery in his hometown of Falls City. His ever-faithful wife joined him in eternal bliss on December 10, 1991, at the age of 81.

PAUL WANER (1903–1965)

Always a threat to break up a ball game but never a party, Paul Waner had the sharpest bloodshot eyes in baseball. He hit doubles and triples during games and drank them afterward. It's amazing that he was able to amass 3,152 hits with all the alcohol he consumed.

One year Warner announced he was on the wagon, but when his batting average hovered around .250, his manager personally shepherded him to his nearest watering hole. Within a few weeks, he was back over .300. His father wanted him to be a teacher, but he dropped out of college to join San Francisco of the Pacific Coast League, where he compiled batting averages of .369, .356, and .401. Purchased by the Pirates in 1926, he batted .336 and had a league-leading 22 triples his rookie season. Joined by his brother Lloyd in the Pirate outfield the following season, Paul had career highs in batting average, with .380, and RBI, with 131, as the two siblings helped lead their team to the 1927 pennant.

Legend has it that Paul received his nickname from a frustrated Brooklyn fan, who complained about the two brothers, saying, "Them Waners! It's always the little poison [person] on thoid [third] and the big poison [person] on foist [first]!" From that point onward, Paul and

Lloyd were "Big Poison" and "Little Poison," respectively. Waner refuted this claim, stating that the nicknames where actually conceived by a Giant fan at the Polo Grounds.

Like his brother, Paul was a speedy outfielder who possessed perhaps the strongest arm in a Pittsburgh outfield until the arrival of Roberto Clemente. Waner was also fearless at the plate. He once told a reporter, "I never let them [pitchers] get the better of me. If you flinch and show any fear, you're done." Pirate pitcher Ray Kremer remembered his teammate as one tough customer, commenting,

> I'm telling you now, no pitcher could rattle Paul Waner. Pitchers like Burleigh Grimes would throw at him to intimidate him, but they never got the best of him. Every time Paul got knocked down, he would just get up, dust himself off, and get back in there like nothing happened. Usually he would hit the next pitch somewhere hard, for a base hit.

Waner was not a typical ballplayer of the time. Big Poison once wrote a comedy skit that he appeared in with Heinie Manush, and he read Seneca in his spare time. He was an avid golfer, becoming so good that he shot in the 70s. He also helped organize the first National Baseball Players Golf Tournament and enjoyed hunting and fishing when he wasn't out partying. One day one of Waner's teammates on the Pirates, Fred Lindstrom, stopped by for a morning golf date. He was told by Waner's wife that he had gone out for a loaf of bread. After waiting for a while, Lindstrom inquired, "When did he leave for the store?" "Last night," replied Mrs. Waner. Waner eventually gained a well-deserved reputation for playing hung over. Adam Comorosky remembered a play against the Cubs in Chicago:

> Paul had been out the night before and was not feeling too good when he got to the park. After I took a look at him, I decided that it might be a long day in the outfield for him. Well, I decided to make extra sure to back him up on every play. Hack Wilson came up in the fifth inning and caught hold of one that set me back on my heels. I just turned and ran with my head down, praying to God that he didn't hit it out. Well I heard the crowd roar, and when I looked up, I saw Paul standing there, a few feet from the wall, with the ball in his glove. He had backed me up on the play and hadn't missed a step! From then on I never doubted him.

Waner rarely smiled in his on-field photos. Casey Stengel once noted, "Paul don't smile cause he's too damn tired from being up all night."

After his retirement, Waner found steady employment as a hitting coach for the Milwaukee Braves. Eddie Mathews once saw Waner order a six-pack for breakfast, which he then easily chugged down without a problem. Like Babe Ruth, his distaste for discipline made him an inappropriate candidate for managing. Elected to the Hall of Fame in 1952, Waner joyfully told the press, "I have realized my life's ambition. This is what I have been looking for, for a long time. Thank God I have lived to see the day." Eventually retiring to Florida, he spent most of his time doing what he loved doing best: golfing, hunting, fishing, and, of course, imbibing.

Suffering from a variety of ills during the last few years of his life, Waner passed away from pulmonary emphysema complicated by pneumonia on August 29, 1965, at the age of 62, at his home in Sarasota, Florida. He was laid to rest at Manasota Memorial Park in Bradenton, Florida, in Section L, Lot 164, Space 1.

ROLLIE HEMSLEY (1907–1972)

If Rollie Hemsley had somehow managed to put as much effort and energy into his baseball career as he did his partying, he might have become a star. Born Ralston Burdett Hemsley on June 27, 1907, in Syracuse, Ohio, he made his major league debut for the Pittsburgh Pirates on April 19, 1928. Used as a backup his first few years in the big leagues, he was rated as an excellent handler of pitchers and a good defensive backstop.

An unabashed partier and rabble-rouser who loved tanking it up whenever he got the chance, Hemsley eventually gained the nickname "Rollicking Rollie." Always out for a laugh, he was a practical joker whose gags ranged from ice water attacks on slumbering teammates to throwing lit matches in the berths of sleeper cars. He was also known to throw firecrackers, light hot foots, and leave frogs and snakes in the beds of teammates. Good-natured when sober, Hemsley often turned aggressive when under the influence of "liquid muscle." When he got into a fight, he often wound up looking like he had gone 10 rounds with Jack Dempsey. A dangerous habit that he acquired early on was driving drunk. Involved in five separate alcohol-related auto accidents before the age of 25, he once drove his car into a parked car and then drove more than a mile before realizing that his female companion was hurt.

Traded to the Cubs in June 1932, as a backup for Gabby Hartnett, Rollicking Rollie fit in perfectly with a rowdy cast of characters who just happened to be on their way to the National League pennant. Making his only World Series appearances that fall, he went 0-for-3 in three games. It was with his trade to the Browns in June 1933, that he finally got his chance to become a full-time player, batting a career-high .309 the following season. It was also in St. Louis that Hemsley had what he would later describe as his "worst years in baseball," despite the fact that he was selected to the play in the All-Star Game in 1935 and 1936.

Hemsley's carefree, partying lifestyle caused him to be at odds with his manager, Rogers Hornsby. Straitlaced and rigid with the rules, Hornsby butted heads with his catcher, levying fines against him on numerous occasions. He also tried to make an example out of Hemsley by playing him when he was in less-than-stellar condition. He often made him catch games (usually doubleheaders) when he was suffering from hangovers, and Hemsley was even called on to catch the last day of the season with two black eyes, both of which were acquired in a brawl the night before.

Hemsley admitted that he often went looking for trouble. He once stated,

> Why one night in San Antonio, I walked right into the Browns' hotel, with a bottle sticking out of each pocket, and smack into Hornsby, Mr. Barnes [business manager], and Bill DeWitt [owner]. Did I try to duck? I told them what I thought of them! A fellow in his senses doesn't do things like that.

Despite the brawls and partying, Rollie remained a highly effective catcher whose pitchers swore by him. Russ Van Atta recalled, "With the Yankees, my catcher was Bill Dickey, one of the best. When I was traded to St. Louis, I got to throw to Rollie Hemsley, and without a doubt, he was as fine a catcher as I ever had the pleasure of throwing to."

Traded to the Indians in February 1938, Hemsley immediately ran into trouble during spring training, which was held in New Orleans. Tribe manager Ossie Vitt briefly suspended him for getting involved in a nasty barroom brawl, one in which he received—you guessed it—two black eyes. "I remember being in a bar with a few friends," he later commented. "I remember starting for the door, and that was the last thing I remember." One of his teammates on the Indians, Hal Trosky, called him the "worst fighter" he had ever seen, likening him to a human punching bag.

Vitt put up with Hemsley's player histrionics long after most managers would have sent him packing. Rollie was always sincere when it came to trying to get on the wagon but always failed miserably. He once tried a "cure" that made him so sick that he didn't care if he lived or died. It was during spring training of 1939 that Hemsley hit his low point. On the night of April 14, while traveling on a train from Richmond, Virginia, to New York, he began drinking and carousing. He played practical jokes and made a general nuisance of himself the entire night. This stunt, although tame in comparison to others he had pulled in the past, brought the ire of Indian management. Ordered to Cleveland to explain his conduct to Indian president Cy Slapnicka, Hemsley was worried. Not only did he have a $5,000 bonus in his contract for good behavior, which was now in jeopardy, but there was a strong possibility that he could be released or sent to the minors. Unbeknownst to him, his luck and life was about to change.

Stepping off the train in Cleveland, he was approached by two men in business suits. These two strangers were not just ordinary businessmen, but members of Alcoholics Anonymous (AA). Apprehensive at first, Hemsley listened intently as the two men gave him his first real hope that he might be able to conquer his demons. Said Hemsley,

> I had tried everything else, and these fellows at least weren't giving me theories. They themselves had conquered the same weakness which was ruining me. They told me about dozens of other fellows— some of them prominent citizens—who had the same experience. I could see they were sincere—and I was desperate. I went with them. It was the most fortunate decision of my life.

There is still some contention as to who sent the two men to meet with him. Whether they were simply two baseball fans who went out of their way to help a player on their favorite team or they were sent to intervene on behalf of Cleveland management remains a mystery. Hemsley traveled with his new friends to Akron to check into a local hospital, and during the next several days he was immersed in the world of AA, spending most of his time resting and listening to the stories of others who had also been helped. Released after just four days, he reported back to the Indians a changed man. Reflecting on what he had learned, he stated, "I realized that I needed help with my disease. The association gave me what I needed to change my life. God knows where I would have ended up if not for them."

Taking over the starting catcher's duties after Frankie Pytlak went down with an injury, Hemsley appeared in 106 games, batting .263, good enough to be selected for the All-Star team for a third time. The next year, Rollie became the only catcher in major league history to catch an Opening Day no-hitter when he caught Bob Feller's gem against the Tigers. After the game, the team gathered at Cleveland's Del Prado Hotel to celebrate the historic event. As a throng of reporters and cameramen interviewed players and snapped pictures, everyone asked, "Where's Rollie?" Vitt, without hesitation, proudly announced, "In the bar, I just saw him go in there." Hemsley was in the bar alright, celebrating with the rest of his teammates by drinking soft drinks.

Hemsley batted .267 for the year and was selected to play in his fourth All-Star Game. He, of course, gave full credit for his resurgence to his sobriety. "I can go at top speed, chase fouls all over the lot, back up first and third—and be as fresh at the end of a game as I am at the start," he once stated. Rollie would remain a staunch member and supporter of AA for the rest of his life, and he would often counsel other people who were in dire straits. He also stirred up a bit of controversy when, in 1940, he admitted to the press that he was a member of AA, becoming the first participant to break their rule of anonymity on a national level.

Sold to the Reds in December 1942, Hemsley was released on July 17, after batting just .113 in 36 games. Signed two days later by the Yankees, he batted .294 in 31 games, as he became the main backup for Bill Dickey. A member of two Yankee pennant-winning squads, in 1942 and 1943, he split catching duties with Mike Garbark in 1944, until he entered the U.S. Navy. Sold to the Phillies during spring training of 1946, Hemsley retired as a player after his release in April 1947. He later became a highly successful minor league manager, being named Manager of the Year twice by *Sporting News*, and started a successful real estate business in Langley Park, Maryland. He also coached and scouted with the Athletics in 1954, as well as the Senators in 1961 and 1962. His final stop in baseball was with Waterloo in 1969.

When Hemsley died from a heart attack on July 17, 1972, at the age of 65, he was remembered not just as a former player, but as a person who, in his darkest hours, was able to turn his life around, and who also gladly helped others in need. Rollie Hemsley was buried at Washington Cemetery in Adelphi, Maryland.

CASEY STENGEL (1890–1975)

A true American folk hero, Casey Stengel will forever be looked upon as one of baseball's greatest managers, a larger-than-life personality whose zany antics both on and off the field often overshadowed his on-field accomplishments. A fun-loving firebrand who could drink with the best of them, he was part clown and part baseball genius.

Born Charles Dillon Stengel on July 30, 1890, he received the nickname "Casey" as a bastardization of Kansas City, his home town. As a child, he showed the type of spunk and outgoing personality that would eventually personify his playing career. A multisport star in high school, he eventually left school to start his professional career with the hometown Kansas City Blues of the American Association. According to Stengel, his father wanted him to have a second career in case he failed as a ballplayer. Saving his money from his baseball earnings, he attended dental school, where he struggled mightily, because most of the instruments were designed for right-handed students. "As soon as I made my first set of dental plates, I knew right then and there that I was going to be better as a ballplayer than as a dentist," he reflected. Drafted by the Brooklyn Dodgers from Aurora of the Wisconsin-Illinois League in the 1911 Rule 5 Draft, he was assigned to Montgomery of the Southern Association for the next season, where he batted .290.

Called up by the Dodgers that September, Stengel made his major league debut on September 17, in a 7–3 win over the Pirates, going 4-for-4, with three steals. Becoming the full-time right fielder the following season, he quickly became a fan favorite due to his consistent play and zany antics both while playing baseball and in his personal life. Sportswriters always knew that they would get a good quote as long as

Casey Stengel. Courtesy of the Library of Congress.

they talked to "Ole Casey." Stengel loved playing the part of the clown and thoroughly enjoyed pulling stunts and gags to please the crowd.

While playing for Montgomery, he lowered himself into an outfield manhole during batting practice when no one was looking. When a fly ball sailed in his direction, he popped out and grabbed it, The crowd gave him a standing ovation. As a manager, to show his displeasure after an umpire had refused to call a game because of darkness, he sent one of his players up to bat holding a flashlight. He once protested the continuation of a rain-soaked game by coaching at third base holding an open umbrella. In addition, he was once offered $10 to end an extra-inning game by a Brooklyn fan who wanted to get home for dinner. With dollar signs in his eyes, Casey shouted to the man, "Don't go very far away, brother, because it won't be long now." Stengel supposedly smacked the first pitch onto Bedford Avenue. With the crowd cheering, he hurriedly rounded the bases to "collect" his "dough."

As a manager, Casey staged races between his players so he could win bets with reporters. While a coach at the All-Star Game, he took an errant throw that had gone into the dugout, examined the ball, and exclaimed, "This is much too hot to handle." To the fans' delight, he proceeded to drop the ball into a bucket of water to cool off. His most famous on-field stunt, however, happened after he was traded to the Pirates in January 1918. That June, he returned to Ebbets Field for the first time as an opposing player. Stengel recalled the incident years later:

> The one that's remembered the most was the time I came to Ebbets Field in 1918, after being traded from Brooklyn to Pittsburgh over the winter. Those Brooklyn fans were riding me. They cheered you as long as you were playing for them, but when you went away you weren't any good, see.
>
> One of my old Brooklyn buddies, Leon Cadore, was out in the bull pen. He was a cutup—loved to do card tricks. Loved to do coin tricks. He was very agile with his hands, and he'd caught this young sparrow in the bull pen that day. Just before my first time at bat, I got it from him and put it under my cap. I could feel it moving, you know, inside there on my scalp.
>
> So I walked up to the plate swinging three bats very hard. And the crowd yells, everybody gets excited, and they're booing me to death. Then I threw the bats down and grabbed my eye as if there was something in it, and said "Time." Cy Rigler was umpiring behind the plate, and he called time. Then I turned around to face the crowd and lifted my hat off and made a big bow. And when the bird flew out, the crowd just went, "Oh-h-h-h-h-h-h."

Traded to the Phillies in August 1919, Stengel was eventually traded to the Giants in July 1921, in a multiplayer swap. Excelling under manager

John McGraw's platoon system, he batted .368 in the 1922 regular season and .407 in the World Series against the Yankees. The next season, he batted .339, while leading the Giants with a .417 batting average in a World Series rematch with the Yankees. He also clubbed two homers, the first one being a Game 1 inside-the-park shot that broke a 4–4 ninth-inning tie. In typical Casey fashion, he scored the winning run minus one cleat (he lost it while running the bases). Traded to the Braves in the off-season, he would make his final major league appearance on May 19, 1925, after which he headed to the minors to start his managerial career.

As a minor league manager, Stengel would find success with numerous clubs. These included Worcester; Toledo, with whom he won a pennant in 1927; Milwaukee, with whom he won a pennant in 1944; Kansas City; and Oakland of the Pacific Coast League, with whom he would win another championship in 1948. The major leagues, however, proved to be a different animal. His first two managerial jobs, with the Brooklyn Dodgers (1934–1936) and Boston Braves (1938–1943), saddled him with the unfair reputation of being nothing more than an inept buffoon. Years later, Casey would jokingly recall those days by saying, "I became a major league manager in several cities and was discharged. We call it discharged because there is no question I had to leave." It was not until he was hired to manage the New York Yankees in 1949 that he finally had the "horses to compete."

Yankee general manager George Weiss, who hired him, knew that the perception that most people in the press had about his new manager was dead wrong and that he was as sound a baseball man as could be found. Stengel, of course, would go on to win an amazing 10 pennants in his 12 seasons as manager, including seven world championships, five straight from 1949 to 1953. His reputation as one of baseball's most endearing personalities was only enhanced during his time as a Yankee manager. Yankee infielder Billy Martin once reminisced about an incident where he tried to outfox the "Ole Perfesser":

> We were in Chicago for a series with the White Sox. Me and Mickey [Mantle] went out after the first game to grab a little dinner. When we were leaving, we both noticed that Casey was in the bar, talking with some writers. Well, we both got back a few hours later and the old man is still in the bar, drinking and talking up a storm. About an hour later, I got a phone call from this girl I knew. She wants me to

meet her at her apartment a few blocks away. Since it was past curfew I took a peek in the bar on the way out to see if Casey was still there. Most people didn't know that Casey could go all night long if he wanted to. Anyway, I got back to the hotel a few hours later, and I don't see him anywhere, and I think to myself, "I'm home free." That afternoon, as I went up to take my batting practice, Casey comes up to me from behind and yells, "Martin, you're fined $20 for breaking curfew." All I can do is stand there, wondering how the hell I got caught. Finally I yell back at him, "How the hell do you know I was out last night?" Casey looks at me and winks and says with that grin of his, "Oh, I know everything." Well I paid the $20, but the story doesn't end there. A couple of weeks later, I pinned him down as to how he caught me. "Well, the night manager is an old friend of mine," he says. "We had breakfast together that morning and he mentioned to me that he just so happened to see a certain player of mine coming in about 3 a.m." So that's how he caught me, but I should also mention that he used my $20 fine to help pay his tab at the bar.

Stengel's favorite postgame activity as Yankee manager was holding court in bars until all hours of the night with sports scribes, whom he called "my writers." Famous for his long monologues and double-talk that came to be known as "Stengelese," his various quotes and ramblings have become legend.

In July 1958, Stengel appeared before a hearing of the U.S. Senate Subcommittee on Monopoly and Antitrust, which was investigating baseball's exemption from federal antitrust laws. Casey delivered what would become his most famous and hilarious speech. When asked why baseball teams should be granted the reserve clause that binds a player to his team, Stengel replied, "I wouldn't know, but I imagine to keep baseball going as high as baseball is as a sport, they [the owners] have gone into baseball and from the baseball angle." It was part of a mock diatribe that left the audience laughing and the committee's chairman, Estes Kefauver, shaking his head.

Released as Yankee manager after a 1960 World Series loss to the Pirates, Stengel resurfaced two seasons later as manager of the expansion New York Mets. Hall of Famer Richie Ashburn, an outfielder for the expansion Mets, once said

Playing for Casey Stengel was one of the most enjoyable things I ever did in the game. It was my last year as a player and the team was just dreadful, and Casey knew we were going to be dreadful, but that didn't stop Casey from being Casey. He had more energy as a 72-year-old than most of the players. He was first to the park and the last one to leave.

As manager of the Amazin' Mets, he used his promoting skills to gain a new legion of fans for both him and his team. On July 24, 1965, as he prepared to celebrate his 75th birthday, Casey broke his left hip and underwent hip-replacement surgery. Relegated to civilian clothes, he retired from the game he loved for good five weeks later.

When the Hall of Fame Veterans Committee waived the normal five-year waiting period the following year, Ole Casey got a chance to wow the crowd one final time with his induction speech. A shrewd businessman, he had invested his money wisely throughout the years. His wife Edna, whom he had married in 1924, had gotten him involved in the banking business, which made him a millionaire. Diagnosed with cancer in the summer of 1975, Casey Stengel passed away peacefully in his sleep on September 29, 1975, at the age of 85. His beloved wife followed him three years later. He is buried at Forest Lawn Cemetery in Glendale, California, in the Court of Freedom, Long Crypt, 6A, Block 7060.

MICKEY MANTLE (1931–1995)

There is a distinct difference between a hero and a role model, and the two often become intertwined. Such was the case with Mickey Charles Mantle. Like Babe Ruth before him, he was a larger-than-life personality who became a hero to millions of fans. Born in Spavinaw, Oklahoma, and raised in Commerce, he was one of baseball's all-time great players and certainly one of its all-time free spirits. Literally a "Rube" among men when he joined the Yankees in 1951, at the tender age of 19, it was Mantle's teammate on the Yankees, Hank Bauer, who supposedly gave him his first drink, a beer, which he chugged as if it were soda pop. Whether taking that first drink was a turning point in his young life is a point of contention. So much has been written about Mantle and his wild escapades that it can be hard to differentiate fact from fiction.

Mantle possessed the type of charisma and all-American good looks that attracted women to him like flies to honey. His good buddy, Billy Martin, once commented, "When Mickey walked into a room, the whole place would just light up. All the women would just stare at him and go ahhhh!" Always the joker, Mantle loved to laugh and kid around with his teammates and enjoyed playing practical jokes on them. He once let a live mongoose loose inside the Yankee clubhouse at Tiger Stadium and planted a live snake inside the uniform of teammate Marshall Bridges. Phil Rizzuto was often the brunt of his practical jokes and was always weary of the assorted snakes, frogs, or bugs that Mantle might leave in close proximity to him—and we can't forget to mention the ice water attacks on unsuspecting teammates in the clubhouse shower.

In 1973, as part of the 50th anniversary of Yankee Stadium, Mantle, along with other former Yankees, was sent a letter by the Yankee public relations department asking him to mention his most memorable moment at the facility. The quotes were to be published in a special, limited edition pamphlet celebrating 50 years of Yankee Stadium. True to form and in typical Mantle style, Mickey wrote back that his favorite moment was when he received oral sex from a female fan under the right field stands. It was just another case of Mickey being Mickey. More than anything, however, Mantle wanted to be known as a great teammate. Yankee first baseman Joe Collins remembered Mantle not just as a great teammate, but as an equally caring human being. According to Collins,

> Mickey was the type of guy who always cared about you as a person. As a teammate, he never complained about his injuries and always tried to lead by example. He always had that country boy attitude that made you feel at ease. He was a huge star, but he never treated you like he was better than you.

If it had not been for his off-field habits, especially drinking, there's no telling what records he would have smashed. His rationale for his hard-living lifestyle was that all the men in his family, including his father, Elvin "Mutt" Mantle, had died young as a result of Hodgkin's disease. One of his most famous lines was, "If I'd known I was gonna live this long, I'd have taken better care of myself." His 18-year career saw him play in 2,401 games (more than any other Yankee player), garner three

MVP Awards ('56, '57, and '62), and win the Triple Crown in 1956, not to mention hit 536 lifetime home runs. Mantle also appeared in 12 World Series, winning seven championships. His 18 home runs, 42 runs, 40 RBI, and 43 bases on balls are still World Series records. Retiring after the 1968 season, he was inducted into the National Baseball Hall of Fame in 1974.

After his retirement, Mantle worked as a spring training instructor for the Yankees, as a baseball broadcaster for both the Yankees and NBC, and in customer relations for Dallas Reserve Life Insurance Company. Taking a job with the Claridge Hotel and Casino in Atlantic City, he was suspended from baseball by Commissioner Bowie Kuhn but later reinstated. A mainstay of sports memorabilia shows during the 1980s and early 1990s, he became one of the most in-demand personalities on the circuit. He loved to relate a story where, after his death, he would be standing at Heaven's Gate, waiting to get in. He would say, "St. Peter is looking at me and he's shaking his head and says to me, 'Mick, we checked your records. We know what went on down there. Sorry, but we just can't let you in. But before you go, God would like to know if you could sign these baseballs for him.'"

Although his personal battles had been known for years, those same frailties made him even more popular to his millions of adoring fans, as

Grave of Mickey Mantle. Courtesy of Bill Lee.

his weaknesses showed him for what he was, a mere human being. As he entered his 60s, Mantle finally attempted to clean up his life. Entering the Betty Ford clinic in 1993, he would eventually become an outspoken opponent of both alcohol and drugs.

In early 1995, he was diagnosed with cancer and cirrhosis of the liver. Further tests also revealed that he was suffering from hepatitis C. Doctors at Baylor University Hospital in Dallas, Texas, informed him that he would need a liver transplant to save his life, which he received on June 8. While the transplant was initially declared a success, physicians feared that the cancer would spread. In July, Mantle held a press conference at Baylor, noting that many fans had looked to him as a role model. "This is a role model: Don't be like me," he said, as he implored young people not to follow his example. He also established the Mickey Mantle Foundation to raise awareness for organ donation.

In late July, it was discovered that the cancer had metastasized throughout his body. Doctors at Baylor maintained that it was the most aggressive form of cancer they had ever seen due to the fact that the antirejection drugs he had been taking for his transplant had allowed the cancer to spread. Mantle died on August 13, 1995, at 2:10 a.m., at Baylor University Hospital, with his wife Merlyn and son David by his side. At his funeral, sportscaster Bob Costas described him as a "fragile hero to whom we had an emotional attachment so strong and lasting that it defied logic." Costas added, "In the last year of his life, Mickey Mantle, always so hard on himself, finally came to accept and appreciate the distinction between a role model and a hero. The first, he often was not. The second, he always will be. And, in the end, people got it." Mickey Mantle is interred at Sparkman-Hillcrest Memorial Park in Dallas, Texas, in the Mausoleum, St. Matthew Section, along with his wife Merlyn, who died in 2009, and his sons, Billy and Mickey Jr.

BRIAN TRAXLER (1967–2004)

Despite a major league career that was all but a snapshot in time, Brian Traxler became what his biographer Rory Costello calls a "cult hero" to legions of fans throughout the world. A fan favorite in every city he played in, Traxler was a big, jovial player with a large personality and an absolute love for the game. Known to friends and fans by the nickname

Trax, his physique seemed more suited for a weekend softball league than a professional baseball player.

Born to Sandy and Ruth Traxler in Waukegan, Illinois, on September 26, 1967, Brian was born to play the game, as his parents introduced him to it when he was but a toddler. From sandlot and little league to American Legion and high school ball, Brian played them all and played them well. With the encouragement of his parents, he lived and breathed the game. After high school, Traxler attended the University of New Orleans, where he was primarily a first baseman. Even though he was left-handed, he could play almost anywhere except shortstop and second base. A pure hitter, he was known for a quick and powerful bat and his intensity on the field. Blessed with a superlative baseball IQ, he understood every facet of the game. After his junior year at New Orleans, where he was one of the star players, he was selected by the Dodgers in the 16th round of the amateur draft. Despite the fact that the odds of setting foot on a major league field were against him, Traxler (who was the number 400 overall pick) remained upbeat and confident.

Trax started his professional career in 1988, with the Class A Vero Beach Dodgers of the Florida State League. The following year, he split time with the Double A San Antonio Missions of the Texas League and Triple A Albuquerque Dukes of the Pacific Coast League. True to his personality, Brian remained his usual fun-loving self. Once the game began, however, his competitiveness shined brightly, for there was only one way he knew how to play the game—what many people call the "right way." On the field, Trax was a leader, known for his never-say-die attitude. Despite the ups and downs that go with playing professional baseball, nothing seemed to really bother him. After all, he was doing what he loved to do, and in his words, "what more could I ask for."

Trax finally got his shot at the majors when the Dodgers purchased his contract from Albuquerque in April 1990. Making his major league debut on April 24, against St. Louis, he entered the game in the seventh inning as a replacement for Eddie Murray (who had been tossed by umpire Harry Wendelstedt). Facing Cardinal right-hander Bob Tewksbury, Trax wound up striking out on one of Tewksbury's patented changeups. During the course of his one-month stay in "The Show," Trax would appear seven more times as a pinch hitter, while making just one start at first base. His only major league hit (he lost a second one when a double, off of the Mets' David Cone, was erased by a rainout) came when he doubled off Expos right-hander "El Presidente," Dennis Martinez, in a game at Montreal on May 10. His last appearance on a major league field took place on May 21st, in a 12–3 loss to the Mets at Dodger Stadium.

When he was optioned back to Albuquerque a few days later, Trax had no reason to believe that his big-league career was over and that he would never have another chance to play in the majors. Many of Traxler's friends and defenders now believe that there was an underlying prejudice that kept him from getting a second chance. Despite the fact that he could hit in his sleep, his round, paunchy build was usually held against him. Even though he would never be given a legitimate shot at making a major league club, Trax persevered and continued his career in the minors. The list of minor league teams he played for includes the San Antonio Missions of the Texas League, Albuquerque Dukes of the Pacific Coast League, Fargo-Moorhead Red Hawks and Sioux Falls Canaries of the Northern League, and Somerset Patriots of the Atlantic League. He also spent the 1994 season with the Fukuoka Daiei Hawks of the Japanese Pacific League and, in 1998, played briefly with the Chinatrust Whales of the Chinese Professional Baseball League, in Taiwan. Traxler also played winter ball in the Dominican Republic, Venezuela, and Puerto Rico.

No matter where he played, Brian was a fan favorite. His relationship with fans was such that he enjoyed being in their company as much as they liked watching him. Never one to turn down an autograph request, he would usually stand and sign for fans until every last one was taken care of. In an age where professional players were becoming more and more arrogant and reclusive, Trax stood out. The *Home News Tribune* described Traxler's personality as "gregarious and approachable, the type of player that fans of all stripes could relate to."

Traxler's career as a player ended with his retirement in 2000, but his career in baseball didn't stop there. Finding work as a minor league hitting instructor for the Dodgers, he used his knowledge of the game and acumen to help young players learn the finer points of hitting. Not only did he excel as a hitting coach, he seemed happier than ever, as he was able to stay in the game he loved so dearly. Trax was such a great teacher that many in the Dodger organization felt that he would be a perfect candidate to one day manage, but alas, the opportunity would never come.

After the 2004 season, the Dodger front office decided not to renew his contract. It was then that he planned to travel to that year's baseball winter meetings in the hopes of finding work. Sadly, it was not to be. His years of heavy beer consumption, which he was known for, had finally taken their toll. On November 4th, Trax was taken to North Central Baptist Hospital in San Antonio. He would eventually slip into a coma and pass away on November 19th. He was just 37 years old. He was survived by his ex-wife Gabby, his daughter Ashley, now serving in the U.S. Army as a medic, his mother Ruth, and sisters Kelly and Stacey, and, of course, countless friends who cherished their friendships with him.

It would take an encyclopedia—and then some—to sum up the life of Brian Traxler. One obituary for him stated that, "he was the 'life of the party' and always made people laugh." While this may be true, it only tells half the story. His is the story of the everyday man playing for the love of the game. Fans can see through fakes and phonies, one thing Trax never was. He was as genuine as the grass he played on. True to his love of the game, Traxler's family had him cremated and his ashes scattered at Privateer Park at New Orleans University and V. J. Keefe Stadium in San Antonio.

3

CONSUMED BY CONSUMPTION

Since its inception, the national game has been plagued by the "white plague"—tuberculosis. The disease itself has been around for thousands of years and killed millions of people. It was referred to by several names, including consumption, phthisis, phthisis pulmonalis, phthisis florida, scrofula, Pott's disease, and the aforementioned white plague. Professional baseball players, like the general population, were not immune to it. Of the ballplayers who died from 1872 to 1967, more than 250 died from the disease. This, of course, does not include the list of minor leaguers who also succumbed to the illness.

Cases of TB are not always relegated to the lungs. Players like Addie Joss and Hughie Jennings, both members of the National Baseball Hall of Fame, died from tubercular spinal meningitis. Longtime catcher Lou Criger died as a result of TB that first affected his left knee joint, necessitating the amputation of that same leg above the knee. Another famous player from baseball's halcyon days, Fred "Sure Shot" Dunlap, died in a most ghastly fashion from a tubercular distended rectum. Others, for instance, Carl Weilman, whom Ty Cobb rated as one of the toughest pitchers he ever faced, and Jake Stahl, who managed the Red Sox to the 1912 World Series championship, died from complications resulting from tuberculosis of the throat. TB can also cause pulmonary hemorrhages and general sepsis (infection) within the body.

Major league players were dying from the disease well into the 1950s, with the last known case of a former major leaguer passing from it being Mike Chartak in 1967. Some players were lucky enough to beat it. When former Giant great Larry Doyle contracted the disease in 1942, he entered the Trudeau Sanatorium in Saranac Lake, New York, the same place where his former teammate, Christy Mathewson, went to convalesce more than 20 years earlier. Unlike Mathewson, who died at the young age of 45 in 1925, Doyle, with the help of new antibiotics that were unavailable to his old friend, was not only cured, but he lived to the ripe old age of 87. Doyle's case was the exception to the rule, however, as the majority of players who contracted TB had a slim chance of surviving it before such antibiotics as Streptomycin, and later Isoniazid, were developed. By the 1970s, TB was almost looked at as an afterthought. Today, mostly due to the fact that there are new strains resistant to antibiotics, tuberculosis is still ranked as one of the most common causes of infectious disease-related deaths in the world.

ELMER WHITE (1849–1872)

Little is known of the early life of Elmer White, the first major leaguer known to have died from TB. The son of Benjamin and Minerva White, he was born on December 7, 1849, in the sleepy town of Caton, New York. Elmer had two younger sisters, Ada (born circa 1852) and Ina (born circa 1862). White learned the rudiments of the game playing in local town contests, along with his cousin, James "Deacon" White, who was two years older, and Deacon's brother Will, who was five years younger. By the mid-1860s, Elmer was already thinking of following in the footsteps of his cousin James and making baseball his livelihood, but this would be no easy task, as his parents regarded playing baseball as a waste of time. This didn't stop him, however, as he signed on to play with the amateur Cleveland Forest City team beginning in 1868, joining James there.

In 1869, a new professional Forest City team was organized that included the likes of Art Allison and Al Pratt, along with Jim and Elmer. The Forest Citys of this period featured players who were both professional and amateur. White was a member of the Forest Citys when the team joined the new National Association (National Association of Professional Baseball Players) in 1871. He made his major league debut on May 4, 1871, in the first-ever game played in the National Association. The contest, which was called in the top of the ninth inning due to rain, ended in a 2–0 loss to Bobby Mathews and the Ft. Wayne Kekiongas. White, the starting right fielder, wound up having a horrendous debut, striking out three times in as many at bats.

White played just one season in the National Association, appearing in 15 of the Forest Citys 29 scheduled league games in 1871. Primarily an outfielder, City manager Charlie Pabor also used him as a catcher in three games. It was while manning the catcher's position that he broke his arm after running into a fence while attempting to intercept a badly thrown ball from the outfield. The incident happened on Monday, June 19, in a 10–6 loss against the New York Mutuals at Cleveland's Union Grounds. White's injury kept him out of action until August 30, when he returned against the Troy Haymakers in a 17–12 loss.

White's final appearance in a major league game occurred on September 27, the final day of the season, in a 9–7 loss to the Boston Red Stockings. He would go 2-for-5, with 2 RBI and 1 run scored. Elmer would finish his major league career with a lifetime .259 batting average, with 18 hits, 9 RBI, and 9 runs scored in 79 plate appearances. Fielding he made 7 errors and accrued a .788 fielding average.

White returned to upstate New York after the season, fully confident that he would make the Cleveland club the following season. Unfortunately, it was not to be. Sometime during the winter of 1871–1872, he contracted tuberculosis, which was a rampant killer of the times. Confident that he would beat the disease, he gamely fought what his cousin Deacon later recalled as the "good fight." White passed away from pulmonary tuberculosis on March 17, 1872, in the town of Scio, New York, giving him the distinction of being the first active major leaguer to die.

While Elmer White's career was all too brief, his cousins Will and James, on the other hand, would both go on to have successful careers in the national game. Will pitched 10 seasons in the majors, accruing a 222–166 record that included four 40-win seasons. He died from an accidental drowning in Port Carling, Ontario, Canada, on August 31, 1911, at the age of 56.

James "Deacon" White went on have an excellent 20-year major league career that saw a lifetime batting average of .312, with 2,012 lifetime hits and 998 RBI playing for nine different teams in three leagues. Deacon, who died in Aurora, Illinois, on July 7, 1939, at the age of 91, was eventually inducted into the National Baseball Hall of Fame by the Veterans Committee in 2013, 74 years after his passing.

There is one final footnote to Elmer White's passing. As of this writing, his final resting place remains unknown, although there is some evidence that his body was brought back to his hometown of Caton for burial. There are few, if any, public records available to confirm this. Hopefully the mystery of Elmer White's final resting place will soon be solved.

CHARLIE HODES (1848–1875)

A versatile performer, Charlie Hodes played every position during his big-league career except pitcher and left field. Hodes, whose parents were German immigrants, was born in Manhattan and moved with his family to Brooklyn when he was five. After making a name for himself with several local amateur clubs, he joined the famous Eckfords of Brooklyn beginning in 1868. He joined the Chicago White Stockings in 1870, staying with them when they joined the newly formed National Association in 1871. Chicago's primary catcher, Hodes appeared in 20 of the team's 28 scheduled games that season. Stockings manager Jimmy Wood, a fellow Brooklynite, used Hodes's versatility to his advantage, as he also logged time at third base, shortstop, and outfield. At the plate, he batted .277, with 25 RBI in 130 at bats, and hit the only two homers of his major league career. With the disbanding of the Chicago franchise after the season, Hodes, along with teammates George Zettelin and Michael "Bub" McAtee, followed Wood when he took over the reins of the Troy Haymakers the following season.

Hodes appeared in 13 of the Haymakers' 25 games that season, making appearances at catcher, third base, shortstop, and outfield. The move to Troy proved to be ill-fated, as club ownership was forced to cease operations on July 23rd because they were unable to pay the players. This left Hodes and several other members of the team—including local products Michael McAtee and Steve and Marshall King—looking for work. With no team to play for, Hodes headed home to Brooklyn to plan his next move.

Even before he arrived home, there was talk on the street that the Brooklyn Eckfords had interest in signing several of the former Haymaker players. These rumors eventually proved to be true, as no less than six former Troy players signed on with Brooklyn. Sadly for Hodes, he was not one of the players chosen to perform at Brooklyn's Union Grounds. Undaunted, he focused on catching on with one of the local semipro teams in the city, of which there were many.

Hodes finally returned to the National Association a year and a half later when he signed on to play with the local Brooklyn Atlantics. Almost from the start of the season, Hodes suffered from bouts of tiredness and sluggishness on the field. He made his final major league appearance as a player on Monday, July 13, 1874, in a 6–4 win over the Hartford Dark Blues at the Hartford Ball Club Grounds in Connecticut. Playing second base, he went 0-for-5.

After deciding that a period of rest would be the best thing for his player, Atlantic manager Bob Ferguson sent Hodes to the bench. His final active appearance on a major league field occurred as an umpire in an October 3rd game between the Atlantics and Baltimore Canaries (Hodes umpired four games in 1874).

Diagnosed with tuberculosis in mid-October, Hodes's lethargy and weakness worsened with the coming of cooler fall weather. Manager Ferguson took it upon himself to raise funds to help with his player's rehabilitation. The *Brooklyn Eagle* reported the following story in the November 13th evening edition: "A benefit hop on behalf of Charlie Hodes, a sickly member of the Atlantic Base Ball Club, was not so successful as might have been desired. There was a game of ball for the same purpose on the Union Grounds yesterday afternoon."

Hodes's battle with the white plague continued well into the winter months. During this time, Ferguson and several of his teammates visited him at his home in the hopes of rallying his spirits, but to no avail. He died on February 14, 1875, at his home, located at 474 Humbolt Street in the Williamsburg section of Brooklyn, which was located in the old 18th Ward. He was buried at Lutheran All Faiths Cemetery in Queens, New York, in the Hodes family lot 4769, two days later.

SILVER FLINT (1855–1891)

Philadelphia-born Frank Sylvester Flint was rated as one of the top catchers during his time in the majors. Born on August 3, 1855, he moved with his family to St. Louis at an early age. Gaining notoriety as an amateur, he played with the Elephant Base Ball Club of St. Louis in the early 1870s. He eventually left the "pachyderms" for the hometown St. Louis Red Stockings of the National Association at the age of 19. Playing a season with the Indianapolis Blues before joining the Chicago White Stockings in 1879, it was in the Windy City that he would make his mark on the game.

Playing during the days when catcher's equipment was crude at best, Flint was known as a defensive wonder. Catching barehanded, he was known for being fearless and tough, almost oblivious to pain. During his career, Flint broke every joint of every finger in both hands, had his nose broken several times, and injured his knees and hips. Despite his injuries, which also included split lips and broken teeth, he was known as a man of iron, a player who could go the distance. Every spring, as part of his training regimen, Flint would lay his hands on top of buckets of sand and have a teammate beat him in the palms with a baseball bat. When asked why he allowed himself to be put through this excruciating process, he replied that it helped his hands to become more "limber." A great handler of pitchers, he was credited with nurturing a young Larry Corcoran into becoming a star hurler. Never much of a hitter, his best seasons were in 1879, when he batted .284 with a career-high 41 RBI, and 1881, when he batted .310.

An unabashed partier, drinker, and man about the town, Flint enjoyed going out with his teammates to local establishments after games to imbibe. The handsome, mustachioed Flint, who also had an eye for the ladies, was a dapper figure in his three-piece suit, his pockets full of cash and a gold watch fob hanging from one of them. Staying out all night and carousing with his buddies was standard fair. Teammate Billy Sunday felt that there might have been a more calculated method to his teammate's madness: "Frank would go out with the rest of the boys and drink heavily. I believe that his body took so much punishment that it was the only way to rid himself of the pain. Of course, the drink brought its own demons. Still, he was as fine a catcher as I have ever seen."

Flint went on the wagon many times during his playing career, but his thirst always got the best of him. Refusing to go on Chicago owner Albert Spalding's world baseball tour of 1888–1889 with the rest of his teammates, he had, by this time, also put himself in bad standing not just with Spalding, but also his manager, Cap Anson, who had grown

Silver Flint, 1887, Old Judge Baseball Card. Courtesy of the Library of Congress.

weary of his catcher's night-crawling habits and lack of sobriety. Retiring after the 1889 season, Flint opened a saloon in Chicago, a business that would eventually fail due to his lack of discipline and knowledge of business matters. Always a free spender who never watched over his money, his days of hard living finally began catching up with him.

Diagnosed with consumption, which it was suspected that he had contracted while tending bar, he was found by his ex-wife living on the streets in the fall of 1891. He was also showing signs of liver cirrhosis. Taking pity on her former husband, she brought him to her home on 25th Street in Chicago, where she cared for him in his final days. During the last week of his life, Flint, by now a mere skeleton, was too weak to recognize even his most intimate friends. The end came on the evening of January 14, 1891. Upon his death, Flint was remembered throughout the country for being one of baseball's all-time great catchers.

At his funeral, which was attended by many of his former teammates, a grief-stricken Cap Anson wept uncontrollably. King Kelly remarked about his old comrade that, "he lived life to the fullest and was game to the last." Flint, who had also lost two brothers to consumption, was laid to rest next to his parents in St. Peter's Cemetery in St. Louis in the Bethany Division, Section F, Lot 73.

SPIDER CLARK (1867–1892)

Brooklyn native Owen F. Clark was on his way to a promising career when he was cut down by TB. Clark, born to Irish immigrant parents on September 16, 1867, learned and honed his baseball skills on the streets and sandlots of Brooklyn. He started his professional career in 1887, with a brief three-game stint with the Nashville Blues of the Southern League. He split time with the Manchester Maroons of the New England League and Hazelton Pugilists of the Central League in 1888.

Clark, who was nicknamed "Spider" (the first major leaguer to be associated with that nickname) due to his lanky 5-foot, 10-inch, 150-pound frame—and also due to the fact he was quite rangy in the field—became known for his versatility and willingness to play where needed. He appeared at every position except pitcher during his minor league career, something that did not go unnoticed by baseball executives and fans as he made his way forward in his career.

In 1889, Spider signed on with the National League's Washington Nationals, where he continued his role as a jack-of-all-trades. He appeared in 38 games that season, batting .255, with 3 homers and 22 RBI, as well as 8 stolen bases. He would have appeared in more games if not for a freak injury to his catching hand. *Sporting Life* reported on it in the May 8, 1889, edition, saying,

> A peculiar accident happened to catcher Owen Clark, of the Washingtons, at Staten Island Thursday. He didn't know his hand had been split till his glove filled with blood. He wondered where the blood came from and, taking off the glove, discovered a gash between the third and little fingers.

Joining the Buffalo Bisons of the newly formed Players League the following season, Clark again made an impression on management and fans alike. He played the outfield and each infield position, including one game as pitcher. *Sporting Life* reported on page 10 of its August 9th edition that, "Owen Clark's first base playing has caught the crowds. He is deservedly a favorite."

The 1890 Bisons will never be confused with the '27 Yankees, as they finished with a putrid record of 36–96, good enough for last place, 45 games behind the league champion Boston Reds. A hand injury once again played a part in Clark's season, as he "split a finger" while catching in a game against the Cleveland Infants. Despite the injury, which limited him to just 69 games, he still batted a respectable .265, with 2 homers and 25 RBI.

With the demise of the Players League after the season and the folding of the Buffalo franchise, Clark found himself in need of a job for the coming campaign. Unfortunately, during the fall and winter of 1890, he contracted tuberculosis. While it is unknown where or how he contracted the disease, what is for sure is that he missed the entire oncoming season battling it. Despite a game effort on his part, Clark didn't have a chance. He passed away from phithisis pulmonalis (pulmonary TB) at his home at 93 Wythe Avenue in Brooklyn on February 8, 1892. Single, he was buried at Calvary Cemetery in Woodside, Queens, in Section 9, Plot 914, Grave 15/16.

Spider Clark, 1887, Old Judge Baseball Card. Courtesy of the Library of Congress.

EDGAR SMITH (1862–1892)

Born and raised in Providence, Rhode Island, Edgar Eugene Smith played for four teams during the course of his limited four-year major league career, appearing in just 26 games for the Washington Nationals of the American Association, as well as the Philadelphia Quakers, Providence Grays, and Cleveland Spiders of the National League. Smith was a well-known amateur player in the New England area because of his versatility in the field (he pitched, played both corner outfield positions, and also manned first base when needed).

Smith made his major league debut with the hometown Grays on May 25, 1883, in a 9–6 win over the Chicago White Stockings at Lake Front Park III in Chicago. He appeared in two games for the Grays, both at first base. Smith would reappear in the majors less than a month later when he started one game for the Philadelphia Quakers on June 20th against the Boston Beaneaters at South End Grounds in Boston. This forgettable start saw him pitch 7 innings, while giving up 18 hits and 17 runs, of which 12 were earned. Boston won the game, 29–4. In 1884, Smith played 14 games for the Washington Statesman of the American Association, where manager Holly Hollingshead used him in three games as a pitcher (he went 0–2 in two starts) and 12 games in the outfield.

On August 5, 1885, Smith was pressed back into service by his old team, the Grays, after all three of the club's starting pitchers, Joe Start, Charlie Radbourn, and Dupee Shaw, came down with a mysterious illness. There was some speculation that the three men were "laying down," but this narrative has never been proven. With nowhere else to turn, Providence manager Frank Bancroft hurriedly signed Smith, who was pitching for a local amateur squad. His opponent would be the St. Louis Maroons, a weak-hitting lot whose three best players were shortstop Jack Glasscock, second baseman Fred Dunlop, and first baseman Alex McKinnon.

The 500 people in attendance at the Messer Street Grounds that day had grim doubts about whether an amateur would be able to pitch the home team to victory, but Smith surprised and delighted by twirling a fine game, scattering 9 hits and giving up just 1 earned run as the Grays won, 4–3. As the *New York Times* reported in its August 6th edition, "The Providence club played without the services of Start, Shaw, and

Radbourn yesterday. They were on the sick list. Edgar Smith, a young amateur, did the pitching, and the champions managed to win by one run. Sharp fielding gained the victory."

After his stint with Providence, Smith would not make another major league appearance until the 1890 campaign, when he appeared in eight games for the Cleveland Spiders. During his major league career, the adaptable fielder appeared in 26 games, 11 of them as a pitcher, where he accrued a 2–7 record with a 5.05 ERA. He appeared in 17 games as an outfielder and two as a first baseman, and batted .184 lifetime, with 18 hits and 6 RBI in 98 at bats. By contrast, his career in the minors was somewhat longer, as he played for the Brooklyn Greys of the Interstate Association, Columbus (Georgia) Stars of the Southern League, Providence Grays of the Eastern League, Boston Blues/Haverhill of the New England League, and Detroit Wolverines of both the International League and International Association.

Smith died as a result of a pulmonary hemorrhage due to consumption at his home, located at 18 Dexter Street in Providence, on November 3, 1892. He was buried at Swan Point Cemetery in Providence, Rhode Island.

NED WILLIAMSON (1857–1894)

It was none other than the great Cap Anson who once called Ned Williamson the "greatest all-around ballplayer the country ever saw." Another son of the City of Brotherly Love, Edward Nagle "Ned" Williamson made his major league debut on May 1, 1878, with the Indianapolis Browns, in a 5–4 loss to his future team, the Chicago White Stockings. Williamson, who came up to the majors as a third baseman, was regarded as a "heady" fielder in the days of barehanded play, leading the National League in assists seven times, fielding average four times, double plays six times, and putouts twice. It was at the plate, however, where Williamson was to make his mark.

Joining the Chicago White Stockings in 1879, Ned entered an ensemble of talented, hard-nosed, and hard-partying players. An average hitter in the beginning of his career, it was when the White Stockings moved into their new home at Lake Front Park II during the 1882 season that he began setting records. To say that Lake Front Park was a bandbox would be an understatement at best. Only slightly larger than a present-day softball field, left field was 180 feet, center field 300 feet, and right field just 196 feet.

Lake Front Park's ground rules originally called for any ball hit over the left and right field fences to be called a ground rule double. Williamson, who smacked a career-high 27 doubles in 1882, outdid himself in 1883, when he set a single season record, with 49. Prior to the 1884 season, a change in ground rules allowed for balls hit over the right and left field fences to be called home runs. On suggestion of Cap Anson, Williamson and the rest of his teammates began swinging for the fences. Ned blasted a National League record 27 homers that season. The record, which stood for 35 years, was finally broken by Babe Ruth in 1919, when the Bambino was good for 29.

Williamson, much like the rest of his compadres, was an unabashed partier who often played hung over—not the easiest of things to do under the notoriously brutal Midwest sun. Stocking second baseman Fred "Fritz" Pfeffer once recalled a rather hysterical episode where Williamson was brought relief during a game by teammate King Kelly after a hard night of partying:

> Ed was looking rather poor in the field that day. The heat and humidity were making it really tough on all the boys. It was about the fourth inning. Ed was sitting in the dugout, and he didn't look like he was going to get back out there. Kelly saw what bad shape he was in and, without saying a word, vanished from the dugout. When he comes back he has a cold beer in his hand. He walks over to Williamson and tells him, "Here, drink this and you'll feel like a new man." Well, the elixir must have worked because he was back out there the next inning, better than ever.

Williamson, who also became the first major leaguer to hit 3 home runs in a game, could usually be found after games hanging out with some of his teammates in the saloons on and around State Street. Staying out all night with his chums was standard fair for Ned, who was looked upon by his teammates as a good man and loyal friend. His skills began to decline in 1889, not because of his lifestyle, but due to a knee injury suffered that August. Never the same player afterward, he was able to hang on for one more season, finishing out his career with the Chicago Pirates of the Players League in 1890.

Remaining in Chicago after the end of his career, Williamson opened up a saloon with former minor league player Billy Woods. It was while working in that very establishment that he contracted tuberculosis, possibly from a customer. To make matters worse, his years of hard partying caused his body to break down at an alarming rate. Diagnosed with both dropsy of the liver and heart disease, his health deteriorated to such an extent that he traveled to Hot Springs, Arkansas, for treatment. Arriving there in January 1894, hoping that the rejuvenating powers of the town's hot springs would somehow magically rid him of his dreaded ills, his would last a little less than two months. He passed away in nearby Willow Springs on the evening of March 3rd, at the age of 36. His body was brought back to Chicago for burial, and he was laid to rest in an unmarked grave in Roseland Cemetery, in what is now known as the Paupers Section, located along Peterson Avenue.

WILLIAM BROWN (1866–1897)

Nicknamed "Big Bill" because of his 6-foot, 2-inch, 190-pound frame, and "California" because he hailed from San Francisco, William Brown played seven seasons in the majors, from 1887 to 1891 and 1893 to 1894. He was a catcher who also played first, second, third, and outfield. He played with the New York Giants, Louisville Colonels, Philadelphia Phillies, Baltimore Orioles, and St. Louis Browns. In New York, Brown was the primary backup for future Hall of Famer Buck Ewing, and it was there that he became known for his defensive ability and gamesmanship, as he would often talk to batters when he was behind the plate in an effort to get them off their game. A favorite receiver of Giant pitchers Tim Keefe and Mickey Welch, he especially enjoyed using sarcasm to rattle baseball's top hitters, especially future Hall of Famer Mike "King" Kelly.

While with the Giants, Brown appeared in two World Series, in 1888, versus the St. Louis Browns, and 1889, against the Brooklyn Bridegrooms. He jumped to the New York Giants of the Players League in 1890 for better money. When the Players League folded, he joined the Philadelphia Phillies for the 1891 campaign. Playing 91 games at first base that season, he batted .278, with a career-high 4 home runs and 43 RBI. Brown headed back to the minors in 1892,

Grave of William Brown. Courtesy of G. Royston Morlidge.

where he split time between the San Francisco Metropolitans and Oakland Colonels of the California League. He made it back to the majors the following season, when he caught on with the Baltimore Orioles.

After appearing in just seven games with the Orioles, Brown's contract was sold to the Louisville Colonels. It was with Louisville that he posted career highs in batting average (.305), RBI (85), hits (140), runs (85), walks (50), and triples (9). Despite his breakout season, he was supplanted the next year at first base by newcomer Luke Lutenberg. After appearing in just 13 games for the Colonels in 1894, his contract was bought by the St. Louis Browns, with whom he would appear in the final three games of his big-league career.

Contracting consumption in 1895, he traveled to Arizona, Hawaii, and Southern California in an effort to find a climate that would be more beneficial to his condition, but his efforts proved fruitless. Even as his condition worsened, Brown held out hopes of returning to the majors. In an interview with the *San Francisco Call* a few months before his death, he proclaimed, "Don't count me out just yet, I'll be back, just you wait and see."

In 418 major league games, William Brown accrued a lifetime .281 average, with 6 homers and 252 RBI in 1,569 at bats. In three World Series games, he went 6-for-13 for a batting average of .462, with 1 homer and 2 RBI.

Brown died at his home in San Francisco on the evening of December 20, 1897. Originally buried in Calvary Cemetery in San Francisco, his body was later moved to Holy Cross Cemetery in Colma when the San Francisco City Council ordered a stop to all burials inside the San Francisco city limits and a relocation of bodies in Calvary Cemetery. He was reinterred in Section B, Row 15, Area 23, Grave 3.

HENRY PORTER (1858–1906)

Born in Vergennes, Vermont, in June 1858, Henry Porter later moved with his family to Brockton, Massachusetts. It was in this town that he started gaining the necessary baseball skills to make it to the major leagues. Porter gained notoriety playing for semipro clubs in Webster, Massachusetts; Woonsocket, Rhode Island; and Holyoke, Massachusetts, before beginning his pro career with Bay City of the Northwest

League in 1883. In late September 1884, after Bay City's season ended, he was given a tryout with the Union Association's Milwaukee Grays, also known as the Brewers. Porter would go 3–3 with a 3.00 ERA in six games, with an amazing 71 strikeouts in 51 innings of work. On October 3rd, he struck out 18 Boston Reds in a 5–4 loss at Milwaukee's Wright Street Grounds.

Moving to the American Association the following season, he became the toast of Brooklyn, as he led that city's entry in wins, with a 33–21 record and a 2.78 ERA. The next season, he went 27–19, with a 3.42 ERA.

New York's *National Police Gazette* reported on Porter in its August 15, 1885, edition, mentioning his, "giant work for the Brooklyn Club . . . in the pitcher's box." Beginning with the 1887 season, when he went 15–24, with a 4.21 ERA, Porter would pitch to sub-.500 records for the remainder of his major league career. On January 22, 1888, he was sold to the Kansas City Cowboys for $7,000 as part of a nine-player transaction.

Statistically speaking, Porter would have the worst year of his career in 1888, when he went 18–37, with a 4.16 ERA, in 474 innings. His 37 losses led the American Association. Despite his dismal season, Henry accomplished a wondrous feat when he became just the 26th pitcher in major league history to throw a no-hitter. Porter's no-no happened in a 4–0 win over the Baltimore Orioles in a game played at Oriole Park on June 6th.

In its June 7th edition, the *Baltimore Sun* writes,

> A game played by 18 galvanized corpses is a spectacle unexpected in any baseball city, and yet that was the sight to which the spectators of the Baltimore–Kansas City game at the Huntingdon Avenue grounds yesterday were treated. Baltimore was defeated, but there was nothing remarkable in that. Baltimore was shut out, but that has happened before. But it never before occurred when every Baltimore player was doing fairly good work that they were shut out without a single hit.

Amazingly, Porter's no-hit gem only brought his record to 10–24 for the season. On June 17, 1889, with his record standing at 0–3 for just four games, Kansas City gave him his unconditional release, after which he signed on with Hartford of the Atlantic League in mid-July. He appeared in eight games for the London (Ontario, Canada) Tecumsehs of the International Association in 1890, going 2–5 before finally retiring from pro ball, although he would continue to pitch semipro ball for many years. He also worked in a shoe factory in Brockton, Massachusetts.

While working in the confines of the shoe plant, Porter came down with tuberculosis. He died from the disease at his home at 615 North Montello Street in Brockton on December 30, 1906. Porter, who was married, was buried at Calvary Cemetery in Brockton. He was laid to rest on January 2, 1907.

HERMAN LONG (1866–1909)

A member of the famed Boston Beaneaters dynasty of the 1890s, Chicago native Herman Long was considered to be one of the best shortstops of his era. In fact, many of his peers rated him as being heads above all other shortstops of that time. Long played two years of minor league ball in the Western League and Western Association before signing with the American Association's Kansas City Cowboys. Boston purchased his contract from the cash-strapped Cowboys on January 5, 1890, for a purchase price that was reported to be between $5,000 and $6,000. Boston brought Long in to replace the previous season's starting shortstop, Joe Quinn, who had jumped to the ill-fated Players League for 1890.

During his 13 years with Boston, Long, who was known by the nicknames "Germany" and the "Flying Dutchman," would go on to become an integral part of five Boston pennant-winning teams. One of the team's on-field leaders, he was a smart, heady player who knew that Boston manager Frank Selee counted on him both offensively and defensively. A .277 lifetime hitter, Long drove in 1,055 run, despite hitting just 91 homers. Known for his speed and aggressive baserunning skills, he stole 537 bases and scored 1,457 runs during his career, including six straight seasons of 100 runs or more between 1891 and 1896. He also had a lifetime .718 on-base plus slugging (OPS) average that included four straight years (1894–1897) with an OPS of .800 or better (77th all-time).

Herman Long, New York Highlanders. Courtesy of the Library of Congress.

Despite the fact that he holds the all-time record for most errors made during a career, with 1,096, of which 1,030 were made at short-stop, Long was considered a good defensive player, leading the league in errors only twice in his career, with a career fielding average at shortstop of .906, three points higher than the league average of .903.

Jumping to the American league in 1903, Long was the Opening Day shortstop for the newly christened Highlanders franchise. On June 10, 1903, after appearing in just 22 games for New York, he was traded, along with Ernie Courtney, to the Detroit Tigers for Kid Elberfeld. Elberfeld would go on to play the next seven seasons with New York, while Long was almost done. He would finish his major league career after appearing in just one game for the Phillies in 1904, after which he went back to the minors, where he also managed. His last stop in pro-fessional baseball was with the Omaha Rourkes of the Western League in 1906.

Long, who made decent money from the game, should have had a happy retirement; however, sadly, he contracted tuberculosis. Thinking that a change in climate would improve his health, he moved to Denver, Colorado, where he would eventually settle at the Oakes Home, a resi-dence for people suffering from consumption. He died there on Sep-tember 17, 1909, at the age of 43. His body was brought back to Chica-go for burial in Concordia Cemetery in Forest Park, Illinois, in Section 8, Lot 1425, Second from South.

An interesting postscript to Long's career happened in 1936, when the first-ever Veterans Committee vote for the National Baseball Hall of Fame took place. Long accrued the eighth most votes (15.5) among players considered, and he had a higher vote total than King Kelly, Amos Rusie, Hughie Jennings, Fred Clarke, Jimmy Collins, Charlie Comiskey, and George Wright, all of whom are now in the Hall of Fame. Long, on the other hand, has been virtually forgotten.

GEORGE KAISERLING (1893–1918)

Pitcher George Kaiserling, a native of Steubenville, Ohio, was a career minor leaguer except for 78 games spent in the ill-fated Federal League. Born May 12, 1893, to German immigrants Fred and Johanna Kaiserling, he started his professional career in 1910, with the Class D

Great Bend Millers of the Kansas State League, after which he made stops for teams in the Illinois-Missouri League and Central League, as well as Indianapolis of the American Association.

Before the 1913 season, Kaiserling signed to play with the Indianapolis Hoosiers of the Federal League, which, at the time, was still considered an independent league and not a major league. He officially made his major league debut on April 20, 1914, as the winning pitcher in a 7–2 win over the Kansas City Packers. Kaiserling had a successful season for Indy, as he threw to a 17–10 mark, with a 3.11 ERA, helping the Hoosiers to the pennant. His personal highlight of the season was when he hurled a one-hitter against St. Louis on July 19th.

The Hoosiers were a strong team that boasted such notable players as Edd Roush, Bill Rariden, Bill McKechnie, Frank LaPorte, George Mullin, and the highly touted Benny Kauff. Kaiserling remained with the club when it moved to Newark, New Jersey, the next season, going 15–15, with a stingy 2.24 ERA. After the Federal League shut down, he played for Toledo of the American Association and Chattanooga of the Southern Association. It was while playing for Chattanooga in the summer of 1917 that he was forced to quit baseball due to ill health. He died on March 2, 1918, in his hometown of Steubenville from pulmonary tuberculosis and was buried at Union Cemetery in Steubenville on March 4th.

MAURY UHLER (1886–1918)

An outfielder who batted and threw right-handed, Maurice William "Maury" Uhler appeared in 36 games for the 1914 Cincinnati Reds. The son of Nicholas and Anna Rebecca (Spurrier) Uhler, he was born in Pikesville, Maryland, where, prior to his baseball career, he worked in the Office of the Board of Fire Commissioners as a fire department clerk. Before his engagement with Cincinnati, Maury played baseball with the Maryland Athletic Club, Western Maryland Club, and B&O Railroad baseball team.

Uhler made his major league debut on Opening Day, Tuesday, April 14th, in a 10–1 rout of the Chicago Cubs at Redland Field in Cincinnati. Red manager Buck Herzog had Uhler pinch-hit for left fielder Armando Marsans after the game was well out of hand. The contest, which lasted two hours and ten minutes, was played in a steady drizzle that kept Opening Day attendance to a disappointing 12,000 hardy fans.

It was a tale of two pitchers, as Cub starter Larry Cheney, who was obviously not enthralled with the wet conditions, allowed eight Reds to reach base via walks and threw four wild pitches to boot. Cincinnati starter Rube Benton, however, was nearly perfect, pitching a two-hitter and allowing the lone Cub tally to come via a Heinie Zimmerman sacrifice fly in the ninth inning after he walked the bases loaded. As for Uhler, he was used mostly in a utility role during his stay in the Queen City, which saw him bat an unimpressive .214. He was released to Minneapolis of the American Association on July 24, 1914.

Uhler lived at 1742 Warwick Avenue in Baltimore and was working as a stenographer/clerk at the time of his death on May 4, 1918. The cause of his passing was tuberculosis of the lungs. He was buried at Druid Ridge Cemetery in Pikesville, Maryland, on May 7th in the Linden Section, Lot 21, Grave 3. Maury Uhler, who was just 31 years old, was survived by his wife Myrtle and his parents.

JERRY HURLEY (1875–1919)

There were two Jerry Hurleys who played in the major leagues. The first one, Jeremiah Joseph Hurley, played 33 games for three teams in three leagues from 1889 to 1891, and died in Boston, Massachusetts, on September 17, 1950, at the ripe old age of 87. The second Jerry Hurley had an even shorter major league career, and, unfortunately, a brief life. Hurley's parents, Daniel and Ann, were Irish immigrants who settled in Manhattan. Young Jeremiah played amateur and semipro ball before making his professional debut at the age of 23 with Class C Utica of the New York State League, where he would play for the next three seasons. In 1901, he played with the Schenectady Electricians of the New York State League. After the minor league season concluded, his contract was transferred to the Cincinnati Reds.

Hurley made his major league debut on September 23, 1901, as the starting catcher for the Reds in a 25–6 loss to the Brooklyn Superbas at League Park in Cincinnati. The amazing thing about the game was that, despite all the runs scored, it was played in just two hours. Hurley batted an abysmal .048 during his nine-game stint, getting 1 hit in 21 at bats, with a stolen base. The next time he got a chance to play in the majors was six years later, ironically with the same team he debuted against, the Brooklyn Superbas.

On Monday, April 15, 1907, Hurley managed one walk in three at bats in a 3–2 loss to the Boston Doves at the Sound End Grounds in Boston. Nap Rucker was Hurley's battery mate, as Boston scored all their runs in the third inning on just one hit and a steal of home. The game was played in just an hour and 35 minutes. That was it as far as the major leagues were concerned for Hurley. His contract was sent to the Toronto Maple Leafs of the Eastern League after the game. Hurley would soldier on in the minors until 1911, after which he played semi-pro and amateur ball in the New York City area.

Hurley was single and living in Manhattan when he died at Roosevelt Hospital on December 27, 1919, from the effects of pulmonary TB and tuberculosis peritonitis. Just 44 years old, he was laid to rest at Calvary Cemetery, in Woodside, Queens, on December 31st, in Section 7, Range 34, Plot C, Grave 12.

BILL LATTIMORE (1884–1919)

Known more for his slowness afoot than his pitching prowess, Bill Lattimore was given the nickname "Slothful Bill." He was so slow that teammates often referred to him as an "Ice Wagon," a popular term that was used to describe painfully slow baseball players. Some players ascertained that he was even slower than Slow Joe Doyle, who was regarded as the slowest of the slow in baseball.

William Hershel Lattimore was born to Joseph and Clementine Lattimore on May 25, 1884, in Roxton, Texas. A left-handed pitcher, he started his pro career in 1906, with the Class C Webb City (Missouri) Goldbugs of the Western Association. He graduated to the Class A Toledo Mudhens of the American Association in 1907. In September of that year, he was drafted by the Cleveland Naps in the Rule 5 Draft. Invited to spring training the following season, he made his major league debut on April 17th against the Ty Cobb-led Detroit Tigers at Bennett Park in Detroit. Cleveland won, 12–8, in a 12-inning slugfest. Lattimore, who started the game, gave up eight runs in eight and two-thirds innings of work, walking four and striking out three. Addie Joss came in relief of him and got the win when Cleveland plated four in the top of the 12th. Lattimore appeared in four games total, going 1–2 in 24 innings before being sent back to Toledo. Slothful Bill finished his pro career in the minors, where he would later play in the Central League with the Wheeling, West Virginia, club and the Fort Worth Panthers of the Texas League.

After his baseball career came to an end, Lattimore became a highly successful clothing merchant, starting a business in his hometown of Roxton, where he was the coowner of a store. Unfortunately, around 1916, he caught tuberculosis. Feeling that a change in climate would be better for his disposition, he moved to Colorado. He was living at Nob Hill Lodge in Colorado Springs with his wife Grace when he died on October 30, 1919, from pneumonia due to a pulmonary hemorrhage caused by his TB. His body was brought back to Texas, where it was interned at Evergreen Cemetery in Paris in Section 17, Block 75, Grave 4.

GERMANY SCHAEFER (1876–1919)

One of the nuttiest, if not the nuttiest, characters in baseball history, Chicago native Herman "Germany" Schaefer is probably best remembered for helping to institute a rule change because of one of his baserunning stunts. Schaefer was the master of "stealing" first base. This may sound a bit odd, but there was actually a method to the Schaefer madness. One summer day not so long ago (or maybe it was), Detroit was playing the Indians. The Tigers had the speedy Davy Jones on third base and Schaefer on first in the ninth inning and tried a delayed double steal, but Cleveland catcher Nig Clarke, didn't throw. Schaefer ran back to first base on the next pitch and shouted to Jones that he was going back to second base. Clarke became undone and threw down to second, while Jones scored the winning run. Schaefer tried the play a couple more times before it was outlawed.

Germany, or "Dutch" or "Schaef" as he was known to his friends, was a ruddy-faced, good-natured gent with a heart of gold. A free spirit in a time of free spirits, he befriended a young Ty Cobb and became one of his closest friends. Schaefer was a low-average hitter but a jack-of-all-trades in the infield, sort of an early-day super sub. His fielding versatility kept him in the majors for 13 seasons.

A hard-partying, two-fisted drinker, Schaefer's dream was to one day own a saloon where his former teammates could come to hang out. His manager in Detroit, Hughie Jennings, once said of him, "Schaef can always be counted on to pick up the spirits of the boys . . . nothing rattles that bird."

As starting second baseman for the Tigers during his first two years with the club, Schaefer led the American League in putouts in 1905, and total chances per game in 1906. He had only one more season where he played 100 games at a single position. His best season offensively was probably 1908, when he reached career highs with 96 runs (third in the American League), 40 steals (third in the league), and 20 doubles, as the Tigers won their second of three consecutive American League pennants (1907–1909). Traded to the Senators in mid-1909, he had one more significant season, hitting a career-high .334 in 125 games in 1911.

By 1912, Schaef began to spend more time on the coaching lines, where he teamed up with fellow clown Nick Altrock. An earlier vaudeville act with Tiger teammate Charley O'Leary was the inspiration for the MGM musical *Take Me Out to the Ball Game*, starring Gene Kelly and Frank Sinatra.

Schaefer was known for being a master heckler and bench jockey. No one was safe from his one-liners and practical jokes, not even his own teammates. Teammate Wild Bill Donovan saw him light a "hot foot" on an unsuspecting Red Downs, who was snoozing away after having one too many.

One of Schaefer's most well-known stunts happened when a game was being played during a torrential downpour. In the third inning, Germany stepped up to the plate wearing a raincoat and tall boots, with an umbrella in one hand and a bat in the other. Much to the delight of the crowd, the umpire called the game.

Schaefer, who served as a player/coach for the Yankees in 1916 and Indians in 1918, contracted tuberculosis after the 1918 season. Warned by doctors that he needed to lay off the liquor and get maximum rest, Schaef, as per his personality, decided to go a different route, instead accepting a scouting job from his old friend John McGraw.

On Friday, May 16, 1919, Dutch caught a New York Central Railroad train bound for Lake Placid. As the train approached Saranac Lake, he suffered a hemorrhage due to his TB. He was rushed to a hospital in Saranac, but died within the hour. He was only 42 years old. When news of Schaefer's death reached his old friend Ty Cobb, the Georgia Peach wept. Cobb later remembered his friend, saying, "Schaef was a good friend and a great teammate. When I first came up to the Tigers, he was one of the few veteran players who welcomed me with open arms. He never showed me anything but kindness."

One interesting footnote to Schaefer's passing: When he died, eyewitnesses at the hospital said that there was a hint of a grin on his face. If that story is true, then Germany Schaefer died just as he lived. Schaefer's body was brought to Chicago, where he was laid to rest at St. Boniface Cemetery in Chicago, in Section T, Lot 109, Grave 6.

BILL GREVELL (1898–1923)

The son of William and Mary (Morgan) Grevell, William Joseph "Bill" Grevell was born March 5, 1898, in Williamstown, New Jersey. He made his mark in the Independent League and semipro circles before being discovered by Philadelphia Athletic owner Connie Mack. Grevell, who pitched in 12 innings in five games during the 1919 season, made his major league debut on May 14th during a 12–0 slaughter at the hands of the St. Louis Browns. His last appearance was in a 9–2 loss to the White Sox at Comiskey Park on July 9th. He remained under reserve by the A's and was invited to spring training in 1920.

Feeling that his young pitcher needed more seasoning, Mack sent him to play with the Jersey City Skeeters of the International League on April 28th. Grevell went 4–14, with a 4.37 ERA in 19 games, and was one of four International League pitchers to go errorless for the season. Grevell would later go back to playing semipro ball in the Philadelphia area, most notably with the South Phillies. In 1922, it was reported in several newspapers that Grevell had been sent to the Chattanooga Lookouts by the Athletics, who supposedly still owned the rights to him, but the story was likely a fabrication, as Grevell never played for the Lookouts and was still playing semipro ball at the time.

Grave of Bill Grevell. Courtesy of Dr. Fred Worth.

Grevell's life and career were forever changed when he came down with tuberculosis. Where he contracted the disease is anyone's guess, as he was known for having fairly temperate habits and rarely frequented cramped establishments like saloons, where the chances of catching the white plague were greater. One theory is that he contracted the disease while playing ball, but the exact when and where will forever remain a mystery. Grevell died at the Home for Consumptives, located in Chestnut Hill, a suburb of Philadelphia, on June 21, 1923. Just 25 years old, he was buried in Lot 97 in First United Methodist Church of Williamstown Cemetery in Williamstown, New Jersey, on June 25th.

POP BOY SMITH (1892–1924)

A good pitcher in the minor leagues, Clarence O. "Pop Boy" Smith got his nickname when he was a youngster in Alabama selling soda pop at the ballpark. He also had a bit of pop in his pitches, as he excelled in the minor leagues. After pitching to a 15–8 record for the Birmingham Barons in 1912, the White Sox signed him to a contract. Smith went 0–1, appearing in 15 games in 1912, mostly in relief. In early July, he got into a bit of trouble while playing ball with a semipro team, the Coulon Athletics, a no-no for a player signed to a pro contract. Due to his age and lack of experience, he was only reprimanded.

Smith continued his winning ways in the minors with the New Orleans Pelicans, and he was purchased by the Cleveland Indians late in the 1916 season. He pitched five games for the Tribe that season, going 1–2, and six games the next, twirling to a 0–1 record. After his major league service was over, he pitched in the minors with the Salt Lake City Bees of the Pacific Coast League and New Orleans Pelicans of the Southern Association.

After serving in World War I, Pop Boy moved to the Lone Star State, where he managed Sweetwater and Ballinger of the West Texas League. He died suddenly from a pulmonary hemorrhage due to pulmonary tuberculosis at his home in Sweetwater on February 16, 1924. His body was taken to his native state of Alabama, where he was laid to rest at Elmwood Cemetery in Birmingham, in Block 5, Lot 10 in an unmarked grave.

DUTCH ULRICH (1899–1929)

Originally signed to his first pro gig by the Baltimore Orioles under Jack Dunn, Dutch Ulrich was initially ineffective because of his wildness. After Baltimore released him, he moved on to Waynesboro of the Blue Ridge League, where he finally found success. The Philadelphia Phillies took an interest in him and signed him to a contract.

Used mostly in relief, Ulrich was never able to have a winning season in the majors, the closest being his 3–3 rookie season of 1925. Considering that he had the bad luck of twirling for several dreadful Phillie teams (the 1927 club lost 103 games), the fact that he had a 19–27 lifetime record, with a 3.48 ERA, was quite amazing. His 3.17 ERA in 1927 was sixth in the National League.

Ulrich was unable to play in 1928 due to illness. In February of that year, he contracted TB and wound up with a case of double pneumonia (the tuberculosis was not made known to the general public). Because of his condition, he was forced to stay at Franklin Square Hospital in Baltimore for several weeks. His recovery was so slow that it took him several months until he was able to start a training regimen. In the fall, Dutch had a slight relapse, and his condition deteriorated as the winter approached.

In late January 1929, Ulrich's health declined rapidly. He died at his stepparent's home, located at 823 North Montford Avenue in Baltimore, on February 11, 1929. Newspapers reporting on his death stated that he died as a result of pneumonia and pleurisy, but his death certificate states that he died as a result of pulmonary tuberculosis with cardiac exhaustion. Ulrich, who was single, was just 29 years old. He was buried at Bohemian National Cemetery in Baltimore on February 14th in Section O, Block 2, Grave 2A.

RIP HAGERMAN (1888–1930)

Also known as "Rip Zip," Zerah Zequiel "Rip" Hagerman pitched during parts of four seasons for the Chicago Cubs and Cleveland Naps. The Cubs obtained him after he pitched for Des Moines of the Western League and Topeka, Kansas. Hagerman pitched in Cuba during the winter of 1908 and did so well that Cuban League officials informed the Cubs that they would gladly accept his services for the year if he was farmed out.

Hagerman made his big-league debut on April 16th in a 3–1 loss to the Cardinals at Chicago. He pitched a splendid game, except for a three-run sixth inning, during which St. Louis bunched three of their five hits. He appeared in 13 games in 1909, going 4–4. He was sold to Louisville of the American Association on April 19, 1910, spending the next four seasons in the minors, where he also spent time with the Portland Beavers of the Pacific Coast League. He was sold by Portland to the Cleveland Indians in January 1914. Hagerman was never able to find his winning ways with the "Cuyahoga County Nine," as he suffered through two losing seasons. On May 22, 1916, after appearing in just two games for the Tribe, he was sold back to Portland. Hagerman played in the minor leagues until 1925, with his last stop being the Oklahoma City Indians of the Western League.

In 1927, Rip Zip contracted TB, which induced a move to New Mexico the following year. Sadly, the drier climate of the Southwest did not improve his health. In addition to tuberculosis, Hagerman also suffered from myocarditis during the last few weeks of his life. He passed away with his wife Margaret at his side on January 30, 1930, at his home at 311 South 6th Street in Albuquerque. He was buried at Mount Calvary Cemetery in Albuquerque a few days later. His grave has remained unmarked.

REGGIE RICHTER (1888–1934)

Originally scouted by the White Sox, pitcher Emil "Reggie" Richter appeared in 22 games for the 1911 Cubs. Acquired by Chicago from the Louisville Colonels of the American Association for Jack Pfiester on May 15, 1911, he made his major league debut on May 30th in the second game of a morning–afternoon split doubleheader against the Pirates. Richter, who had a 1–3 record, with a 3.13 ERA in 22 games, was used mostly out of the bull pen by Cub manager Frank Chance, this despite the fact that the future Hall of Famer once remarked to the press that his young right-hander had a "million dollar arm."

Sent back to Louisville for the 1912 season, Richter experienced a serious injury to his throwing arm when he was hit by a fastball. When doctors informed him that he would no longer be able to pitch to his old form, he moved back to Chicago to rehab. He spent the 1913 season out of pro ball and took a job working for the Western Electric Company as a clerk. Even though he was unable to pitch in the majors, Richter was still good enough to pitch Western Electric to a Chicago Commercial League championship. He spent his final two pro seasons splitting time with the International League's Newark Indians and the Montreal Royals.

Retiring after the 1914 season, Reggie returned to full-time work as a clerk for Western Electric, while continuing to pitch for the company's baseball team. In August 1933, he played in an old-timers game at Mills Stadium, located on Chicago's West Side. The contest featured former major leaguers versus former semipro stars.

Richter was living at 548 West 61st Place in Chicago when he passed away from pulmonary tuberculosis on August 2, 1934, at the age of 44.

Survived by his wife Mary, he was buried at Oak Hill Cemetery in Blue Island, Illinois, in Division 3, Plot 15, Grave E of Northwest 4th on August 6th.

RUBE LUTZKE (1897–1938)

Walter John "Rube" Lutzke was considered to be the best third baseman in the minor leagues when he was purchased from Kansas City of the American Association by the Cleveland Indians on November 4, 1922. Lutzke, who had previously played with Indianapolis in 1920, was coming off a .325 season in 1921. The Tribe touted him as an up-and-coming star at third base as spring training of 1923 approached. Unfortunately, Lutzke was never able to make the transition to the majors. He only batted .256 in his first season, with 65 RBI. His fielding was not much better, as he committed 35 errors. He batted a disappointing .249 lifetime, with only 4 home runs and 223 RBI, and ended his career in 1931, with the Chattanooga Lookouts of the Southern Association, after which he went back to Milwaukee, where he played semipro ball, mostly in the Milwaukee City League.

Lutzke opened a successful tavern in Milwaukee and did quite well until pulmonary TB overtook him just a little more than a year before his death. Doctors surmised that he caught the disease from one of the customers who frequented his saloon. Rube Lutzke died at 11:45 a.m. on March 6, 1938, at his home in Granville, Wisconsin. Also suffering from pernicious anemia, he was survived by his wife Clara and brother Fred. He was laid to rest on March 9th at Valhalla Memorial Cemetery in Milwaukee, Wisconsin, in the main mausoleum, Crypt 526.

DICK COTTER (1889–1945)

Brooklyn native Dick Cotter's story is much like that of many players who made it to the "show" for an all-too-brief period. The son of William and Mary (O'Donnell) Cotter, both Irish immigrants, Dick was born October 12, 1889, in Manchester, New Hampshire. He moved with his family to Brooklyn at the age of 10, where he later attended

Erasmus High School and Brooklyn Prep before enrolling in Manhattan College.

A catcher by trade, Cotter played 20 games for the 1911 Philadelphia Phillies and another 20 for the 1912 Chicago Cubs. In 1912, he played in the American Association and, after serving in World War I, for the Reading Marines of the International League from 1920 to 1921. Dick went on to join the New York-Penn League's Binghamton Triplets from 1923 through 1924.

Financially well off, Cotter and his wife Marion eventually purchased a 4,916-square-foot Tudor-style revival home designed by famous architect John J. Petit in 1904. The house, located at 1203 Albemarle Road in the Prospect Park South area of Flatbush, still stands today, looking much the same as it did when the Cotters lived there more than 70 years ago. Albemarle Road is still considered one of the most architecturally splendid areas in Brooklyn.

Living in their dream home with no cares to speak of, the Cotters were looking forward to a long life of leisurely retirement. Fate, however, has a way of mucking up the works. In 1941, Dick was diagnosed with pulmonary tuberculosis. While not an immediate death sentence, as it had been decades earlier, the odds of a full recovery were against him. Refusing to move to a more accommodating climate to rehabilitate, with the help of Marion, Cotter battled the insidious disease for four years, finally succumbing on the morning of April 4, 1945. He was

Grave of Dick Cotter. Courtesy of the author.

only 55 years old. He was laid to rest three days later in Holy Cross Cemetery in the St. Theresa Section, Range 12, Plot 1 to 4. But if you think the story ends there, you're wrong.

In the early morning hours of August 8, 2007, 62 years after Cotter's passing, an EF2 tornado with wind speeds of 111 to 135 miles per hour touched down in Brooklyn. Heading north-north east, it eventually hit part of Holy Cross Cemetery, causing severe damage to several stones. Cotter's stone, a magnificent granite Celtic cross, suffered the most extreme damage. Lifted from its three-tiered pedestal mount as if being shot from a mortar, it landed several hundred feet away, breaking into three large sections.

In the aftermath of the storm, attempts were made by the staff at Holy Cross to contact members of Cotter's family to have the cross restored to its original glorious condition. Unable to locate family in the area and with no other alternative, the broken and battered monument was returned to the Cotter family gravesite, an eternal testament to Mother Nature's wrath. One can now firmly state that poor Dick Cotter will, forever more, rest in pieces.

POL PERRITT (1891–1947)

A highly underrated pitcher who excelled under the tutelage of John McGraw, William Dayton "Pol" Perritt spent a little less than two seasons in the minors before joining the St. Louis Cardinals in early September 1912. A son of Louisiana, his nickname was pronounced like the name Polly, in conjunction with his last name, which sounded like the word *parrott*. After a 16–13 season with the Cardinals in 1914, Perritt signed a Federal League contract. The Cardinals then sold his rights to the New York Giants on February 18, 1915. Giant manager John McGraw talked Perritt into returning to the National League, where he became a mainstay of the Giant pitching rotation. He won 18 games in 1916 and 1918, and was 17–7 in 1917, when the Giants won the National League pennant.

During the course of 11 seasons, Perritt accrued a lifetime record of 92 wins and 78 losses, with 8 saves and a 2.89 ERA. He pitched in the minors until 1922, after which he became an oil operator in Shreveport. He remained active in the game, pitching semipro baseball whenever he got the chance. His occupation at the time of his death was listed as lease broker. Perritt died on October 15, 1947, at Charity Hospital in Shreveport from respiratory failure due to advanced tuberculosis and was buried at Arcadia Cemetery in Arcadia, Louisiana.

BUCK FREEMAN (1896–1953)

Not to be confused with the power-hitting outfielder of the same name, right-handed pitcher Alexander Vernon "Buck" Freeman joined the major leagues as a 27-year-old rookie in 1921. A native of Mart, Texas, the five-foot, 10-inch Freeman had served as a sergeant in the U.S. Army with the 160th Depot Brigade during World War I, hence the delay in his career. Discharged in December 1918, he would go on to play with the Class B Beaumont Exporters of the Texas League in 1920, where he pitched to a 3–6 record in 12 games. Including Freeman, the Exporter roster had no less than 18 players who had either played or would go on to play in the majors.

Freeman made his major league debut for the Chicago Cubs on April 13, 1921, in a 5–2 win over the Cardinals. He came into the game in the seventh inning in relief of Grover Cleveland Alexander, after "Old Pete" was pinch-hit for. Buck pitched in 38 games that season, logging a 9–10 record, with a 4.11 ERA and 3 saves. He appeared in 11 games the following season, his last being on June 10th in a 13–0 loss to the Brooklyn Robins. On July 8th, he was released outright to Denver of the Western League. He continued to pitch professionally in the minors until 1929, after which he moved back to his native Texas. Settling in San Antonio, he lived at 101 North Flores Street for the last five years of his life.

A widower, Freeman passed away at Brooke Army Hospital at Fort Sam Houston on February 21, 1953, from the effects of pulmonary tuberculosis, which he had suffered from during the last three years of his life. At the time of his death, he was also suffering from a variety of other ailments, including gangrene of the right foot and heart disease, which made his recovery from TB nearly impossible. Freeman, who was 59 years old, was buried at Fort Sam Houston National Cemetery on February 25th in Section N, Grave 191.

BUCK HERZOG (1885–1953)

Throughout the history of the national game there have been many players known for being the proverbial jacks-of-all-trades and masters of none. The complete contrast of that moniker was Baltimore native Charles Lincoln "Buck" Herzog. During the course of his 13-year major league career, Herzog played third base, second base, and shortstop with equal adroitness and reliability, so much so that to this day he is generally regarded as one of the most versatile infielders in the history of baseball.

Born in the Monumental City on July 9, 1885, Herzog's family moved to rural Ridgley, Maryland, when he was still a child. He attended Maryland Agricultural College (now the University of Maryland), where he played shortstop next to future Hall of Famer Frank Baker. He started his professional career in 1907, when he signed on to play with the popular York White Roses of the Tri-State League. Herzog stayed with the White Roses when the franchise moved during the season to Reading, Pennsylvania. It was during his first pro season that he began garnering a well-deserved reputation for versatility, as he played both third base and shortstop for manager Curtis Weigand's team. Despite batting a paltry .204 in 431 at bats, he was signed by John McGraw's New York Giants on September 1 in that year's Rule 5 Draft.

When Herzog joined the Giants the following spring, reports indicated that he got along well with his new boss. Herzog's rookie campaign saw him finish with a .300 average in just 64 games. In the field, he appeared in 42 games at second base, 12 at shortstop, 4 at third, and 1 in the outfield. McGraw noted that while his rookie player had showed "good form," he still had a "lot to learn." Aside from his player's versatility, McGraw also loved the fact that Buck was quite adept at doing the little things that were so important to "inside baseball," which, of course, was the prominent style of play at the time. A terrific bunter, he was fast on the bases and exceptional at both stealing bases and taking the extra base. Almost from the start of his rookie season, Herzog showed an energetic and fiery disposition. In modern terms, he was a cross between the Energizer Bunny and what old-time hockey players called a "shit disturber." Herzog eventually earned the nickname "Choke 'Em Charley" because of his motto, "When you get 'em down, choke 'em," speaking of the opposition.

Herzog took a gigantic step back the following season, as he became mired in a season-long slump that saw him bat only .185 in just 42 games. Relegated to the bench by McGraw, his constant chirping and whining with regard to his playing time so grated on the manager that they became estranged. Despite the fact that McGraw brought him to camp the next season, he was not about to spend another season listening to Herzog's complaining.

On April 4, McGraw engineered a trade of Herzog and rookie outfielder Bill Collins to the Boston Doves for David "Beals" Becker. Herzog had no problem acclimating himself to Boston due to the fact that he got along exceptionally well with manager Joe Kelley. While McGraw was known for being a strict disciplinarian, Kelley, his old teammate on the Baltimore Orioles, was known for being a "players' manager" who got along with everyone. This did not lead to good play by the Boston team, however, which finished with a 63–91 record. Buck spent a season and a half with Boston before he surprisingly found himself traded back to the Giants in a July 22nd deal that saw Boston receive Al Bridwell and Hank Gowdy.

When Herzog reported to New York, McGraw told him in no uncertain terms that he didn't care about what the two thought of one another, all he cared about was winning the pennant. Knowing that his pepper-pot infielder wanted to win as much as he did, McGraw decided to put personal feelings aside for the good of the team. Readily agreeing to this baseball version of détente, Herzog, as he always did, played his heart out for the rest of the season, batting .267, with 26 RBI, 22 stolen bases, and 37 runs scored in 69 games. Herzog's high-energy game seemed to bring new life to McGraw's minions, who wound up winning the pennant by five games over the rival Cubs.

The Giants' opponents in the World Series would be the Philadelphia A's, led by their $100,000 dollar infield of Stuffy McInnis, Eddie Collins, Jack Barry, and Frank Baker. For years, A's manager Connie Mack had rankled over the way his team was masterfully vanquished in the 1905 series by McGraw and his all-world pitcher, Christy Mathewson, who had pitched three shutouts. To go along with the ageless Matty, McGraw had future Hall of Famer Rube Marquard, Doc Crandall, and Red Ames at his disposal. The A's would counter with Eddie Plank, Chief Bender, and Jack Coombs, as tough a trio as could be found anywhere. When Mathewson won the first game, 2–1, over

Bender, many experts predicted a repeat of the 1905 debacle for the A's. But the Athletics were simply too good of a team to go down without a fight. Led by Frank Baker's 2 home runs and 5 RBI, the Athletics dispatched the Giants in six games. Herzog, like many of his teammates, would have a miserable series, batting .190.

The next season, Herzog appeared in 140 games, all at third base, and batted .263, with 47 RBI, 37 stolen bases, and 72 runs scored. He redeemed himself in that year's Fall Classic against the Red Sox, when he batted a hefty .400 for the series, which the Giants once again lost. Herzog's 12 hits set a record that stood for more than a half-century. The following year, injuries relegated him to just 96 games, as he split time with Tillie Shafer at third.

In the World Series against the Athletics, Herzog was shut down, going just 1-for-19 for a horrendous .043 average. To be fair, all of the Giants had trouble in the series. After Mathewson bested Eddie Plank in the first game, 3–0, Connie Mack's crew went on a run, taking four straight to become world champions. After the series, McGraw congratulated Mack and his team, opining that he was still proud of his team despite the loss. Herzog, on the other hand, was none too happy with his performance, vowing to friends and teammates that he would be back stronger than ever the following spring.

In December, while major league owners gathered at the Waldorf Astoria in New York, a trade was announced between the Reds and Giants. Engineered by Giant owner Harry Hempstead, the agreement sent Herzog to the Reds, along with catcher Grover Hartley, for speedy outfielder Bob Bescher. The deal was made without the knowledge of McGraw, who was on a trip around the world. While McGraw had been interested in Bescher for some time, he was described as "incensed" when he learned of the trade. When he finally met up with Hempstead, he lambasted the owner, telling him, "I'll do the thinking around here. The next time a deal is made on this ball club, I'll make it."

Herzog, on the other hand, was delighted with the move, for he was immediately named the Reds' player/manager. He would be replacing Joe Tinker, who had been traded to Brooklyn during the same meetings where Herzog's deal had been made. A December 15th article in the *New York Times* warned that Herzog would have his hands full because of insubordination of Red players the previous season. Former Red outfielder Jimmy Sheckard, who had just finished up his final major league season, warned about the slackers, commenting, "No matter who gets Tinker's place, the new manager will have to get rid of the 'knockers' on that club before he can hope to succeed. There is no chance to win with players who think more of their own records than they do of the success of the club." Interestingly, Bescher was one of several players whom Sheckard accused of "laying down."

In Cincinnati, Herzog, as per his personality, battled with management and players, and was otherwise his usual gruff self. His tenure as Red manager was subpar at best, as he guided his teams to records of 60–94 and 71–83 his first two seasons in the Queen City. In July 1916, with the Reds again playing lackluster ball, rumors abounded that McGraw was interested in obtaining his old nemesis. "Little Napoleon" was so enamored with the thought of obtaining Herzog that he wired Red president Gary Herrmann himself to tell him that he would personally travel to Cincinnati to handle negotiations. On July 20th, it was announced that Herzog had been traded back to New York, along with Bill Killefer, for Christy Mathewson, Bill McKechnie, and Edd Roush, as well as $40,000 in cash. Herzog, who had grown weary of the problems in Cincy, was ecstatic about returning to the Polo Grounds. Almost immediately, McGraw named Herzog team captain and inserted him as starting shortstop. Herzog's style of "firebrand" ball had an immediate impact, as the Giants went on to win 26 games in a row.

The following spring, Herzog was involved in what would become his most famous altercation. The incident occurred during a three-game exhibition series between the Giants and Tigers at Dallas, Texas. When Ty Cobb arrived late for the first game because he had played two rounds of golf that morning, the Giant bench, led by McGraw, Art Fletcher, and Herzog, started in on him. Newspapers reported that Cobb was called, among other things, a "showoff" and "swellhead," while, Joe S. Jackson of the *Detroit Free Press* maintained that the language was much rougher, including McGraw calling Cobb a "lazy son of a bitch." When the bench jockeying continued in game two, Cobb decided to exact his revenge. With two outs in the top of the second inning, Cobb singled to center. With Bobby Veach at bat, he took off for second base, and Giant catcher Lew McCarty made a strong throw that beat Cobb to the bag by 10 feet. As Herzog stood with the ball in his glove, Cobb came in like a freight train, spikes high, leaving Herzog torn and bloody. As Herzog and Cobb tangled with one another, both benches emptied, led by McGraw and Detroit manager Hughie Jennings. A squad of Dallas police officers hurriedly ran onto the field to help restore order. When Cobb took his usual position in right field in the bottom of the inning, McGraw complained to umpire Bill Brennan that he needed to be tossed because he had started the fight. Rather than listen to McGraw's whining, Brennan threw Cobb out of the game. As it turned out, this would only be the start of the proceedings.

With both clubs staying at the Oriental Hotel, it was almost a forgone conclusion that fireworks were in the cards that evening. As Cobb ate dinner in the hotel dinning room, Herzog walked up to him and challenged him to a fight. An hour later, both men met in Cobb's room to, as Herzog biographer Gabriel Schechter writes, "finish their business." The Giants' Heinie Zimmerman and Detroit catcher Oscar Stanage were allowed into the room as seconds, with Tiger trainer Harry Tuthill refereeing the match.

Before Herzog entered the room, Cobb had cleared the furniture and sprinkled water on the floor to gain an advantage. Wearing leather-soled shoes to get better footing, he easily manhandled Herzog, who was wearing tennis shoes. Knocked down a half dozen times or so, Herzog looked like he had gone 20 rounds with heavyweight champion Jess Willard. After a half hour of fisticuffs, Zimmerman and Stanage finally intervened. The *New York Times* later reported that afterward, the two men "shook hands and declared a truce." Herzog did gain a moral victory of sorts, as he managed to knock Cobb down once, later stating to his teammates, "I got hell kicked out of me, but I knocked the bum down, and you know that swell head, he'll never get over the fact that a little guy like me had him on the floor."

Moral victories aside, for Herzog, his business with Cobb was over; however, McGraw, who verbally accosted Cobb in the lobby later that night, vowed revenge. On the advice of Hughie Jennings and Detroit management, Cobb did not play in the final exhibition games, opting to go to Cincinnati, where he continued his spring training regime with the Reds, now managed by his good friend Christy Mathewson. Interestingly, Cobb would always maintain that he had the highest respect for Herzog because of how "game" he was when they fought. It was the same attitude that Cobb had been shown by former teammate Boss Schmidt when the two had fought nearly a decade earlier.

Despite the thrashing he took from Cobb, 1917 would be another memorable year for Herzog and the Giants, as they would go on to win the pennant. In the World Series, against the White Sox, Herzog made an error in Game 5 that allowed Chicago to tie the score. The White Sox would go on to win the game and the series, four games to two. Once again out of favor with McGraw, Herzog was traded to the Braves the following January in a deal for Jesse Barnes and former Giant Larry Doyle. Buck batted just .228 in 1918, and he was traded midway through the following season to the Cubs, where he finished out his major league career.

After his release from Chicago in January 1921, Herzog returned to the minors, splitting the 1921 season between the Louisville Colonels and Columbus Senators of the American Association. In 1924, he was named manager of the Newark Bears of the International League but was given his release that March before managing a regular-season game. His final two seasons of professional baseball were spent as manager of the Easton Farmers of the Eastern Shore League. After coaching the U.S. Naval Academy team for a time, he found work as a passenger agent with the B&O Railroad and later worked at a Maryland racetrack. During the ensuing year, he was mentioned in numerous articles regarding the Giants and baseball in general.

When McGraw died in 1934, Buck had nothing but kind words to say. He spoke with the Associated Press, stating, "He was the best manager I ever played for." Herzog lived in relative obscurity throughout the next two decades, occasionally meeting up with old teammates who visited the Baltimore area. In 1952, bad luck befell the former Giant great. In the April 17th edition of the *New York Times*, it was reported that Buck had been struck by a car in downtown Baltimore and treated at Mercy Hospital for "multiple lacerations." Less than a year later, on January 14, 1953, the *Times* reported that Herzog was found "penniless" in the lobby of a Baltimore hotel, suffering from what doctors later diagnosed as advanced tuberculosis. Taken to Baltimore City Hospital, he would fight the disease for the next eight months. When the news of Herzog's plight reached baseball commissioner Ford Frick, he, without hesitation, made funds available to help with Herzog's hospital stay. Herzog, who was known for being one of the tougher players of his generation, never stood a chance against the insidious disease that had been ravaging him for several years. Worn out and run down, he succumbed to its effects on September 4, 1953. At the age of 68, Herzog was buried at Denton Cemetery in Denton, Maryland, next to his beloved wife Mattie, who had preceded him in death in 1942.

4

HEADHUNTERS

Brushbacks. Skull balls. Dusters. Chin music. Throughout the history of baseball, pitchers have sought to establish command of the strike zone by throwing high and inside to let hitters know who owns the full width of the plate. Some hurlers went much further than that, throwing up and in so many times, often with such dubious intent, that they garnered reputations as "headhunters." They made it abundantly clear that you crowded the plate at your own risk. Off the field, many were naturally ornery and some surprisingly cordial. On the mound, all were somewhat feared by opposing batters, who considered these brazen beanballers to be more annoying than the last mosquito of summer.

Deliberately throwing at batters or administering close shaves with regularity was a more acceptable part of the game years back. The practice has become more and more taboo in recent decades. What would merely have drawn choice words and dirty glares years ago will incite bench-clearing brawls amongst today's players.

In the majors, there has been one death directly related to a batter being struck by a baseball thrown from the pitcher's mound. When Carl Mays plunked Cleveland Indian shortstop Ray Chapman on the temple at the Polo Grounds on August 16, 1920, Chapman was helped off the field and died the next day at the hospital.

Considering the sheer number of pitches that have made their way toward so many heads, it's surprising—and incredibly fortunate—that there haven't been more fatalities and grave injuries in the big leagues. Simply put, the brushback pitch will always be part of the game—it's just that things aren't so simple anymore. The level of tolerance isn't what it used to be for aspiring headhunters, especially if there's no designated hitter to hide behind.

Looking at the comments and records of headhunters who are no longer with us, one can spot a distinct line of influence through such players as Adolfo Luque, Sal Maglie, and Don Drysdale. The up-and-in mindset had a tendency to be contagious.

The following is a smattering of the hurlers who reveled in their ability to wind it up and knock 'em down. They are arguably more infamous than famous now. It's a reputation they would have welcomed.

PAT MALONE (1902–1943)

A fierce competitor on the mound, Pearce "Pat" Malone was a ruddy-faced, right-handed hurler who pitched 10 seasons in the majors. A favorite of Cub manager Joe McCarthy, he was also drinking and brawling buddies with Hack Wilson. Born in Altoona, Pennsylvania, in 1902, family legend had it that he despised his real first name of Pearce (a variant of the name Percival) so much that he began using the more Irish-sounding name Pat.

Malone began his professional career in 1921, with the Class D Knoxville Pioneers of the Appalachian League. Sold to the Giants for $5,000, he would remain in the minors for the next six years. Malone was always of the belief that Giant manager John McGraw was the main culprit when it came to him not getting even a sniff for a shot with the parent club. As luck would have it, his big break would come when his contract was purchased by the Chicago Cubs before the 1928 season. The move to acquire Malone proved to be a happy omen for the Chicago front office, for under the tutelage of Cub skipper Joe McCarthy, he would pitch to an 18–13 mark, with a 2.84 ERA, during his rookie season, despite the fact that he lost his first seven decisions. He also gained a reputation that season as a pitcher who threw with a purpose. He was the type of hurler who wouldn't hesitate to throw high and inside to opposing batters. In an era where throwing "dusters" and "skull balls" was the norm, Malone excelled. Known for his control, he could pretty much pitch the ball where he wanted it, hence the reason why he only hit 45 batters during his career.

According to Charlie Grimm, "Malone never had problems busting one inside, especially if he thought the batter was getting too comfortable up there. He'd throw one high and tight, and if you didn't move, he'd throw another one."

Said Billy Jurges,

> Everyone always talks about the Gas House Gang and how they were maybe the toughest team in the National League at the time, but let me tell you, we had some pretty tough players on the Cubs, even before I got there in 1931. All of our pitchers had been around the block a time or two and all of them could be rough customers when they wanted to be. Guys like Charlie Root, Lonnie Warneke, Guy Bush, and Pat Malone. They were real bulldogs on the mound. They never took nothing from no one. If you dug in on them, you were taking your chances. Malone might have been the toughest of all of them.

Malone also gained a reputation during his rookie season as a prankster of the first order. When he wasn't drinking or brawling, he was usually pulling a fast one on one of his teammates. His first roommate in the majors, Percy Jones, asked for a new roommate when Malone put some pigeons that he had caught on a hotel ledge in Jones's bed while he slept. He was also a master of the hot foot and enjoyed engaging in the practice of towel whipping an unsuspecting teammate in the showers.

Malone's sophomore campaign saw him lead the National League in wins, with 22, and strikeouts, with 166, helping the Cubbies to the 1929 World Series. His outstanding pitching continued the next season, as he again led the National League in wins, with 20. By 1931, however, his drinking, a vice he had since he was a teenager, and late night carousing with his inseparable best friend Wilson, had begun to take a toll. It was during the '31 campaign that Malone's (and Wilson's) off-field escapades reached an ill-fated high-water mark, when the two were involved in an altercation with two sportswriters, Harold Johnson of the *Chicago American* and Wayne K. Otto of the *Herald Examiner*.

Depending on who you believe, the fight, which occurred at a Cincinnati train station, was either started by the two writers, who were getting on Malone and Wilson for their poor play and drinking habits, or by the hungover Wilson, who, even before the fight, was in a detestable mood due to his being benched for poor play by Cub manager Rogers Hornsby. Either way, a brawl ensued, with Malone pounding both scribes as if they were punching bags. After the fight, Cub catcher Gabby Hartnett commented that both Otto and Johnson had gotten in over their heads when they took on the two ballplayers. Hartnett stated, "Everybody in the league knows not to mess with either of them. Hack is as strong as they come, and Pat, with that Irish temper of his, he wouldn't hesitate to punch a bull right between the eyes. They really should have known better." Malone and Wilson showed no remorse.

Malone would finish the season with a 16–9 record for the North Siders, not bad considering that his number of strikeouts dropped to 112. The Cubs traded Wilson to the Cardinals in December 1931. The reason for the move was twofold. They had long grown tired of Wilson's antics both on and off the field, and they also reasoned that Malone, who still had something left in the tank, would settle down and focus more on baseball with his carousing buddy traded away. Malone averaged 14 wins a season from 1932 to 1934, going 15–17 in the Cubs' pennant winning season of 1932, while pitching 2.2 innings of scoreless relief in Game 3 of that year's Fall Classic, the game during which Babe Ruth supposedly called his shot.

Cub management finally tired of him after the '34 campaign, trading him to the Cardinals for Ken O'Dea that December. He never played a single game for St. Louis, as the Yankees acquired him for $15,000 in March 1935. Reunited in New York with his old manager, Joe McCarthy, Malone was used almost exclusively in relief, since he enhanced an already potent bull pen that included relief ace Johnny Murphy. His best season for the Yanks came in 1936, when he went 12–4 and led the American League with 8 relief wins and 9 saves. He also appeared in two games in the 1936 World Series against the Giants, going 0–1, with a stingy 1.80 ERA in five innings of work. Malone spent three seasons in New York, going 19–13, with a 4.67 ERA and 16 saves. Released on January 20, 1938, he signed a contract with the Red Sox three weeks later but never pitched a game for them. He spent his last season of professional baseball in the minors, split between three teams, the Minneapolis Millers, Chattanooga Lookouts, and Baltimore Orioles.

Malone retired from the game after the '38 season with a Major League Baseball record of 134–92, with a 3.75 ERA and 26 saves. One can only wonder what he could have accomplished if he had not had such a love affair with the bottle and the nightlife. With his baseball career behind him, Malone became a restaurateur and lived in his wife's hometown of Milan, Ohio, for several years, before moving back to Altoona to live with his father Christian.

On the morning of Thursday, May 13, 1943, Malone was stricken with severe abdominal pain at his father's residence, located in Hollidaysburg, Pennsylvania. Advised by a local physician, he checked himself into Altoona's Mercy Hospital, where he died at 11:45 p.m., at the age of 40. The cause of death was acute pancreatitis caused by his lifetime of heavy alcohol abuse. Malone was survived by his wife Marion, an 18-year-old daughter, and his father. His body was taken to Pittsburgh, where it was cremated, and the remains were sent back to Milan for burial in Milan Cemetery in Section HO, Lot 28, Grave 3.

EARL WHITEHILL (1899–1954)

Pound for pound, Earl Whitehill might have been the meanest pitcher of his era, parlaying his assets of a hair-trigger temper and vituperative personality (both on at off the field), along with a devastating curve and exceptional changeup, into a combination that helped him win 218 games during a 17-year big-league career. Strikingly handsome, the five-foot, nine-inch, 175-pound left hander was born in Cedar Rapids, Iowa, on February 7, 1899. Known for being fearless on the mound, he had no problem throwing high and tight to opposing batters, especially if they made the mistake of digging in against him. One only has to look at Whitehill's lifetime mark of 101 hit batsmen to realize that he used the skull ball as an effective deterrent against enemy sluggers. If an opposing batter took a toe hold against him, he did so at his own risk.

Whitehill's personality was such that no one was safe from his wrath, not even his own teammates, whom he would often berate for what he deemed poor play. He also had a well-known extreme dislike for umpires, whom he regarded as a necessary evil. Whitehill's personality can be compared to that of Johnny Allen, a highly talented and equally temperamental pitcher who played from 1932 to 1944. Earl's personality was so prickly that Babe Ruth referred to him as "that little son of a bitch" on several occasions.

Ruth and Whitehill became members of Connie Mack's barnstorming tour of Japan in 1934. Whitehill's wife Violet, a gorgeous woman who for years was erroneously known as the Sun-Maid Raisin girl, was befriended on the tour by Ruth's wife Claire, a beautiful woman in her own right. The two couples would eventually become good friends.

Despite his pitcher's nasty disposition, Detroit manager Ty Cobb admired Whitehill for his tenacity and reliability. "I don't have to worry about Whitehill turning Bolshevik on me. I can always rely on him. He goes out and does his job, and is ready for every challenge. He fears no one and never gets unnerved. I wish I had 10 pitchers like him," said Cobb.

In 1930, Whitehill proved that an old dog could learn new tricks. With his record standing at a miserable 3–9, he decided to change his disposition and display a less combative nature on the mound. The results were astounding, as he reeled off 11 straight wins, while winning 14 of his final 18 decisions, finishing with a 17–13 record.

After 10 years with the Tigers, "The Earl," as he was often known, was traded to the Senators in a two-for-one deal that saw Detroit receive pitchers Firpo Marberry and Carl Fischer. The timing of the trade could not have been more perfect, since the Senators would go on to win the pennant.

Whitehill's move to DC didn't mellow him much, and his propensity for headhunting continued with regularity. He suffered major consequences when he beaned Yankee slugger Lou Gehrig, actually knocking him out for a few minutes. The incident occurred on April 23, 1933, in the first game of a three-game set at Griffith Stadium. This would lead Yankee manager Joe McCarthy, who felt that the beaning was intentional, to unleash his "enforcer," Ben Chapman, to seek revenge. Two days later, in the final game of the series, all hell broke loose when Chapman and Senator second baseman Buddy Myer were involved in a fourth-inning play that escalated into a full-scale donnybrook that included both teams, along with several hundred fans and dozens of DC policemen. As Chapman attempted to leave the field through the Senator' dugout, he was confronted by an angry Whitehill. Taking no chances, Chapman hit Whitehill with a haymaker that knocked him down. Whitehill was suspended and fined (along with Myer and Chapman) by American League president William Harridge. Chapman would continue his tormenting the following May 30th, when he broke up Whitehill's attempt at a no-hitter with a ninth-inning single in the first game of a Memorial Day doubleheader played at Yankee Stadium. Washington won the contest, 1–0, on a Fred Schulte RBI single in the eighth.

Whitehill's best year was his first year in the Capital District, going 22–8, with a 3.33 ERA. Named the Game 3 starter by player-manager Joe Cronin in that season's World Series, he shut out the New York Giants on five hits, as Washington won, 4–0.

Whitehill was traded to the Cleveland Indians as part of a three-team deal on December 10, 1936, the Senators receiving Jack Salveson from the White Sox and the Indians sending Thornton Lee to Chicago. Despite the fact that his career was winding down, Earl still maintained a professional attitude whenever called upon, which was usually as spot starter and reliever. He was also quite happy that he was getting a chance to play with his buddy, Hal Trosky. Whitehill would go 17–16 playing for the Cuyahogas.

Signing with the Cubs in 1939, he went 4–7, with a 5.14 ERA, in what turned out to be his last season as a player. Released after the season, Whitehill was hired by his old team, the Indians, to be part of the coaching staff under manager Ossie Vitt. The 1940 Indians became infamous as the "crybaby Indians," due to the fact that several players petitioned team owner Alva Bradley to fire Vitt because of the critical and often heavy-handed way he treated his players.

Despite the distractions, Earl, along with Johnny Bassler, did a good job coaching what appeared to the public to be a dysfunctional team. Let go at the end of the year in a general housecleaning, he would coach in the International League for a season before taking his last big-league job as a coach with the Philadelphia Phillies in 1943. He then took a job as a traveling sales representative with the A. G. Spalding Company, which proved to be fruitful financially, since he was able to use his name and reputation as a former major league player to great success. In an interview shortly after the end of World War II, Whitehill exclaimed, "I think I've signed more autographs now than I ever did when I was playing. It seems like everyone wants a piece of old Earl."

As the 1950s approached, it appeared that Earl and Violet were on the high road to a happy ending, an ending that unfortunately was never to be. In October 1954, Whitehill was involved in an auto accident at an intersection in Omaha, Nebraska, when another car ran through a stop

Grave of Earl Whitehill. Courtesy of Dr. Fred Worth.

sign and broadsided him. Ever defiant, he refused to go to the hospital, opting instead to "shake things off." Still not feeling well the next day, he went to see a doctor, who, after close examination, concluded that he had suffered a skull fracture. He was admitted to St. Joseph's Hospital in Omaha, where x-rays showed that he had actually suffered a basal skull fracture, a fracture at the base of the brain. Doctors were initially optimistic that he might make a full recovery, but complications soon set in. He died as a result of a cerebral hemorrhage on October 22nd, leaving behind his wife Violet and a daughter, Earlinda. He is buried at Cedar Memorial Park in Cedar Rapids in Evergreen Section, Lot P, Grave 4.

During the course of 17 seasons, Earl Whitehill went a respectable 218–185, with a 4.36 ERA. He gave up 1,726 earned runs in 3,564 2/3 innings pitched, while recording 1,350 strikeouts. He pitched in 541 games, 473 of them starts. His lifetime ERA of 4.36 is higher than any other 200-game winner.

DOLF LUQUE (1890–1957)

Originally signed by the Boston Braves after a 22–5 season for Long Branch of the New York-New Jersey League in 1913, Cuban-born Adolfo Luque pitched 20 years in the majors. Making his major league debut with Boston on May 20, 1914, he appeared in five games during the next three seasons, as he was relegated to the minors, pitching in such venues as Toronto, Jersey City, and Louisville. In July 1918, his contract was purchased from Louisville by the Cincinnati Reds.

Luque made his debut for the Reds against his old club, the Braves, in a rainy July 24 contest in Boston. With the Reds already trailing, 4–0, manager Christy Mathewson sent Luque in to relieve starter Mike Regan in the eighth inning. The *Boston Globe* proclaimed that Luque "looked pretty good too," as he gave up no hits in his lone inning. For the rest of the season, Luque worked as a spot starter and out of the bull pen, earning a 6–3 record. Mathewson saw something in the hot-headed Spaniard. He was not only tenacious on the mound, never wanting to give an inch, but he possessed a curveball that reminded Matty of his own. All he needed was a little more experience at the big-league level.

It was supposedly one of Luque's teammates on the Reds, catcher Ivey Wingo, who told his batterymate, "Kid, all ya gotta do is throw it inside once in a while to show 'em who's boss." Although he didn't need any coaxing, Luque apparently took the advice to heart, for as his career progressed, he gained a reputation for being an aggressor and a head-hunter. Luque knew that throwing inside allowed him to establish the inside part of the plate, something all pitchers must do if they are to be successful.

With the start of the 1919 season, Luque and the Reds had a new manager, Pat Moran. Luque was once again used as a spot starter and reliever, going 10–3, with 3 saves in 12 games. He also made two appearances during the 1919 World Series, gaining no decisions. It was in 1920 that he became a full-time member of the rotation, going 13–9 in 23 starts.

During the next several seasons, Luque's career had its share of ups and downs. In 1921, he lost 19 games and, in 1922, led the National League with 23 losses. He rebounded nicely the following season with a

Dolf Luque, Cincinnati Reds. Courtesy of the Library of Congress.

22–7 mark, a career best. The Red clubs of the early to mid-1920s were usually quite competitive, seldom finishing out of the first division.

After a 5–16 record in 1929, Luque was traded to the Brooklyn Robins for Doug McWeeney. Spending two seasons in Brooklyn, he chalked up an overall record of 21–14. While Luque's temper didn't always sit well with managers, he got along fine with Brooklyn manager Wilbert Robinson, a laid back Georgian. During one game, a heckler in the stands started loudly chanting, "Lucky Luque! Lucky Luque!" Having finally had enough, Dolf went over to the Dodger dugout and told Robinson, "I tell you, Robbie, if this guy don't shut up, I'm gonna shut him up." Robinson replied, "Aw, come on, Dolf. He paid his way in, let him boo." Robbie had barely finished getting his words out when the heckler started in on him, yelling, "Hey, fat belly!" Robinson looked over at the heckler, turned to Luque, and said, "Okay, Dolf, go ahead and clobber the jerk," to which Luque gleefully obliged.

When the Dodgers released him on January 22, 1932, he considered retirement, mostly because injuries had slowed him down the previous season. He had also grown tired of the commute between his native land and the United States. Less than a month later, Luque was approached by Giant manager John McGraw. McGraw had always admired the feisty Cuban and felt that he still had something left in him. "My intention is to use him out of the bull pen," McGraw revealed. "He still has a wonderful curveball and a presence on the mound. He should do just fine for us."

At the Polo Grounds, Luque found new life, along with a new nickname, "Papa," due to his "advanced" age. McGraw's investment in Luque proved to be a fruitful one, as he appeared in 38, 35, and 26 games, respectively, all in relief, during the next three seasons. The highlight of his stay in New York was a relief appearance in the fifth and final game of the 1933 World Series. Coming into the contest in relief of Giant starter Hal Schumacher, Dolf threw four and one-third shutout innings, which earned him the win in the 10-inning affair. Mel Ott blasted a home run in the 10th inning to win it for the Giants.

In 1935, Papa appeared in just two games, eventually becoming a coach, a position he would hold on and off for the next 12 seasons. As a pitching coach, Luque always stressed the importance of throwing inside, encouraging pitchers to use the brushback pitch when the opportunity arose. He also was a master at correcting faults in pitcher deliveries.

Luque's greatest pupil was none other than Sal Maglie, who completely took his instructor's advice to heart, especially when it came to throwing inside. He was later given the nickname "The Barber" due to the close shaves he gave opposing batters. After he asked for, and was given, his release from the Giants, he began a career as manager of minor league teams in Latin America, most notably Cuba and Mexico. Even though he was in his mid-50s, he was still as combative as ever. One doozy of a story is that he once got into an altercation with one of his own pitchers, who had refused to take the mound for a game. Instead of threatening the pitcher with a fine or suspension, he pulled a revolver from his desk and proceeded to escort the pitcher to the mound, at gunpoint.

In 1954, Luque was honored with a gold medal for his years of service in the Cuban Winter League. He died from a heart attack in 1957, at the age of 66. He is buried at the Christopher Columbus Necropolis in Havana.

CHARLIE ROOT (1899–1970)

Known more for being the pitcher who gave up Babe Ruth's supposed called shot, Charlie Root was one of the all-time great pitchers in Chicago Cub history. He was a highly underrated pitcher who won 206 games in the majors, while being part of four pennant-winning teams.

Also known by his nickname, "Chinski," the Middletown, Ohio, native originally signed with the Browns in 1921. After two seasons in the minors with Terre Haute, he finally made his major league debut on April 18, 1923. He appeared in 27 games that season, only two of which he started, going 0–4 in the process. Sent back to the minors the next season, he was eventually traded to the Los Angeles Angels of the Pacific Coast League. It was in Los Angeles that he finally came into his own, winning 46 games during the two seasons he was there. This brought him to the attention of Cub manager Joe McCarthy, who was looking for a young pitcher to help fortify his staff. Making the parent club in 1926, he went 18–17 and managed to impress McCarthy with his guts and aggressive attitude on the mound.

Almost from the beginning, Root became the type of pitcher that opposing batters needed to be wary of. Hall of Fame Giant first baseman Bill Terry once remarked,

> When he was in a good mood, he was pretty easy to get along with, but heaven help you if he was having a bad day. I remember one day, I was standing behind the batting cage at Wrigley Field, talking to my old buddy Joe McCarthy, who was the Cubs' manager. We were shooting the breeze when along comes "Ole Charlie." One of the boys, I think it was Freddie Lindstrom, yells out, "How's it going Charlie," and Root replies, "Go to hell." I look over at Mac, and I ask him who's pitching, and he gives me a wink and says, "Root." I just rolled my eyes, because I knew it was going to be a long afternoon.

Truth be told, Root never needed to have a "bad day" as an impetus to pitch aggressively. From the moment he stepped on the field, he was all business. Chinski won 14 games or better eight straight seasons, with a career high of 26 in 1927. Making opposing batters "do a dance" was simply an accepted part of the game.

As far as Ruth and the called shot were concerned, Root always insisted that the Babe never called anything, implying that he simply pointed into the Cub dugout before the fateful pitch. Charlie once commented, "If he had pointed to the stands, he would have gone down on his fanny. I'd have loosened him up. Nobody facing me would have gotten away with that." Gabby Hartnett agreed: "If Ruth had really called his shot, Charlie would have thrown one down his damn throat."

In the days before newspaper writers would "clubhouse" to get a story, there was not a single mention of the incident in any of the newspapers of the time until almost three days later. Such is the fodder that legends are made of. Root and the legend of the called shot will forever be entwined and remain a part of baseball lore.

After his major league career, Ole Charlie went back to the minors, pitching, coaching, and later managing Hollywood of the Pacific Coast League. He later managed at Des Moines, Billings, and Columbus, and served as a coach with the Braves and Cubs. Root's last year in uniform was 1960, after which he retired to his family's cattle ranch in Paicines, California, where he spent the remainder of his days occasionally reminiscing about his past glories and telling anyone who would listen about a legend that had no basis in fact. He died on November 5, 1970, from complications of pneumonia and leukemia.

CARL MAYS (1891–1971)

The story of Carl Mays is a tale of two pitchers. One is about a right-handed, submarine sinkerballer who won 20 games five times, totaling 207 wins during his 15-year major league career. The other is of a hurler who threw the pitch that resulted in the only on-field fatality in major league history. The incident, which occurred at the Polo Grounds on August 16, 1920, cost Cleveland Indian shortstop Ray Chapman his life and solidified Mays's reputation as one of the most notorious head-hunters in baseball history. Truth be known, even if Mays's high and tight fastball had not found its fatal mark, he would still rank as one of the nastiest SOBs in baseball.

Although he never had a high ranking when it came to hitting batters, mostly due to his pinpoint control, Mays still had the reputation as someone not to dig in against, as he successfully used intimidation to enhance his game. Ty Cobb, who had a running feud with Mays, wanted him banned for life after Chapman's death (it should be known that Cobb liked Chapman, a fellow southerner and all-around good guy). Mays, who began his career with the Boston Red Sox in 1915, was never popular with teammates. Hall of Fame outfielder Harry Hooper, one of his teammates on the Red Sox, once spoke about Mays, remarking that, "Carl had an odd disposition."

Born in Liberty, Kentucky, the son of a Methodist minister, Mays first joined the Red Sox at spring training in Hot Springs, Arkansas, in 1915, after spending the previous season with the Providence Grays. Impressing Boston management with his "rise ball," he pitched well enough to make the final cut. Mays was used sparingly during his rookie season, going 6–5 in only 38 games for the fabulously talented Boston pitching staff. Always full of self-confidence, he knew it would only be a matter of time before he would get a full chance to show his wares. During the next three seasons, Mays's star shone bright, as he won 18, 22, and 21 games, respectively.

On July 29, 1919, he was traded to the Yankees for a package that included Allen Russell, Bob McGraw, and $40,000. The trade was not

Carl Mays, New York Yankees. Courtesy of the Library of Congress.

unexpected, as Mays had gone AWOL during a Boston road trip because he felt that he lacked support from his teammates in the field (he was a pedestrian 5–11 at the time of the trade). His trade to the Yankees invigorated him, and he went 9–3 to even his overall record for the season at 14–14. While his career will be forever linked with Chapman and the beaning, the fact is he was having one of his best seasons at the time, eventually finishing with a 26–11 mark, with a 3.06 ERA and 2 saves.

Yankee pitcher Bob Shawkey once remarked:

> He was always trying to get over on someone. He was not a friendly fellow at all. Most of the boys didn't care for him. He was usually sullen and had the kind of attitude that didn't mix well. I remember once he was getting smacked around pretty good by the Indians. Huggins goes out to get him, and the two start having a discussion on the mound. Finally Mays leaves, and all you had to do was read his lips. You could see he was swearing under his breath. Hug eventually sits down next to me on the bench and looks like he wants to kill someone. I asked him what's wrong, and he looks at me and says, "Bob, that son of a bitch is trying to tell me how to manage!" That's the kind of person Mays was.

On the field, Mays didn't allow the Chapman incident to affect him.

The next season, 1921, saw him post a career-high 27 wins, helping lead the Yankees to their first American League pennant. Shawkey remembered Mays giving advice to some of the young pitchers at spring training that season: "Mays is telling them to throw inside to batters, to dust them off. This after he killed a man. Unbelievable." Controversy continued to haunt Mays during the 1921 World Series against the Giants. After pitching a five-hit shutout in Game 1, he took a 2–0 lead into the eighth inning of Game 4. He suddenly gave up four hits and three runs, en route to a 4–2 loss. After the game, New York sportswriter Fred Lieb was contacted by a man who "spilled the beans" on Mays, claiming that Mays had been offered a "substantial sum in cash" if he lost the game. He further explained that Mays's wife Marjorie was to flash a signal to him at the start of the eighth inning by wiping her face with a white handkerchief to indicate that she had received the money. Lieb took the story to the commissioner's office, where it was investigated.

Mays was eventually exonerated of any wrongdoing by a detective agency hired by Commissioner Landis. (Years later, Lieb revealed that Miller Huggins and the Yankees' part-owner, Colonel "Cap" Huston, had told him that they both thought Mays had thrown games in the '21 and '22 World Series.) Mays, who lost his only start in the '22 Fall Classic, eventually fell out of favor with Yankee management. Huggins, who considered Mays nothing less than a bastard, sold him to Cincinnati on December 11, 1923. Many members of the press questioned the move, especially after the Yanks finished 1924 in second place, behind Washington.

Carl, on the other hand, flourished in his new surroundings, as he rebounded with a 20–9 season. He continued to pitch until 1929, finishing with a lifetime 207–126 record, surely good enough for consideration for the Hall of Fame.

After his playing career ended, Mays turned to scouting, where he worked for the Indians and Braves. Tragedy befell him in February 1934, when his wife died from eye surgery complications. He eventually remarried, settling in Oregon. In his later years, he would winter in San Diego, where he also helped his stepson coach little league. The one thing that seemed to rankle him was his exclusion from the Hall of Fame. "I think I belong. Just because I killed someone in an accident, they keep passing me up," he lamented. According to relatives, Mays never really got over what happened that fateful day at the Polo Grounds, preferring to keep his true feelings hidden from the public.

Years after the Chapman beaning, Mays's former teammate, Roger Peckinpaugh, commented, "I don't know how he did it. I really don't. He had to live all those years knowing that he killed a man in a ball game." Mays was 79 when he died on April 4, 1971, at Valley Hospital in El Cajon, California, from pneumonia and heart disease. He was buried in Riverview Cemetery in Portland, Oregon, in Section 13, Lot 49, Grave 7.

LEFTY GROVE (1900–1975)

Lefty Grove is generally considered the greatest left-handed pitcher in American League history. Born in Lonaconing, Maryland, on March 6, 1900, legend has it that he developed his arm speed by throwing rocks as a youngster. Although he did not reach the majors until the age of 25, he still won 300 games, earning eight 20-win seasons. He led the American League in strikeouts seven consecutive seasons. With a temperament as mean as his fastball, he was 31–4 for the 1931 Athletics, compiling a 16-game winning streak in the process.

In 1931, Grove was en route to his 17th straight victory, which would have broken the American League record then shared by Walter Johnson and Smoky Joe Wood. Al Simmons had taken the day off, and the rookie outfielder subbing for him misjudged a fly ball, leading to an unearned run; Grove lost, 1–0. He said, "After that game I went in and tore the clubhouse up. Wrecked the place. Tore those stall lockers off the wall, giving Al Simmons hell all the while."

Grove regained his composure, won another eight straight, was named MVP, and ended the season 31–4, possibly the single greatest season enjoyed by any hurler. The dominant pitcher of his era, he was the American League's strikeout leader his first seven years in the majors, led in ERA a record nine times, and went on to compile a won–lost record of 300–141 for a winning percentage of .680. Normalized for league average and adjusted for home park, his 3.06 ERA is quite simply the best in baseball history.

Although Lefty was known to throw at batters, one player he learned to stay away from was Lou Gehrig. "You can never tell what that big fellow will do if you get him mad at you," Grove admitted. Lefty also had an unknown soft side when it came to kids. He "adopted" a sandlot team that he used to drive past on his way home from games. He bought the kids new uniforms and equipment with no fanfare.

Grove started in organized ball with Martinsburg, West Virginia, of the Blue Ridge League and joined the International League Orioles when Baltimore bartered for him, paying cash for Martinsburg's new center field fence. Owner Jack Dunn knew what he had in Grove and delayed his entry into the big leagues until the southpaw was 25 years old. He sold Grove to Connie Mack's A's for $100,600.

Like Sandy Koufax after him, Grove had his troubles early on, winning 10 and losing 12 in 1925, his rookie year. The following year, his ERA improved from 4.75 to 2.51, good enough to lead the league for the first time. By 1927, he was ready for his first 20-win season and tied George Pipgras for the league lead in wins (24), while losing only eight.

From 1929 to 1931, Grove was an awesome 79–15, and the A's won pennants each year, as well as the World Series in the first two. By the time he was sold to the Red Sox for $125,000 in 1933, he had won 20, 24, 20, 28, 31, 25, and 24 games, respectively, in seven consecutive seasons. Yet, success didn't mellow him. During batting practice, a Boston teammate once hit a ball back through the box; on the next pitch, the batter hit the dust.

Grove was elected to the Hall of Fame in 1947. He died from a heart attack at his daughter-in-law's home in Norwalk, Ohio, on May 22, 1975. Fittingly, Grove was sitting in a comfortable lounge chair watching a baseball game on television when he passed. He was interred at Frostburg Memorial Park in Frostburg, Maryland, in Section 9, Lot 94.

BURLEIGH GRIMES (1893–1985)

Gruff, aggressive Burleigh Grimes was the last of the legal spitballers. He won 270 games in 19 seasons for seven major league teams, reaching 20 on five occasions. He helped Brooklyn to the championship in 1920, the "Gas House Gang" Cardinals to pennants in 1930 and 1931, and the Cubs to the flag in 1932. Known as "Ol' Stubblebeard" for his habit of not shaving on the day he was scheduled to pitch, Grimes would glare at his opponents with a scowl and reveal a mouth filled with yellowed teeth, giving him an even more menacing look.

Grimes was born in 1893, in Clear Lake, Wisconsin. He started his baseball career in 1912, with Eau Claire of the Class D Minnesota-Wisconsin League. Using the spitball almost from the start of his career, he favored slippery elm for doctoring the baseball. Grimes made it to the Pittsburgh Pirates in 1916, going 2–3 in six games. The next season, he lost 13 straight, en route to a 3–16 record. In January 1918, the Bucos traded him to the Brooklyn Robins in a deal that sent outfielder Casey Stengel to the Pirates. Grimes went on to a 19–9 record his first year hurling for "Uncle Robbie's Minions," racking up four 20-win seasons and an overall 158–121 mark during his nine-year stay in Flatbush. Almost from the beginning, Grimes gained a reputation as a pitcher with a win-at-all-costs attitude. Before a Giants–Robins game late in the 1924 season, he called a team meeting and announced, "Anyone who doesn't want to play today's game to win, let me know right now." Grimes then went out and knocked down the first New York batter on the first pitch of the game.

A difficult character, Grimes was usually at odds with Robin manager Wilbert Robinson. Robby, known for his laid back style of managing, would use a clubhouse boy to tell Grimes when he was starting so as to not have any interaction with his hotheaded hurler. In 1926, after Grimes fell to 12–13, Brooklyn traded him to the Giants, where he went 19–8 in 1927. In 1928, New York traded him back to the Pirates, where he went 25–14, leading the National League in wins, complete games, innings pitched, and shutouts. His greatest personal achievement came in the 1931 World Series against the Philadelphia Athletics. He won two games, including Game 7, a torturous affair that saw him pitch to two outs in the ninth inning with a dislocated vertebra.

It was said that the only players that Burleigh could not intimidate were Paul "Big Poison" Waner and Frankie Frisch. Burleigh would often dust off Paul or the "Fordham Flash" and, almost always, on the next pitch, Big Poison or Frankie would smash a line drive. After his retirement in 1934, Grimes managed the Brooklyn Dodgers for two years. Succeeding Stengel as Dodger skipper, his teams finished sixth in 1937 and seventh in 1938. He then went back to the minors to manage for several years, eventually scouting for the Yankees, A's, and Baltimore Orioles.

Elected to the Hall of Fame in 1964, Burleigh Grimes, baseball's most aggressive spitballer, died after a lengthy battle with cancer on December 6, 1985, at the age of 92. He is buried in Clear Lake Cemetery in Clear Lake, Wisconsin, in Block 88, Lot 3, Space 2.

VAN LINGLE MUNGO (1911–1985)

Hall of Fame catcher Ernie Lombardi might have summed up Van Mungo's pitching style best when he said, "Van was mean too—and wild to go with it." Mungo (Lingle was his mother's maiden name) intimidated opposing batters with a fierce scowl, burning fastball, and fiery disposition, and he was never one to turn down the chance to dust someone off. In the mid-1930s, Mungo's talent was considered by many to be equal to that of Dizzy Dean and Carl Hubbell. Unfortunately, the big right-hander from Pageland, South Carolina, became enamored with the strikeout, so much so that his fast one tended to lose velocity in late innings.

Originally an outfielder, he started off his professional career in 1929, with the Charlotte Hornets, soon switching to the mound. In just two short seasons, Mungo made the majors as a member of the Brooklyn Robins. He gained a place in the hearts of the Flatbush Faithful when he knocked the hated cross-town Giants out of the pennant race on the last weekend of the 1934 season. That 5–1 win came back to haunt Giant manager Bill Terry, who had jokingly commented before the season began, "Brooklyn? Are they still in the league?"

Pitching for losing clubs usually made Mungo's volatile temper worse. Easily upset by the ineptitude of his teammates, his most famous temper tantrum came after one of his outfielders, Long Tom Winslett, dropped a ninth-inning fly that cost him a game. Mungo went ballistic, smashing and overturning various items in the clubhouse, leaving it looking as if a tornado had come through. He then went to the Dodger telegraph office and sent the following wire to his wife: "Pack up your bags and come to Brooklyn, honey. If Winslett can play in the majors, it's a cinch, you can too."

Van, who was famous for his contract disputes, was the 1936 National League strikeout leader, fanning 238 batters. He also led the National League in walks three times. In an era when starters were expected to go the distance, Mungo, who led the league in games started in 1934 and 1936, only finished 47 percent of his career starts. Between 1932 and 1936, he averaged 16 wins a year, achieving 18 victories twice. An arm injury incurred during the 1937 All-Star Game dramatically changed his career. Continuing to pitch with a bad arm, he won just 13 games in his next six seasons.

Mungo was involved in a wild off-field incident at the Nacional Hotel in Havana during spring training of 1941. He was in the midst of a ménage à trois with famed Latin dancer Christiana Careno and another woman when Careno's husband and dancer partner, Colandra, burst into the room wielding a machete. Mungo briefly scuffled with him and then hightailed it out of the room, followed by an incensed Colandra. Apparently it was improper etiquette to sleep with another man's wife in Cuba. In fear for their pitcher's life, Dodger officials smuggled Mungo off the island. He supposedly pondered, "Don't anybody ever get into trouble but me?" Colandra filed a personal damages suit against the pitcher for $20,000 and also charged him with battery.

Back in the United States, Mungo was immediately fined and suspended for "breaking training rules." After his reinstatement on April 6, he pitched in just two games before being given his release. He played for the Montreal Royals of the International League and later in the American Association before being picked up by the Giants, for whom he pitched parts of three seasons. He compiled one of his best winning percentages during his final year in the big leagues, pitching to a 14–7 record in 1945. The following spring, he was suspended indefinitely by Giant manager Mel Ott for breaking training rules. Given his unconditional release in April, it was rumored that he was going to jump to the Mexican League, but he signed with the Class D Clinton Blues of the Tobacco State League. On July 30, he was named manager, replacing former skipper Willie Duke. In mid-August, Mungo was involved in a brawl with Wilmington manager Gus Brittain that caused a near riot. W. G. Branham, president of the National Association of Minor Leagues, had no choice but to fine him $50 and suspend him for the remainder of the season, ending his baseball career.

Retiring to his native Pageland, Mungo opened a movie theater, dry goods business, and trucking company. After battling ulcers in the latter half of his career, he had to undergo emergency surgery in March 1956, for a perforated ulcer. In 1970, his colorful name was prominently used in a nostalgic bossa nova ballad, *Van Lingle Mungo*, by David Frishberg. Van Mungo died at his home in Pageland on February 12, 1985, at the age of 73, and was buried at First Baptist Church Cemetery in Pageland.

SAL MAGLIE (1917–1992)

By the time Sal Maglie made his major league debut in August 1945, he was already a veteran of almost nine years of minor league ball. On August 4, 1945, at the ripe old age of 28, while pitching for the Giants' International League affiliate in Jersey City, New Jersey, he finally got the long-awaited call up to the parent club. Five days later, on August 9, Maglie made his major league debut in relief of New York starter Harry Feldman in a 5–3 loss to the Cardinals at the Polo Grounds. Used primarily as a starter for the remainder of the season, the Niagara Falls native impressed Giant management by displaying a gutsy attitude on the mound, while going 5–4, with three shutouts.

On the suggestion of Giant coach Dolf Luque, Maglie pitched during the off-season in the Cuban Winter League for the Cienfuegos team, which just so happened to be managed by Luque. Thus began a friendship that would help transform Maglie into one of the most competitive and aggressive pitchers in baseball history. During spring training of 1946, Maglie showed good form but felt that he was not being given a fair shake by Giant manager Mel Ott. Tired of being sand-bagged and feeling he had little chance of making the Giants' Opening Day roster, Maglie took a major gamble.

On March 31st, a little more than two weeks before the start of the season, the tranquility of the Giant spring training complex in Miami was suddenly broken. Giant secretary Eddie Brannick announced to the press that Maglie and two of his teammates, George Hausmann and Roy Zimmerman, had decided to "jump" their contracts to play for the newly formed Mexican League. The news was not a complete surprise to Giant owner Horace Stoneham, who had already seen outfielder Danny Gardella head south of the border. This new "Outlaw League," led by Mexican promoter and businessman Jorge Pasquel, hoped to lure away major league players who were dissatisfied with their current contracts with the promise of a bigger contract and signing bonus.

Maglie's new deal was reported to be worth $10,000, plus a whopping $5,000 signing bonus, along with $1,000 in travel expenses. When Commissioner Happy Chandler barred Maglie and the rest of the contract jumpers from organized baseball, it appeared that the six-foot, two-inch right-hander had made a disastrous career move. Truth be told, the move to Mexico proved to be the best thing that could have happened to him, as he was quickly assigned to the Puebla team.

As luck would have it, the team, nicknamed the Parrots, was to be managed by none other than Maglie's mentor, Luque. Under his tutelage, Maglie became a favorite with Mexican fans, who learned to appreciate his aggressive style of pitching. Maglie took his manager's philosophy to heart, understanding that a pitcher needed to be aggressive to be successful.

A noted headhunter during his time in the majors, Luque was known as much for his temper as he was for his biting curveball. Luque helped Maglie with his curve, which eventually became his main "out" pitch. Years later, Maglie remembered his coach's teachings fondly, stating, "Dolf always stressed to me that you had to show the opposing batter who's boss. Never let them take advantage of you. If you have to throw inside, do it. If you have to take someone down, you do it." After two successful seasons in the Mexican League, Sal left.

After doing some barnstorming with other former jumpers, Maglie returned home to Niagara Falls to operate a gas station that he had bought using his baseball earnings. In 1949, he signed with the Drummondville Cubs of the Quebec Provincial League. The Provincial League, although not technically an outlaw league, did not operate within the rules of organized baseball, in particular, the National Commission, which oversaw Minor League Baseball in the United States. Drummondville, whose roster featured the likes of Danny Gardella, Roy Zimmerman, Tex Shirley, Max Lanier, Vic Power, and Negro League star Quincy Troupe, would go on to win the Provincial League championship. Maglie was the leading pitcher on the team, sporting an 18–9 record.

In January 1950, after Chandler lifted his suspension, Maglie signed a contract to return to his old team, the Giants. From the beginning, it became apparent to manager Leo Durocher that his new pitcher's time in Mexico had been well spent. At 32, he was not just older, but also wiser, since the last time he had donned a New York uniform. His newfound command of the edges of the plate, coupled with a willingness to "dust" opposing batters, gave him supreme confidence each time he took the mound. The combination of his pitching style and a trademark five o'clock shadow eventually led to the nickname "The Barber" for his practice of throwing close to (shaving) the batter's chin. For Maglie, intimidation was the key to pitching. "When I'm pitching," he explained, "I own the plate."

The start of several successful seasons in a row for Maglie began in 1950. He would eventually become the most successful of the Mexican League returnees, going 18–4, with a 2.71 ERA. (He also led the National League in winning percentage.)

The next year, 1951, developed into the greatest campaign of his career. Maglie pitched to a 23–6 mark, with a 2.93 ERA, while helping the Giants to their first pennant in 14 years. The 1951 Giants are remembered for their 13 1/2-game comeback against the Dodgers, which culminated with the most famous home run in baseball history—Bobby Thomson's "shot heard 'round the world" off Dodger reliever Ralph Branca at the Polo Grounds.

Always good in a pressure situation, Durocher once said of Sal, "If I had to win one game, I would go with Maglie. He reminds me a lot of Whit Wyatt. He's not afraid of anything." Maglie's habit of throwing dusters made him the type of pitcher opposing fans loved to hate, especially those from Brooklyn. Although he was always tough to face, most opposing hitters respected him. Richie Ashburn, in an interview a few years before his death, recalled facing Maglie, commenting, "I never had a problem facing a guy like Sal. You knew when you went up there that you might get knocked down, but it was never, ever personal with him."

After a bad back limited him to just an 8–9 record in 1953, Maglie vowed to take better care of himself. During the winter of 1953–1954, he began a regiment of osteopathic treatments to improve his balky back. It was during these treatments that the cause of his problem was discovered. Doctors found that his right leg was three-eighths of an inch shorter than his left, causing a strain on his right side and leading to a curvature of the spine that generated back and arm problems. To fix the problem, Maglie was fitted with a heal lift measuring three-eighths of an inch for his right shoe and right spikes. This, coupled with continued osteopathic treatments, proved to be "just the tonic" for his ailing back.

Arriving at the Giant spring training camp in Phoenix, Arizona, on February 27, Maglie proclaimed himself totally healthy and ready to pitch back to his "old form." When Durocher was informed that doctors had advised Maglie "not to cut loose," for a few days, he exclaimed to the press, "When Sal tells me he's ready to pitch, it will be all right with me." Maglie's progression during the spring went so smoothly that Durocher proclaimed to the press just before the team broke camp, "I'm expecting big things from Sal. He is back to where he was two years ago and shows no signs of the back trouble that has plagued him the past few seasons."

Maglie and the Giants would have a comeback year in 1954. Sal was indeed back to his old form, pitching to a 14–6 record, including four wins against the rival Dodgers. His crowning achievement that season happened on September 20, as the Giants clinched the pennant before a mostly hostile crowd of 26,982 at Ebbets Field. Maglie twirled a complete-game, 7–1 victory, scattering just five hits in the process. He even assisted on the final out of the game, when Roy Campanella tapped a pitch back to him and he tossed the ball to first baseman Whitey Lockman for the pennant-clinching final out. The victory was doubly sweet for Maglie, since he was able to beat the rival Brooks in their own backyard, while also securing the National League championship.

In the World Series against Cleveland, Maglie started Game 1, allowing two runs on seven hits during seven innings. The Giants eventually won the game in 10 innings on a homer off the bat of Dusty Rhodes. The Giants won the series over the heavily favored Indians in four straight, giving New York its first world championship in 21 years. During the off-season, Maglie declared, "I feel like I still have a lot of pitching life left in me. I know I have more than a few good years left." Sadly, most of those years would not be in a New York uniform.

The following season, on July 31, 1955, Sal was selected off waivers by the Cleveland Indians. Even though his record at the time was a respectable 9–5, Maglie had been experiencing arm trouble, which signaled a red flag to Giant management. Maglie's stay in Cleveland proved to be less than spectacular. Appearing in just 10 games for the remainder of the campaign, he compiled an 0–2 record. On May 15, 1956, his contract was purchased by the rival Dodgers in a deal that left many members of the press shocked and speechless. Many wondered how the former enemy would be received by the Flatbush Faithful. Maglie had tormented Dodger fans throughout the years with his victories and brushback pitches. In fact, from 1950 to 1954, his record against Brooklyn was an amazing 23–11. Skepticism was soon replaced by cheers, as the hurler pitched brilliantly for his new team, eventually going 13–5, while helping lead Brooklyn to the pennant. His popularity with the Flatbush Faithful rose to new heights on September 25, when he hurled a 5–0 no-hitter against the Phillies at Ebbets Field. The Dodgers' starter and winner against the Yankees in Game 1 of the World Series by a score of 6–3, he pitched even better in Game 5, surrendering only two runs and five hits in nine innings.

Unfortunately for both Maglie and the Dodgers, his great performance came on the day that Don Larsen tossed the only perfect game in World Series history. Even though the Dodgers lost the series in seven games, Maglie was still upbeat about his future. "I still have a few more seasons left in me," he declared that winter.

By now, Sal had become a mentor to an up-and-coming right-handed pitcher from Van Nuys, California, named Don Drysdale. Maglie tutored Drysdale on the finer points of pitching inside, always reminding his young student that intimidation was a necessary part of the game. It was Maglie who told the eager Drysdale, "It's not the first one, it's the second one. The second one makes the hitter know you meant the first one." Maglie's words did not fall on deaf ears, as Drysdale went on to a Hall of Fame career, becoming one of the most aggressive and feared pitchers in baseball history.

Battling back from occasional arm problems during the 1957 campaign, Maglie was eventually sold to the Yankees on September 1, for $37,500. Ineligible for play in that year's Fall Classic, he instead helped Yankee pitchers by giving them scouting reports on Milwaukee Brave hitters. Although the Yanks lost to the Braves in seven games, Maglie was again optimistic about his chances for the upcoming season. While he made the team out of spring training, he was relegated to being a spot starter and long reliever. After appearing in just seven games, he was sold to the Cardinals on June 14th for the waiver price of $20,000. Maglie would remain with the Cardinals for the remainder of the season, sporting a 2–5 record. Signed to a contract by St. Louis the following year, he never made it out of spring training. The arm and back problems that had plagued him for years had finally taken their toll. On April 10, 1959, the Cardinals released him, ending his colorful career on the mound.

Maglie, who had thoughts of staying in the game, didn't have long to wait. On October 20, 1959, he embarked on a new career as a pitching coach for the Red Sox, serving in that capacity until the end of the 1962 season. He later served as deputy commissioner for the New York State Athletic Commission, overseeing boxing and wrestling matches. A second stint as Red Sox pitching coach saw him oversee a talented group of young pitchers, including a right-hander with a reputation for throwing inside, Jim Lonborg. When Maglie was asked what pitcher Lonborg reminded him of, he reportedly smiled and said, "Me."

Released from his duties after the 1967 season, Sal later joined manager Joe Schulz's staff as pitching coach for the Seattle Pilots. Retiring from the game for good after that season, he went back home to live in his beloved Niagara Falls, becoming a favorite at old-timer games. Unfortunately, the happiness and tranquility of his golden years was interrupted by ill health. In 1982, he suffered a brain aneurysm but made a complete recovery. After his adoptive son Sal Jr. died in 1985, his health took a turn for the worse. He suffered two separate cerebral vascular accidents (strokes), which completely debilitated him. Maglie, who would spend the last five years of his life in a nursing home, would eventually show signs of Alzheimer's disease.

Sal Maglie passed away at Memorial Medical Center in Niagara Falls from the effects of pneumonia on December 28, 1992, at the age of 75. The Barber was laid to rest in St. Joseph's Cemetery in Niagara Falls, New York, in the Resurrection Mausoleum, Level 5, Crypt 63.

DON DRYSDALE (1936–1993)

Don Drysdale combined an aggressive attitude with superior pitching skills to become one of the most feared pitchers in the National League. The sidearming hurler not only knocked down opposing batters, he plunked them with regularity. Drysdale led the National League in hit batsmen each year from 1958 to 1961. He also holds the league career mark, at 154. Frank Robinson once said, "He was mean enough to do it, and he did it continuously. You could count on him doing it. And when he did it, he just stood there on the mound and glared at you to let you know he meant it."

Drysdale had learned from a master of aggressive pitching, Sal "The Barber" Maglie, who had learned how to pitch aggressively from former Giant great Dolf Luque. Convinced of the value of keeping hitters off balance, Drysdale hung around the veteran Maglie in Brooklyn when he was just starting out. "What being around Maglie did for me," Drysdale explained, "was to confirm this idea in my mind and refine it. It was part of the game. I watched Maglie, I listened to Maglie, and it all sunk in. It just sort of clicked."

Maglie once remarked about his former student,

> I don't think Don has ever tried intentionally to send someone to the hospital. It's not about trying to hurt someone. I tried to impress upon him, just like Dolf Luque taught me, that a pitcher needs to

pitch inside. And if one of your teammates goes down, you do what you have to do to even the score, plain and simple.

Drysdale agreed wholeheartedly with his mentor: "My own little rule was two for one. If one of my teammates got knocked down, then I knocked down two on the other team." Don showed so much promise as a teenager that the Dodgers signed him right out of high school in 1954. Drysdale was 5–5 in 99 innings in 1956, and he moved into the rotation the following season, going 17–9 in the Dodgers' last year in Brooklyn. In 1959, he led the National League in strikeouts and repeated in 1960 and 1962. He averaged 315 innings a season from 1962 to 1965.

He and Sandy Koufax staged a well-publicized joint holdout. Each wanted a $500,000 three-year contract. The previous year, Koufax, who had 382 strikeouts, and Drysdale, who had 210, set the all-time National League record for strikeouts by two teammates. Dodger vice president Buzzy Bavasi said, "You players are entitled to all you can get. That's the history of baseball. But I'm going to stick to our club's policy of one-year contracts." They both eventually signed one-year contracts, Koufax for $130,000 and Drysdale for $105,000.

Regrettably, a torn rotator cuff ended Drysdale's wonderful career in 1969, but it did not stop him from remaining active in the game that he loved. He eventually went into broadcasting, becoming a consummate play-by-play and color commentator. He became adept at telling stories about his old Dodger days and was in demand for his wit and storytelling abilities on the banquet circuit. Don's aggressive pitching demeanor was exactly the opposite of his off-field personality. He had many admirers inside and outside of baseball, including governor and later president Ronald Reagan. A great all-around guy, he was liked by everyone who met him. His former broadcast partner with the California Angels, Dick Enberg, summed him up best when he said, "Every day was a good day when you were with Don Drysdale."

Drysdale was elected to the Hall of Fame in 1984, and the Dodgers retired his number 53 on July 1 of that year. He died unexpectedly from a heart attack in 1993, while in Montreal. He was only 56 years old. For nine years, Drysdale's cremated remains were held in the Utility Columbarium, located in the Great Mausoleum at Forest Lawn Memorial

Park in Glendale, California. In 2002, his ashes were finally returned to his family and scattered in 2003.

WHITLOW WYATT (1907–1999)

Joe DiMaggio called him the "meanest guy I ever saw"—and for good reason. Whitlow Wyatt was a hard-throwing right-hander who was most famous as the pitcher who won 22 games in 1941, and helped lead the Brooklyn Dodgers to the National League pennant. He also won the Dodgers' only World Series game in '41.

As a high school phenomenon, Wyatt once struck out 23 Oglethorpe University batters in an exhibition game. Originally signed by the Tigers, he had 16 straight victories for Evansville of the Three-I League in 1929, before making his debut with the parent club on September 27. Groomed to be a top of the rotation starter by Bengal management, he was unfortunately hampered by an assortment of injuries. Wyatt's fortunes seemed to brighten, when, in 1931, his 1.53 ERA tied Dizzy Dean for the Texas League crown. In 1932, he pitched to a rather disappointing 9–13 record in 43 games and was traded the following June to the Chicago White Sox for Vic Frazier. A change of scenery to the South Side did not help, as he continued to bounce back and forth from the minors to the big leagues. Drafted by the Cleveland Indians in the 1936 Rule 5 Draft, Wyatt was again relegated to pitching mostly in the minors. At this point in his career, his record stood at a paltry 26–43. Many lesser players might have thought about quitting the game entirely, but not the fiery and always game Whitlow.

His luck finally broke when Cleveland sent him to Milwaukee of the American Association in 1937, in exchange for third baseman Ken Keltner. The trade proved to be a good move for both players' careers. Keltner went on to become one of the premier third basemen in the American League during the next decade, while Wyatt became rejuvenated in Milwaukee. His record stood at 12–6, with six shutouts, when Dodger vice president Larry MacPhail purchased his contract for two players and $20,000 on July 11, 1938.

Pitching for the first time in the friendly confines of Ebbets Field, Wyatt went 8–3 and cemented his reputation as a headhunter. He had a simple philosophy when it came to pitching aggressively: "Never be

Grave of Whitlow Wyatt. Courtesy of Andy Benefield.

afraid to pitch inside. If you have to dust someone, do it." Wyatt actually seemed to enjoy flipping opposing hitters and prided himself on his ability to down an opponent. Dodger manager Leo Durocher began the practice of doling out cash for every batter he knocked down. ("The Lip" would normally leave the cash on top of Wyatt's locker.)

Of course, Wyatt was more than just a headhunter. From 1940 to 1943, he won 70 games. In 1940, he went 15–14 and tied for the National League lead in shutouts, with five. In 1941, he and teammate Kirby Higbe each won 22 games, tops in the majors, leading the Dodgers to the pennant. Wyatt's seven shutouts were a major league high. He threw two complete games in the World Series, beating the Yankees, 3–2, in the second contest, but losing, 3–1, in the finale. He continued his winning ways throughout the next two seasons, going a combined 33–12. He retired in 1945, after two injury-plagued seasons, with a 106–95 career record.

When he later became a pitching coach with the Phillies and Braves, the crusty Wyatt refused to mellow, encouraging his pupils to throw at opposing hitters. Whit Wyatt died on June 19, 1999, at the age of 91, and is buried at Buchanan City Cemetery in Buchanan, Georgia.

EARLY WYNN (1920–1999)

Hall of Famer Early Wynn turned every ball game he pitched into a personal war. Talented, mean-spirited, and nasty on the mound, he never yielded an inch to any hitter he faced. Pitching 23 seasons and winning 300 games for Washington, Cleveland, and the White Sox, he was a five-time 20-game winner, leading the American League in innings pitched three times. He also won a Cy Young Award in 1959, at the age of 39, posting a 22–10 record, while leading the "Go-Go Sox" to the pennant.

Wynn, nicknamed "Gus," short for "Gloomy Gus," used pure aggressiveness, combined with a hatred for each batter, to become one of the most feared hurlers of all time. He established himself against opposing hitters with inside fastballs and an assortment of breaking pitches. His dubious reputation as a headhunter preceded him off the field as well. Ted Williams once refused Early's invitation to go fishing in the Everglades (Williams was a world champion fly fisherman who never turned down an opportunity to relax with his rod and reel). Wynn said, "Admit it Ted! You're afraid to go into the Everglades with me." Williams replied, "No hitter ever would go into the Everglades with a pitcher like you. His body might never be found."

Mickey Mantle probably summed Wynn up best when he said, "Early is so mean he'd knock you down in the fucking dugout." Mantle was not alone in his sentiments. Many players in the American League were wary of the burly right-hander, especially on days when he was pitching on the losing end of the box score.

Phil Rizzuto once commented,

> One time we were playing the Indians in Cleveland. It was like the fifth inning, and we were ahead by a few runs. I hadn't had a hit that day, but I remember that I walked and scored a run. Well, here I am batting, and Early throws one high and tight at me. If I hadn't ducked I would have gotten one in the ear. I just shook my head, wondering why he threw at me, of all people. That's the kind of pitcher he was, he never gave an inch.

Considered to be a good teammate, Wynn had an old-school attitude, believing in an eye for an eye. If an opposing pitcher threw at one of his teammates, he would usually hit two of the other team's batters. It was a practice that his teammates appreciated, for they knew that he had their backs, no matter what.

Wynn always regarded brushback pitches as part of the game and had no problem with opposing pitchers throwing inside to him. He once told the *Cleveland Plain Dealer*, "It doesn't bother me if they throw at me or hit me, I've got thick skin. They just better watch when it's their turn in the box." Because of his aggressive style of pitching, Wynn was labeled a headhunter by the press and opposing players. It was a charge that he always refuted. "I hate losing more than anything," he would say. He told the Associated Press, "It's my job to get the opposing batters out. It's also my job to make them feel uncomfortable in the box. If they can't get out of the way, then that's their problem, not mine. My job is to win games, period."

Wynn, who once said that he would hit his own mother, "depending on how she was hitting," could take it as well as dish it out. During a game in 1956, he was hit in the jaw by a line drive off the bat of Jose Valdivielso. Wynn refused to come out of the game right away. When he finally did leave the field, he needed 16 stitches and lost seven lower teeth.

Using a scowl and a blinding stare to intimidate batters, one of the things that bothered him most was when opposing batters crowded the plate. He once told famed sportswriter Red Smith,

> That space between the white lines, that's my office, that's where I conduct my business. You take a look at the batter's box, and part of it belongs to the hitter. But when he crowds in just that hair, he's stepping into my office, and nobody comes into my office without an invitation when I'm going to work.

Yankee infielder Gil McDougald once described Wynn, stating that he was "one hell of a nice guy off the field, but once he's on the mound, I wouldn't trust him to save my life." Yankee manager Casey Stengel once compared him favorably to Burleigh Grimes, the burly right-handed pitcher whose appearance and demeanor on the mound were similar.

Wynn was also considered one of the best hitting pitchers of his day, as he compiled a .214 lifetime average, with 17 homers and 173 RBI. He also pinch-hit 90 times during his career and is one of only five pitchers to slug a pinch-hit grand slam. Wynn, who won his 300th game in 1963, retired with a lifetime record of 300–244 and a 3.54 ERA. He mellowed somewhat after his playing career was over and became a pitching coach with the Indians and Twins, as well as a manager in the Twin farm system.

Always the battler, Early let it be known to the press his extreme disappointment for not being elected to the Hall of Fame in his first year of eligibility, 1968. When he was told a few years later that some sportswriters looked at him as a compiler and not a Hall of Fame pitcher, he dismissed them as "not knowing a damn thing" about baseball. Finally elected to the Hall in 1972, he told a newspaper reporter, "It's been a long wait, but I finally made it, it's just a shame me and my wife had to wait so long."

After retiring from coaching, Wynn worked as a color commentator for Toronto Blue Jay radio broadcasts, a post he held from 1977 to 1980. He then worked as a color commentator for White Sox radio broadcasts in 1982 and 1983. Retiring to Florida, Wynn lived a contented life until his wife Lorraine passed away in 1994, after which his own health took a serious decline.

Early Wynn, one of the toughest and meanest pitchers of all-time, died from complications relating to a series of strokes on April 4, 1999, at the age of 79. He was cremated and his ashes retained by his family.

THE BOB BOWMAN–JOE MEDWICK INCIDENT

The near-fatal beaning of Hall of Fame outfielder Joe Medwick at the hands of Cardinal pitcher and former teammate Bob Bowman in 1940 has been all but forgotten with the passage of time. Yet, it remains one of the most compelling episodes in baseball history. A member of the famous Gas House Gang, Medwick, nicknamed "Muscles," was known for his aggressive attitude on and off the field. He was often antagonistic, not just toward opposing players, but to his own teammates and the press.

By June 1940, Medwick had grown tired of haggling with St. Louis management about his contract. Labeled a malcontent by both President Branch Rickey and owner Sam Breaden, the two men finally decided that it would be best to trade off their talented outfielder. On June 12, Muscles was traded to the Dodgers in a multiplayer deal that also sent pitcher Curt Davis to Brooklyn in exchange for four players and a cash sum that was reported as being between $125,000 and $200,000.

Although he had not asked for the trade, Medwick was ecstatic to be joining his old friend and Gas House Gang teammate Leo Durocher. He was also just as happy to get out from under the clutches of the penurious Rickey. Many baseball scribes predicted that the trade would add fuel to an already intense rivalry. Medwick was scheduled to face his old team just six days later, when "Dem Bums" and the "Redbirds" were scheduled to open up a three-game series at Ebbets Field.

The first game of the series proved to be rather uneventful. St. Louis won, 3–1, and Medwick went hitless. Facing the Dodgers the next day would be Bowman, who, as a rookie in 1939, went 13–5, with 9 saves. Bowman was known for occasionally showing signs of aggression on the mound. During his rookie season, in a game against the Dodgers, he was accused of throwing dusters. In that same contest, Brooklyn reliever Hugh Casey, who was no slouch when it came to throwing high and tight, was also accused by the Cards of trying to dust off players in retaliation.

The Dodgers were a bit on edge, even before the start of the series. They didn't need an incentive to play the hated Cardinals. Adding to the tension was the fact that the "Brooklyn Nine" was playing without their rookie shortstop, Pee Wee Reese, who had been accidentally beaned by Cub pitcher Jake Mooty on June 1st.

The Dodgers got off quickly in the bottom of the first, notching two runs off Bowman. Dixie Walker singled and Cookie Lavagetto doubled, sending Walker home. Then Joe Vosmik singled Lavagetto in. In stepped Medwick, batting cleanup and looking to do even more damage. Bowman was already in a bad mood due to his first-inning woes, and his first pitch to Medwick struck his former teammate square on the left temple. Medwick crumpled to the ground, and Bowman actually rushed to home plate to see if his former teammate was alright.

Did he feel remorse for having thrown the pitch? Was it intentional? The Dodgers weren't about to wait for an inquisition. Several Dodger players, led by manager Leo Durocher, charged at Bowman. While the crowd roared in anger, umpires and Cardinal players got between the pitcher and the angry mob of players. Dodger president Larry MacPhail had to be restrained by Charlie Dressen and Babe Phelps.

After being examined by Dodger team physician Dr. Henry Classen, Medwick was carried off the field by stretcher and taken to Caledonian Hospital. While waiting in the dressing room for an ambulance, he groggily remarked, "It's funny, that makes two bad days in a row. Yesterday I couldn't get a base hit, and today this thing happens."

After Medwick assured his wife, Isadore, that he would be okay, she stormed from the clubhouse on the arm of Durocher's wife. "Wait till I see that Bowman," Isadore told a reporter. "He's the only Cardinal who ever throws at a batter deliberately. I'll punch him in the face myself."

By this point, the behavior of the crowd had gotten so ugly that two uniformed New York City police detectives in civilian clothing were now sitting in the St. Louis dugout to protect Bowman. MacPhail had both officers removed and sent for more help from the NYPD. Eventually nearly 100 uniformed officers entered Ebbets Field, taking their position near the St. Louis dugout. The game eventually continued, with the Cardinals beating the Brooklynites, 7–5, in extra innings.

Cooler heads did not exactly prevail the next day, as a fistfight broke out between Durocher and Cardinal catcher Mickey Owen. (Owen would go on to play for the Dodgers and achieve baseball infamy for allowing a passed ball during the 1941 World Series.) Meanwhile, Brooklyn district attorney William O'Dwyer started an investigation to find out if the beaning was deliberate.

Bowman flatly denied that he had any ill will toward Medwick, claiming, "I tried to put too much stuff on the ball and it got away. If I live 1,000 years, I'll still think that Joe stood there waiting for the ball to curve, and it didn't."

Although Medwick was diagnosed with a severe concussion, O'Dwyer still sent a staff aide, Burton B. Turkus, to interview the ailing star in his hospital bed. Surprisingly, Medwick placed no blame on his former teammate. "No direct threat had been made to me by Bowman," he said. "I saw the ball leave from his hand, but that was the last I saw of it."

As he recounted the events leading up to the beaning, pieces of the story began falling into place. On the morning of the game, Medwick was in an elevator with his wife at the Hotel New Yorker, along with former teammate Mort Cooper and his wife, another Cardinal teammate, Durocher, Bowman, and a few fans. According to Medwick, Durocher and Bowman began ribbing one another about the merits of their teams. Medwick was adamant about Bowman's innocence, stating that he never heard any threats made by his former teammate.

Meanwhile, National League president Ford Frick announced his own inquiry, calling MacPhail, Durocher, and Dodgers secretary John McDonald into his office. Waiting their turn were most of the Cardinal team, including Bowman and manager Billy Southworth. Durocher and the rest of the Dodger contingent maintained that Bowman's pitch had been intentional. Bowman, who was called into Frick's office twice, reiterated how sorry he was and that it had been an accident. "I never meant to hurt Joe," stated a teary-eyed Bowman. Durocher refused to accept Bowman's apology, telling Frick that Bowman had boldly proclaimed, "I'll get you and Medwick."

As the inquiry, which lasted about four hours, wound down, Frick received a phone call from O'Dwyer's office asking him to send several players and coaches to testify. As the Dodger entourage left Frick's office, a defiant Durocher chimed, "I am confident that we have made a strong case against Bowman."

A few days later, on June 20th, as Medwick was preparing to leave the hospital, O'Dwyer's office ruled the beaning an accident, saying that a thorough investigation "failed to disclose evidence of any criminal intent on the part of Bowman." A livid Durocher proclaimed that the skulling of his star outfielder should have been treated like attempted murder, while the Associated Press proclaimed that baseball's "fathers" had closed ranks and "destroyed evidence" in a cover-up. Others felt that Medwick's absolving of Bowman closed the case. Adding salt to the wounds of the Brooklyn faithful was the fact that the only Cardinal to receive any kind of punishment was catcher Mickey Owen for his fight with Durocher. (Owen was fined $50 and suspended four days for his pugilistic efforts.) As Medwick walked out of the hospital on his own power, he attempted to put the incident behind him, sending a message out to his former teammate, saying, "No hard feelings, Bob."

On June 21st, Ford Frick, after studying 32 pages of testimony, officially closed the case. In a statement, he said, "After careful investigation, the National League office finds no proof of the charge brought by the Brooklyn Club that pitcher Bob Bowman deliberately and with premeditation beaned Joe Medwick in the game played at Ebbets Field June 18. The charges therefore are dismissed."

Medwick's recovery was expected to take a minimum of three weeks, and he returned to the lineup June 22nd. By this time, the Cardinals had moved on to Boston to play the Bees. In the first inning of the first game of a doubleheader on June 23rd, Bowman was accidentally spiked by Sibi Sisti of Boston on a play at first base. When informed of Bowman's injury, which needed four stitches to close the wound, Durocher supposedly mumbled a few obscenities under his breath and halfheartedly smiled. Bowman finished the season with a rather unimpressive 6–5 mark in 28 games

Purchased by the Giants in December 1940, Bowman had another disappointing season, going 6–7 in just 29 games. In December 1941, he was traded to the Cubs for Hank Leiber. Leiber would appear in 58

Grave of Joe Medwick. Courtesy of Bill Lee.

games for New York. Bowman played in just one game for the Cubs that season, appearing in what would be his final major league showing on May 25th, before his contract was sold to the Nashville Volunteers of the Southern Association. He would toil in the minors until 1954, with his last professional stop being the Fargo-Moorehead Twins of the Northern League.

Sadly for Brooklyn, the bad luck continued. Pitcher Hugh Casey was beaned during an exhibition game by former Dodger batting practice pitcher Vince Shupe, and rookie shortstop Pee Wee Reese was lost for the season in July with a heel injury.

Despite the beaning, Medwick soldiered on. By season's end, he had a .301 average and 17 homers, but just 86 RBI. Many baseball scribes wondered out loud if the beaning had affected his hitting. His overall stats suggest otherwise. He still drove the ball with power on a consistent basis and was hitting for average. In fact, the next season, he helped lead Brooklyn to its first pennant since 1920, with an 18-homer, 88-RBI campaign that also saw him bat .318. It was not until 1942 that his home run production dropped noticeably. Although he drove in 96 runs and batted .300 that season, Medwick smacked only four round-trippers. He had only two more seasons in which he appeared in 120 games or more, 1943 and 1944, after which he was a part-time player.

Medwick retired in 1948, with a .324 lifetime batting average and 205 homers, 1,383 RBI, and 2,471 hits—surely good enough for consideration for the Baseball Hall of Fame—but Muscles would have to wait 20 years until finally gaining his place in the Hall in 1968. He went on to manage minor league clubs in Miami Beach, Tampa, and Raleigh, and also conducted an insurance business in St. Louis for many years. In 1966, he was offered a job by the Cardinals as a minor league hitting instructor. Medwick continued in this capacity until his death from a heart attack on March 21, 1975, while working at the Cardinal spring training complex in St. Petersburg, Florida.

Never having fulfilled the promise of his rookie season, Bowman's fate was much sadder. After his baseball career was over, he worked for 12 years for the Fort Lauderdale Recreational Department before ill health forced his retirement. Returning to his native West Virginia to seek treatment, he entered the historic Bluefield Sanitarium in late August 1972. A longtime alcoholic, he was suffering from liver cirrhosis and hepatitis when he was felled by a pulmonary embolism on the

Grave of Bob Bowman. Courtesy of Dr. Fred Worth.

evening of September 4th. Bowman, who was 61, was laid to rest at Woodlawn Memorial Park in Bluewell, West Virginia, on September 7th in Section 12, Lot 14, in the northwest corner of the cemetery.

5

SUICIDE IS PAINLESS

In the age of technology, the "new media," and sabermetrics, much of the human element has been taken out of the game of baseball and how we look at players. This is unfortunate, since major leaguers are subject to the same frailties and problems that we all deal with. It used to be that when a player left the majors, he was all but forgotten, unless he was a star of the magnitude of, say, a Ty Cobb, Babe Ruth, or Ted Williams. There are countless stories of players being unable to adjust to retirement. The fear of not being remembered or wanted became too much for some. Many had to deal with substance abuse and alcohol problems that fueled their already depressive state. Yet, there is no definitive answer as to why someone might want to take their own life. Psychological and emotional problems aside, perhaps it simply comes down to the fact that the pain it took to stay became greater than the pain it took to go.

FRANK RINGO (1860–1889)

Depending on which sources you believe, Frank Ringo is either the first or second professional ballplayer to take his own life. This discrepancy exists because many baseball "purists" do not recognize the National Association (1871–1875) as a professional league, even though the players of that organization were considered paid professionals. If one considers the National Association a professional league, which it was,

Grave of Frank Ringo. Courtesy of Dr. Fred Worth.

then Fraley Rogers was the first professional player to commit suicide, which he did by shooting himself in the chest on May 10, 1881.

Semantics aside, Ringo, a catcher by trade, was talented enough to play both the infield and outfield. Born October 12, 1860, in Parkville, Missouri, his alcoholism prevented him from having success at both the major and minor league levels. Known for his binge drinking, he would go on the wagon for months at a time and then suddenly lose it and start hitting the saloons again. While he may have been a power drinker, he was never considered a mean drunk and was always thought to be quite the genial type.

A top-flight receiver, Ringo was constantly battling with club officials, who had no problem levying fines against him for his drunkenness. He played for five different teams in his four seasons in the majors, in both the National League and American Association. His busiest year, game-wise, was his rookie season of 1883, when he appeared in 60 contests for the Philadelphia Quakers.

Referred to as a "heavy hitter" by *Sporting Life* and other newspapers of the time, his lifetime average was just .192. Released from his last two professional stops with Kansas City of the Western League and St. Paul of the Western Association because of his drinking, he was unable to find work for the 1889 season. As desperation set in, he wrote letters to several of his old teammates asking for help in finding an assignment but received no replies. Severely depressed, Ringo went on a drinking binge during the last two weeks of his life, consuming whiskey and beer at dangerous levels.

His death occurred on April 12, 1889, after he ingested 40 grams of morphine. Ringo, who had been married three months earlier, left his parents and new wife to mourn his passing. He was buried in Elmwood Cemetery in Kansas City in Section D, Block D, Lot 488, Grave 2.

MARTY BERGEN (1871–1900)

During his brief four-year run with the National League's Boston Bean-eaters, Marty Bergen was rated as one of the best catchers in the game. The son of Michael and Ann (Delaney) Bergen, he was born in North Brookfield, Massachusetts, on October 25, 1871. Bergen and his younger brother Bill both became known for their superior defensive skills;

however, even as a young teenager, Marty never seemed to enjoy himself on the field. Always anxious, always worrying, he would catastrophize about every little problem that came his way. Never blessed with self-control, he could be argumentative and defensive when he felt that he was being treated unfairly.

Bergen first played for the independent Brookfields Club, a town team that also featured catcher Connie Mack. He played four years of minor league ball before making his major league debut with the Boston Beaneaters on April 17, 1896, in a 7–3 loss to the Phillies at the Baker Bowl in Philadelphia. Sharing backstop duties with veteran Charlie Ganzel, Bergen appeared in 65 games that season, batting .265, with 4 homers and 37 RBI. He quickly established himself as one of the best, if not *the* best, defensive backstops in the game. A member of two consecutive pennant-winning teams (1897–1898), he became known for his strong arm and exceptional instincts behind the plate. His infield teammates, Fred Tenney, Bobby Lowe, Herman Long, and Jimmy Collins, had nothing but praise for Bergen's defensive abilities. As Lowe put it, "Bergen's throws were always strong and very rarely, if ever, sailed. He positioned himself behind the plate as well as any catcher I have ever seen."

Playing during the days before shin guards, Marty was also exceptional at protecting the plate from opposing runners. He was involved in more than his share of collisions at the plate, although he was never injured seriously, contrary to many published reports of the day. His skills were greatly appreciated by his teammates, management, and the fans. What was not appreciated was his moody and antagonistic behavior.

In the social atmosphere of the Boston clubhouse, the antisocial Bergen stuck out like the proverbial sore thumb. As his career progressed, so too did his "issues." A sullen loner, he was stricken with frequent bouts of depression. If he were alive today, he most surely would be diagnosed with some sort of clinical depression or perhaps borderline personality disorder. By 1899, his last season in the majors, Bergen was showing clear signs of paranoid schizophrenia, as he began having psychotic episodes where he complained of being poked and prodded and chased by unseen people. He also complained of hearing voices, even during games.

Marty Bergen, Boston Beaneaters. Courtesy of the author.

The one place where Bergen found comfort was amongst his family, which included his wife Harriet, whom he married in 1895, and three children. By all accounts, Bergen was a typical doting father who enjoyed home life. While it is not known if Harriet was aware of his mental health "issues" when they first met, one would have to assume that she was made aware of his condition as their relationship progressed. Bergen was also extremely close to his parents and siblings, which included sisters Mary, Margaret, Ann, and Catharine.

The start of the 1899 season was not easy for Boston, as the club played 16 of its first 17 games on the road. On Monday, April 24th, the team was in Washington, where it was finishing up a four-game wrap-around set with the Senators. Sometime after the game, which was won by Boston, 10–1, Marty received a telegram informing him that his five-year-old son, Martin Jr., had passed away that morning from diphtheria. The devastating news turned out to be the "body blow" from which he would never recover. His mind already in a fragile state, he began blaming himself for not being with his son when he passed. Boston manager Frank Selee and owner Art Soden told him to take as much time off as needed to get his affairs in order and give himself the proper amount of rest.

When Bergen returned to the team two weeks later, he was cordially welcomed back by his teammates in a fruitless effort to "bury the hatchet" (no pun intended) with him. But he would have none of it. Instead of accepting their condolences and well wishes, he became vitriolic and paranoid, accusing them of purposely reminding him of his deceased son. He also began making open threats against them. The situation became so bad that by season's end, almost everyone on the club was staying away from him. While Bergen's mental state was such that even a blind man could have seen that he needed help, none was forthcoming. It is important to note that during this time period, there was little in the way of treatment for the mentally ill outside of institutionalization or "exhausting" a patient by overmedicating them with such drugs as opiates or morphine.

In the early morning hours of January 19, 1900, Bergen took an ax and proceeded to kill Harriet and his two remaining children, Florence and Joseph. After the initial carnage was over, he grabbed a straight razor, stood in front of a kitchen mirror, and ended his life by slitting his throat. Bergen's 55-year-old father Michael discovered the bodies the next morning and immediately contacted the authorities.

In their Saturday, January 20th edition, the *New York Times* reports the following:

> Martin Bergen's body and that of the little girl, Florence, six and one-half years old, were lying on the kitchen floor, while in the adjoining bedroom there were the bodies of Mrs. Bergen and her three-year-old son, Joseph. Mrs. Bergen was lying on the bed, with her hands raised as if in supplication or if to ward off a blow. The little boy was lying on the floor with a large wound in the head. Mrs. Bergen's skull was terribly crushed, having evidently been struck by more than one blow by the infuriated husband. The appearance of the little girl also showed that a number of savage blows had been rained upon the top and side of her head. Bergen's throat had been cut with a razor, and the head was nearly severed from the body.

While there is no doubt that the bloody aftermath of Bergen's horrendous act was a gruesome sight to behold, the reference to his head being almost severed was clearly a fabrication by the press. Dr. Stephen Boren, assistant professor of emergency medicine at the University of Illinois in Chicago, has debunked this theory entirely, stating:

> The physician's death certificate does agree with newspaper accounts. It says, "Bergen cut his throat, severing the windpipe and large vessels, dying from the injury." That is very logical. He cut his trachea (windpipe). He cut his jugular veins and carotid arteries. They are not that deep. The newspaper account undoubtedly was an exaggeration. The cervical vertebrae hold the skull on the body. A self-administered razor cut would not have severed all those ligaments around them. However, the razor could have cut the sternocleidomastoid muscles, and with all the blood, the reporter could have come to the conclusion that the head was almost severed.

Interestingly, Bergen's Commonwealth of Massachusetts death certificate states his cause of death as "suicide by shooting," and not a razor. A death certificate is usually amended after an autopsy has been performed. Since no such postmortem procedure was carried out on Bergen, the only explanation for such a contradiction has to be a clerical error.

It is tragic that Bergen never got the help he so desperately needed. The combination of his various mental health issues and lack of treatment was a lethal combination against which he didn't stand a chance. The murder–suicide of Bergen and his family shocked the baseball world and nation at large. Just 28 years old at the time of his death, he and his family were buried in Saint Joseph's Cemetery in North Brookfield, Massachusetts, on January 20th. His grave remained unmarked for many years until his old teammate with the Brookfields, Philadelphia Athletic manager Connie Mack, paid for a headstone. Years after Marty's death, his brother Bill spoke with a local newspaper, commenting, "It was as if he was possessed. The demons got to him and never let him go."

HARRY EAST (1862–1905)

The memory of Harry East is not imbedded in the minds of fans like that of Babe Ruth or Ty Cobb, nor is it enshrined in the National Baseball Hall of Fame at Cooperstown. The only thing to show for his brief career are the statistics that prove he played one game, going hitless in four at-bats for the American Association's Baltimore Orioles in 1882.

The son of William H. East and Ada Virginia Finnegin East, he was born in St. Louis, Missouri, on April 12, 1862. East had two interests growing up, baseball and medicine. Choosing baseball at the start, he made his only major league appearance on June 17, 1882, in a 10–5 loss to the St. Louis Browns at Sportsman's Park in St. Louis. East, who batted and threw left-handed, started the game at third base. In the minors, he played for the Memphis Reds of the Southern League in 1885, and the Lincoln Tree Planters of the Western League in 1886. He played semipro ball until the late 1880s, after which he decided to pursue his other dream of becoming a physician. East attended Barnes Medical College in St. Louis starting in 1890, and, after graduating, set up practice in St. Louis, where he specialized in allopathic medicine. By all accounts, he had a thriving practice.

In May 1905, East was admitted to Alexian Brothers' Hospital in St. Louis for treatment of melancholia, a severe disorder characterized by prolonged sadness, unhappiness, and misery of everyday experiences and thoughts. On June 2nd, he decided to put an end to his suffering by slitting his throat with a straight razor. By the time orderlies found him, it was too late; he had punched his ticket to the "great beyond." East, who had never married, was just 43 years old. He was buried in IOOF Cemetery (International Order of Odd Fellows) in Xenia, Illinois, a few days later.

REDDY FOSTER (1864–1908)

Oscar E. "Reddy" Foster was a star catcher in the Virginia State League when he was discovered by a scout from the New York Giants. A life-long resident of Richmond, Virginia, he was known as a hard-drinking, rough, and ready ballplayer whose temper usually got the best of him. He eventually acquired the bad habit of venting his frustrations on his wife Mary when his teams lost. Exacerbated by his drinking, Foster would go on wild tirades, making threatening gestures toward her. While Mary never admitted to it, there was suspicion that Foster occasionally beat her. Reddy's continued abuse after team losses became so commonplace that his wife came up with the idea for an "early warning system," where she was given a heads up to the outcome of that day's game by friends. If her husband's team won, she would usually stick around, since then he would become a "happy drunk." If, God forbid, his team lost, she would quickly hightail it to a neighbor's house, where she would wait for him to sober up.

Foster appeared in just one major league game, going 0–1 on June 3, 1896, for the New York Giants in a 14–8 loss to Chicago at the Polo Grounds. He also managed in the minors, most notably with Bluefield, West Virginia, and served as player-manager of Portsmouth of the Virginia State League. It was with Portsmouth that he worked his last professional engagement. Foster always demanded the best from his players and teammates on the field; incompetence was something that was totally unacceptable to him. He quit the game for good when his first baseman made a "bone head" play by dropping a pickoff throw that had the runner out by a mile. Utterly disgusted, Reddy threw his catcher's glove and mask on the ground and walked off the field, never to return.

Foster's drinking problems frew worse after his retirement. In December 1908, he went on a bad drinking binge during a two-day period and began making suicidal comments. On December 19th, he walked down to the James River with his friend, Lee Poklington, and a loaded double-barreled, 12-gauge shotgun. He took a swig from a whiskey bottle, looked over at his friend, and said, "Watch me do a trick." He then put the shotgun to his chin and pulled the trigger with his foot, killing himself instantly. He was just 44 years of age. The suddenness of his death shocked Richmond's baseball community, for despite his personal demons and faults, he was a well-liked individual who had made many friends and fans during his 20-year career. He was survived by Mary, his wife of 21 years; their three children, John, Katie, and Julia; and son Joseph from a previous marriage. He was buried at Oakwood Cemetery in Richmond.

HUGH CASEY (1913–1951)

One of the great relievers in Brooklyn Dodger history, Hugh Casey is largely remembered for throwing the pitch that proved to be the turning point of the 1941 World Series. The play in question occurred with two outs in the top of the ninth inning of Game 4. With the Yankees leading the series, 2–1, and the Dodgers holding a 4–3 lead, Casey threw an unhittable 3–2 breaking pitch to outfielder Tommy Henrich. "Old Reliable" swung at and missed what appeared to be a series-tying strikeout. Certain victory immediately turned into disaster, as the Flatbush Faithful saw catcher Mickey Owen, in his first year as Dodger backstop, mishandle the speeding sphere. While Owen chased down the runaway ball, Henrich safely reached first base. From that point onward, it was all downhill. The Yankees went on to plate 4 runs, en route to a 7–4 victory and a commanding 3–1 World Series lead.

Casey's professional baseball career began in a most inauspicious way. As a strapping 18-year-old, he was hired by former Brooklyn skipper Wilbert Robinson as what the *New York Times* described as "his personal chauffeur." After seeing first-hand his talent for throwing a baseball, he decided to coach him. When "Uncle Robbie" took over the presidency of the famous Atlanta Crackers in 1932, be brought his protégé onboard. Casey appeared in 13 games for the Crackers, going

0–3, with a rather hefty 5.77 ERA. Moving to the Charlotte Hornets of the Class B Piedmont League the following season, Casey had a breakout year, going 19–9 in 37 games. Back with the Crackers in 1934, his overall record was hardly impressive, as he went 8–6, with a 4.90 ERA, in 26 appearances.

Drafted by the Cubs after the 1934 season, he made his major league debut on April 29, 1935, in a 12–11 win over the Pirates at Wrigley Field. Casey, who pitched two scoreless relief innings, originally got the win, but National League president Ford Frick stepped in and awarded the win to Fabian Kowalik instead. Casey spent the entire '35 season at the big-league level, appearing in just 13 games for the pennant-bound "North Siders." Sent back to the minors the next season, he would have to wait three years before getting another crack at the majors.

On the recommendation of Charlie Dressen, Dodger president Larry MacPhail selected Hugh in the September 1938 Rule 5 Draft. His first-ever start for the Brooklyn nine came on Decoration Day 1939, against the Giants at the Polo Grounds. The game turned out to be a memorable performance, as Casey bested Carl Hubbell, 3–1, in front of 58,000 fans. The decision to draft the hurler proved to be a prudent one, as he pitched to a 15–10 record. He also opened Brooklyn management's eyes with a tough, aggressive style of play on the mound, as he led the National League in hit batsmen, with 11.

After his rookie campaign, Casey began seeing more and more service out of the bull pen, eventually blossoming into one of the premier relievers in baseball. During his career, he relieved in 287 of his 343 appearances, leading the National League in relief wins three times and saves twice. A consummate professional and loyal friend, he never failed to come to the aid of a teammate who had been dusted.

"Fireman," as he came to be known because he came into games to put out fires, could take it and dish it out. A prime example of this came on July 11, 1940, when he was beaned in an exhibition game at Johnstown, Pennsylvania. Playing right field that day, Casey came to bat in the fourth inning against left-hander Vince Shupe, a former Dodger batting practice pitcher. Shupe's first pitch struck Casey above the left temple, eventually bouncing into the grandstand. Going down as if struck by an anvil, he eventually got to his feet and, with some help, walked off the field on his own. Taken back to his hotel room, he collapsed and was immediately taken to the hospital. Diagnosed with a concussion, he remained there for several days. Casey didn't miss a step after his return. In his first game back, on July 19th, he instigated a brawl at Wrigley Field when he drilled Cub pitcher Claude Passeau in the back. Passeau and Dodger backup first baseman Joe Gallagher were both tossed by umpire Ziggy Sears. Casey got nothing more than a reprimand.

Unbeknownst to most fans was the softer side of his personality. Kindhearted to a fault, he was usually quiet and unassuming when around large groups of people. Pee Wee Reese once remarked that, "Case would give you the shirt off his back and his last dime if you needed it." Few people knew that he was one of the first players to welcome Jackie Robinson when he joined the Dodgers in 1947, even hitting balls to him during fielding practice to help him get acquainted with the area around first base. Casey proudly displayed an auto-graphed picture of Robinson at his restaurant, Hugh Casey's Steak and Chop House.

If Hugh had one problem, it was with the bottle. The jovial Georgian would often run his mouth when drunk, occasionally using racial slurs. This, of course, didn't sit well with his buddy Robinson, who out of respect for their friendship, kept quiet. One of his best friends outside of baseball was Ernest Hemingway. The two drinking buddies would often argue and resort to pugilism to settle their differences. Still, at the end of the day, the two would remain firm friends.

Taking time out of his baseball career to serve in the Pacific theater during World War II, where he served with his friend Reese and Yan-kee shortstop Phil Rizzuto, Fireman returned to the Brooklyn mound in 1946, accruing a splendid 11–5 mark, with a sublime 1.99 ERA, leading the National League in games finished, with 27. Success continued for him the following season, as he posted a 10–4 mark, although his ERA ballooned to 3.99. The Dodgers, winners of the National League pen-nant, again faced the Yankees in the World Series. In one of the great-est Fall Classics of all time, the Dodgers fell to the Bronx Bombers, four games to three. Casey himself had a series to remember, as he appeared in six games, while accounting for two of the Dodgers' three series wins. In 10.3 innings of work, he compiled a miniscule 0.87 ERA. Joe DiMag-gio later reflected on Casey's year by saying, "Hugh was at his best in that series. We just had a really hard time handling him. He pitched as well as anyone I have ever seen."

In May 1948, Casey suffered a serious injury when he slipped and fell down a flight of stairs that led from his apartment, which was located above his restaurant. Wearing loafers at the time, he suffered torn ligaments and tendons, injuries that would shelve him for two months. Never the same after the injury, he was released by Brooklyn after appearing in only 22 games. Signing with the Pirates for the following season, he appeared in 33 games before being given his release on August 10, 1949. Less than a month later, he signed with the Yankees, with whom he gained his last major league win. He appeared in just four games for New York, making his last appearance as a major leaguer on September 23rd. With his release on October 13, his major league career came to a close.

Feeling that he still had something left in the tank, Hugh caught on with his hometown Atlanta Crackers, with whom he posted a 10–4 record in 1950, helping them to the Southern Association pennant; however, the happiness of his comeback season would be short-lived. In late 1950, a paternity suit was brought against him by 25-year-old Hilda Weismann of Brooklyn, who was known for being one of the numerous baseball groupies who hung around Ebbets Field. In late December, a court ruled that he was the father of Weismann's son, and Casey was ordered to pay $20 a month in child support. The paternity scandal not only grated on his nerves, but it also put even more of a strain on his marriage to his wife Kathleen. In late January 1951, Casey was notified by the IRS that he was being fined for $6,759 in back taxes. While he never admitted that anything was wrong, friends could see a change in his demeanor.

During spring training, Casey worked out with his old team, the Dodgers, in hopes of catching on, but nothing materialized. On May 13th, he made his last mound appearance, giving up four hits in five innings of work for the semipro Bushwicks of Brooklyn. In late June, he made plans to organize his own celebrity softball team, which would be comprised of local semipro players and former major leaguers, including ex-Yankees pitcher Marius Russo. In early July, he contacted his old friend Ben Gould of the *Brooklyn Eagle* looking for assistance in finding a playing field, with the intention of playing a series of charity games to benefit the Police Athletic League. It was during this time that he traveled to Georgia on a trip that he told friends was "for business reasons." No one had any reason to believe that there was a problem.

Shortly after midnight on July 3rd, Casey called his friend, Gordon McNabb, a real estate developer, asking him to come to his room at the Atlantan Hotel. "You'll see me, but I won't see you," he told his old friend. After hanging up, he immediately phoned his now-estranged wife. As the two conversed, McNabb rushed to the hotel in a mad dash to save his friend's life. Upon arriving, he phoned Casey's room from the clerk's desk but found that the line was busy. As he rushed upstairs and approached the door to the room, a shot rang out. In a panic, McNabb ran back downstairs for help, returning with a bellhop and policeman. When they opened the door, they found the former pitcher lying on the floor, face down, dead from a shotgun blast to the neck. Lying next to him was a 16-gauge shotgun.

When contacted by police by phone a few minutes later, an emotional Kathleen Casey recalled her last conversation with her husband, placing full blame on Hilda Weismann's shoulders. Kathleen said,

Grave of Hugh Casey. Courtesy of Dr. Fred Worth.

> I begged and pleaded with him not to do it. I tried to tell him it was for God to do and not for him to do. But he said he was ready to die. He was as calm about it as if he was about to walk out on the ball field and pitch a game. My husband was just devastated. He told me, "I can't eat or sleep going through all this embarrassment. And I had to drag you through it, too, but I swear with a dying oath that I am innocent."

Kathleen also told police that the last words she heard her husband utter were, "I am innocent of these charges." She also revealed that her husband had threatened to commit suicide several times since the paternity suit was first filed.

When news of Casey's death reached his friends and colleagues, feelings of shock and grief where mixed with bewilderment, puzzlement, and anger. Probably the hardest hit was Pee Wee Reese, his closest friend on the Dodgers. Said Reese, "I was very close to Casey, after our experience together in the South Pacific, and I can hardly believe this happened to my friend Hugh. Why he was the guy we all relied on in the clutch. He never failed us." Dodgers manager Chuck Dressen was stunned by the news, lamenting, "I can't believe it happened. He must have had terrible trouble because the guy I knew was all heart and could face anything."

On July 4, 1951, as the United States celebrated its birthday with nationwide festivities, Hugh Casey was laid to rest next to his parents at Mt. Parran Cemetery in Atlanta. Two of his old Dodger teammates, Whit Wyatt and Dixie Walker, were pallbearers. At the funeral, he was remembered for being a genial, caring man, who, although he may have had problems, would have done anything for a friend. Maybe *Sporting News* summed it up best when they reported that, "Casey was kind to everybody, except himself."

IRON DAVIS (1890–1961)

George Allen "Iron" Davis will forever be known for throwing a no-hitter in the final month of the pennant-winning 1914 season for the Boston Braves. The son of George Allen and Lillian Grimes Davis, he was born in Lancaster, New York, a suburb of Buffalo. His father, George Sr., was a well-known judge in Buffalo and also a Republican

New York senator. George Sr. was a self-made man who handed down the qualities of hard work and self-reliance to his son. His father's wealth enabled the younger George to attend the prestigious St. John's Military Academy in Syracuse, where he played on the baseball team. An extremely cerebral student, his academic interests varied from science to literature and religion.

In 1908, Davis attended Williams College in Williamstown, Massachusetts. It was there that he gained the nickname "Iron" due to his feats as a weightlifter. A member of the baseball team, which was coached by former major league pitcher Andy Coakley, Davis used his fastball and curve to amass a huge number of strikeouts. According to Buffalo baseball historian Joseph M. Overfield, Davis struck out 20 against Wesleyan, 18 against Trinity, and 15 against both Princeton and Dartmouth; he also beat Yale after it had won 19 games in a row.

In 1912, on a tip from Yankee trainer Doc Barrett (who worked in the off-season for the Williams athletic department), Yank scout Art Irwin signed Davis to a $5,000 deal. Davis signed the contract on July 12th and made his major league debut four days later, against the St. Louis Browns, losing, 3–1. In 10 games, seven of which he started, he went 1–4, with a 6.05 ERA. In the spring of 1913, George joined the Yankees on a spring training trip to Bermuda, but he returned home after only a few days to marry his girlfriend, Georgiana Jones. The move infuriated Yankee manager Frank Chance so much that he threatened to send him to the minors. Davis, who by this time was enrolled at Harvard Law School, could have cared less. When he arrived back in Buffalo, he received a telegram informing him that his contract had been sold to the Jersey City Skeeters of the International League.

Davis would appear in 32 games for the Skeeters, going a horrendous 1–16. On the positive side, he fanned 199 batters in 208 innings of work. Tired of his wildness, New York sold his contract to the Rochester Hustlers of the International League in late August, but before he could throw a pitch for his new team, his contract was again sold to the Boston Braves on August 25th. He appeared in two late-season games, going 0–0 in eight innings of work. Due to his prior commitment to law school, he was unable to join the Braves the following season until early September.

On advice from manager George Stallings, Davis began working on a spitball, which Stallings felt would be a devastating weapon due to the

George "Iron" Davis with his wife, Georgiana. Courtesy of the author.

speed with which he was able to throw the ball. On September 9th, Davis was informed by Stallings that he would start the second game of that day's scheduled doubleheader against the Phillies. Using his spitball to full effect, Davis threw a 7–0 no-hitter. Seven Phillies reached base that afternoon, two on errors by backup third baseman Red Smith and the other five on walks. Of those five walks, three of them came consecutively in the fifth inning to load the bases. George then settled down and promptly struck out Ed Burns and induced pinch hitter Gavvy Cravath to hit into a double play. The only other threat came in the eighth inning, when Burns hit a fly to right, which Possum Whitted corralled with a brilliant shoestring catch. After the game, Brave president John Gaffney sent a telegram to George Sr. that read as follows: "Congratulations! George won his game. No hits. No runs. J. E. GAFFNEY."

The Braves would go on to win the pennant and defeat the heavily favored Athletics, putting the finishing touches on their "miracle season." For the rest of his life, Davis would remain extremely proud of his no-hitter and the fact that he was a part of one of the greatest comebacks in sports history.

Reporting late again the following season due to law school commitments, George started 10 games, ending up with a 3–3 record and 3.80 ERA. Released after making two appearances for the Providence Grays of the International League in 1916, he decided to retire, since he now had his law degree and careers in baseball were uncertain at best. Enlisting in the U.S. Army in early 1918, he reported to Fort Lee, Virginia, where he was commissioned a second lieutenant after three months training. He was so efficient in the use of the bayonet that he was put in charge of bayonet training for new recruits. Discharged with the rank of captain on January 14, 1919, he joined his father's practice, which specialized in real estate law. It should be noted that George's first choice was to become a physician, but George Sr. persuaded him to follow in his footsteps instead.

Davis started his own practice after his father's death in February 1920, and began taking graduate courses in philosophy and comparative religion at the University of Buffalo. It was during this time that he also took an interest in astronomy, eventually accumulating 1,800 volumes in his library. For thirty years, he conducted astronomy classes at the Buffalo Museum of Science and lectured on the subject at the University of Buffalo. The law may have been his profession, but astronomy was his passion.

Throughout the 1920s, George and his family lived a life of means, with no worries or cares. By 1929, he had grown tired of law and decided to change careers and become a stockbroker. As if the timing wasn't bad enough, he also saw much of his savings eaten up by the stock market crash. Confident in his own skills, the always self-reliant Davis joined the prestigious firm of Hodgson, Russ, Andrews, Woods, and Goodyear, whose beginnings traced back to the law offices of Grover Cleveland. A member-at-large of the Buffalo Common Council from 1928 to 1934, he unsuccessfully sought the Republican nomination for mayor. He was also appointed to the Erie County Library Board, serving 14 years in that capacity.

A loving grandparent, George told his grandson bedtime stories, usually about the constellations, and juggled toys for his entertainment. Davis, who owned a six-foot telescope, would go in the backyard with his grandson, and they would identify constellations together. Soon, many of the neighborhood children began gathering in the Davis back-yard on starry nights, forming their own version of an astronomy club. A wonderful storyteller, George would regale the children with myths and legends associated with the galaxies.

George and Georgiana remained deeply in love and happily married until her death in 1952. It was common knowledge that he never recovered from her death and remained horribly grief-stricken, even though he married a second time, to a woman named Grace Butler. As the years went by, he seemed to be slipping into a slow melancholia that he was unable to pull himself out of.

Just past noon on June 4, 1961, Davis walked down into his basement, put a rope around his neck, and hung himself. He was 71 years old. Thus ended the life of Iron Davis, the man who pitched the "miracle no-hitter" for the "Miracle Braves" of 1914. Davis was interred at Lancaster Rural Cemetery in Lancaster, New York, in the Davis family mausoleum, next to his beloved wife, Georgiana.

DONNIE MOORE (1954–1989)

Donnie Ray Moore's 13-season career has been unfairly defined by one pitch that he threw during the 1986 American League Championship Series (ALCS). A native of Lubbock, Texas, Moore attended Monterey High School, where he was a star pitcher on the baseball team. Even though he was the only black student at the school, his outgoing personality, along with his baseball accomplishments, made him hugely popular amongst his fellow students.

Originally a 12th-round draft pick of the Boston Red Sox in 1971, Moore was later drafted by the Cubs as the third overall pick in the 1973 amateur draft. He made his major league debut on September 14, 1975, in a 13–7 loss to the Phillies at Wrigley Field. The first batter he faced in the majors was future Hall of Famer Mike Schmidt, who immediately singled to left. Moore would appear in 141 games for the Cubs during the course of five seasons, going 14–13, with a 4.44 ERA and 5 saves.

Traded to St. Louis in October 1979, he spent the majority of the 1980 season with the Cards' Triple-A affiliate, the Springfield Redbirds. Sent to the Brewers on September 3, 1981, Moore appeared in just three games before being traded back to the Cardinals that November. On February 1, 1982, he was traded to the Atlanta Braves in an even-up swap for pitcher Dan Morogiello. In his three seasons in Atlanta under Joe Torre, he went 9–9, with 23 saves and a 2.74 ERA. While in Atlanta, Donnie developed what would become his signature pitch, the forkball, a pitch sometimes referred to as a splitter. Moore, who appeared in one game of the 1982 National League Championship Series, was chosen by the California Angels as a free-agent compensation pick on January 24, 1985.

Under Angel manager Gene Mauch, who inserted him as closer, Moore blossomed. In 65 games, he went 8–8, with a 1.92 ERA and 31 saves in 103 innings pitched. He also pitched two scoreless innings in that summer's All-Star Game. Becoming a free agent after the season, he re-signed with the Angels for three years at $1 million a year, double the average major league salary. At the start of the season, Moore seemed to be his usual, reliable self, but things slowly began to change. Pains in his rib cage area, which were later diagnosed as shoulder problems, began to hamper his effectiveness. To treat the issue, doctors gave him cortisone shots in the shoulder and rib cage. While the shots killed the pain and somewhat eased the inflammation, they were not a cure. It is truly amazing that he was able to save 21 games, given the condition his shoulder was in.

The Angels won the American League West for the third time in their history in 1986. Their opponent in the ALCS would be the hard-hitting Boston Red Sox, who had sailed through the American League East. Things went swimmingly for the Angels in the first four games, as they jumped out to a three games to one lead. Then came the fateful fifth game. In the top of the ninth, with the Angels leading, 5–2, the Red Sox began to rally. Leadoff man Bill Buckner singled to center off starter Mike Witt. Dave Stapleton came in to pinch-run for the slow-footed Buckner. After Jim Rice was called out on strikes, Don Baylor homered to left-center field to get the score to 5–4. The next batter, Dwight Evans, popped out to Doug DeCinces at third. Mauch then brought in left-handed reliever Gary Lucas to face Rich Gedman. Lucas, known for his pinpoint control, hit Gedman on the right hand with the first pitch.

Mauch then brought Moore in to close the game out. Facing him would be outfielder Dave Henderson, a right-handed hitter who had been forced into the game because of an injury to center fielder Tony Armas. Henderson was looking for redemption because of a play he had made in the sixth inning when he deflected Bobby Grich's warning-track fly ball off his glove and over the wall for a home run that gave the Angels a 3–2 lead. On the seventh pitch of the at bat, Henderson hit a 2–2 forkball that, in Moore's words, "didn't dip." The ball sailed over the left field wall to give the Red Sox a 6–5 lead.

The Angels managed to rally and tie the score in the bottom of the ninth, but they would eventually lose the game in extra innings, thanks to Henderson's sacrifice fly off Moore in the top of the 12th. Final score: Boston 7, Angels 6. The Red Sox would use the win as a springboard for one of the great comebacks in ALCS history, second only to the franchise's comeback of 2004. They would smash a deflated Angels' team, 10–4, in the sixth game and then close out the series with an 8–1 victory in the seventh contest.

Angel fans never forgave Moore for giving up the homer to Henderson, and for the remainder of his tenure with the team, there rained a chorus of boos each time he came into a game. Moore's chronic shoulder problems continued in 1987, as he appeared in just 14 games. Granted free agency in January 1988, he re-signed with the Angels the next month. Around this time, he underwent microsurgery to remove a bone spur located near his spine, which doctors diagnosed as the source of his discomfort. Despite the operation, Moore's shoulder issues continued in 1988, as he was relegated to mop-up duty by new Angel manager Cookie Rojas. In what turned out to be his final major league season, he appeared in only 27 games, going 5–2, with a 4.91 ERA, in just 33 innings of work.

Released by California on August 26th, Donnie signed a minor league contract with the Kansas City Royals before the 1989 season. Assigned to American Association Omaha Royals, he appeared in just seven games before getting his release on June 12th. When he returned to his home to Anaheim, he found it empty, his wife Tonya having packed her bags and taken their three children with her. As the days went by, Moore became increasingly despondent. Friends and family began to worry about him, and there was talk that he might seek help through some sort of rehab, perhaps Alcoholics Anonymous.

On July 18, 1989, Donnie met Tonya at the couple's home, which was located in the Hollywood Hills, to discuss the possible sale of their house. Donnie wanted to move back to Texas, while Tonya was stead-fast in wanting to stay in California. With her that day were the couple's three children, Demetria (17), Donnie Jr. (10), and Ronnie (8). As was par for the course, it didn't take long for the two former sweethearts to start arguing. Sometime during the argument, Moore pulled out a 45-caliber pistol and shot Tonya in the shoulder, stomach, and neck. She somehow managed to make it outside with her children and was hur-riedly driven by her daughter to the hospital. Sometime after the shoot-ing, Moore, in the presence of his son Ronnie, put the gun to his temple and pulled the trigger, killing himself instantly. Even in the midst of tragedy, little Ronnie had the presence of mind to call 911. When authorities arrived, they found him staring down at his father's lifeless body. Tonya, although critically injured, would eventually recover from her wounds and received both a widow's pension from Major League Baseball and a life insurance benefit.

Today, 25 years after his death, there is still much speculation as to what provoked Donnie Moore to shoot his wife and then kill himself. His agent, David Pinter, told the *Los Angeles Times* that he spoke with him only hours before his death and discussed possible minor league assignments, as well as a winter league comeback in Puerto Rico. As Pinter put it, "He wasn't going to give up, he was a fighter." Pinter also believed, as did many, that Moore had never gotten over the Hender-son home run. No one can really say for certain what drove Moore over the edge, but it was most likely a combination of things, including long-standing alcohol problems and the perception that both his marriage and career were over.

Others, for instance, Moore's former teammate with the Angels, Brian Downing, were adamant about who was to blame for his friends' demise, telling the *Los Angeles Times*, "Everything revolved around one (bleeping) pitch. I never, ever saw the guy credited for getting us to the playoffs. All you ever heard about, all you ever read about was one (bleeping) pitch. You (the media and fans) buried the guy. He was never treated fairly."

Donnie Moore is buried at Peaceful Gardens Memorial Park in Woodrow, Texas, in Section C, Lot 58, Space 6.

RON LUCIANO (1937–1995)

One of the most colorful umpires in the history of baseball, Ron Luciano brought an over-the-top style that, in his own words, "people loved or hated." Born in Endicott, New York, on June 28, 1937, the six-foot, four-inch, 260-pound Luciano played college football at Syracuse University (SU), where head coach Ben Schwartzwalder used him as a two-way tackle. Luciano, who majored in mathematics at SU, played in the 1957 Cotton Bowl and was named to the 1958 All-America Team. In 1959, he played on Syracuse's national championship team. Selected by the Detroit Lions in the third round of the 1959 NFL Draft as an offensive tackle, a shoulder injury in the College All-Star Game prevented him from playing a single game for Detroit. Released after the 1960 season, he signed with the Buffalo Bills of the American Football League but retired after two games due to a knee injury. In 1963, he was offered a job with the Detroit Tigers in their minor league system.

While on a trip to Florida, Luciano decided to enroll in Bill Summers's umpiring school so he could better understand the rules. He enjoyed it so much that he decided to go into umpiring full-time. He started his career as an arbiter in 1964 in the Class A Florida State League and was then promoted to the Double-A Eastern League in 1965, the same year he met the man who would become his arch-nemesis, Earl Weaver. The two first met during a four-game series at Reading, Pennsylvania, when Weaver was managing the Elmira Pioneers. Luciano wound up tossing Weaver from all four games, the last ejection coming when the pregame lineups were being exchanged.

After two years umpiring in the International League (1967 and 1968), Luciano's contract was purchased by the American League, where he would remain until his retirement. He became known for his colorful, gregarious, and loquacious personality, as well as his flamboyant calls. His favorite method of calling outs was using a pistol-like motion to "shoot a player out." While some players hated his histrionics, the majority didn't seem to mind. Baseball purists criticized him for being an attention seeker who took away from the dignity of the game, but Luciano could have cared less what anyone thought, least of all his critics. He also conversed with players, managers, and coaches during the games, a practice strictly forbidden by both leagues, although the rule was rarely enforced. Luciano had his share of favorite players during his career, one being Yankee catcher Thurman Munson. Whenever he called a Yankee game, Luciano and Munson could be seen conversing throughout the contest. Another favorite was Baltimore catcher Earl Williams, who hated Weaver more than Luciano.

Despite his run-ins with Weaver, Luciano respected the Oriole players, whom he regarded as true professionals. Weaver's feud with Luciano didn't prevent his players from having some fun at his expense. In the March 1, 1982, edition of *Sports Illustrated*, Luciano recalls that,

> Eventually our relationship got so bad that Weaver's players would establish a betting pool before the game trying to guess what inning I'd throw him out. So I might dump him in the fifth and look into the Oriole dugout, and Mark Belanger or Jim Palmer or Don Buford would be jumping up and down and cheering, "Fifth inning, that's me!"

In spite of all the hoopla surrounding his umpiring style, Luciano was well-respected in the baseball world. In a 1974 Major League Baseball Players Association poll, he was one of just two American League umpires rated as excellent.

While Luciano's career will likely forever be defined by his run-ins with Weaver, it is interesting to note that he only tossed him from six games, with the first ejection coming in 1974, Ron's sixth year in the league. Luciano's umpiring resume included working the 1974 World Series, three American League Championship Series (1971, 1975, and 1978), and the 1973 All-Star Game. He also served two terms as president of the Association of Major League Umpires. Retiring in the spring of 1980 to take a job as a color analyst with NBC on its *Game of the Week* telecast, Luciano did a good job bringing a different point of view to the game. After the 1981 baseball season, NBC decided not to renew his contract. Instead of sulking, he pushed forward and tackled the literary world. Luciano would go on to coauthor five books, four of them with New York writer Dave Fisher. His most well-known is his first, *The Umpire Strikes Back*, released in April 1983. Other works include *Strike Two*, *The Fall of the Roman Umpire*, *Remembrance of Swings Past*, and *Baseball Lite: The Funniest Moments of the 1989 Season*. Popular on the banquet circuit, Luciano was also a frequent guest on sports talk radio.

Married for two years to Polly Dixon, a flight attendant (divorced in 1976), the former ump was extremely close with his immediate family. In the 1970s, his two sisters, Delores (Dee) and Barbara, helped him run a sporting goods store located near Binghamton, New York, called Ron Luciano's Sports World. Unfortunately, the business went belly-up due to "unscrupulous employees" who embezzled money. The most important person in his life was his mother Josephine, with whom he lived, along with one of his sisters. Diagnosed with Alzheimer's disease, Josephine was put into a nursing home in the early '90s. Despite her deteriorating condition, Ron would visit her daily, often taking her to lunch, despite the fact that she did not recognize him.

On the afternoon of January 18, 1995, police responded to a 911 call from Luciano's home, located in Endicott. Entering the garage, they found his lifeless body in the front seat of his Cadillac. The coroner's report states that his death was a result of suicide by way of carbon monoxide poisoning. His passing had many people in the baseball community asking questions, since the persona he showed to the public was the opposite of the type normally exhibited by people who commit suicide. Reports eventually surfaced that he was a long-term sufferer of depression and that he had even checked himself into a clinic the year before for treatment. To this day, no one knows the exact reasons why he took his own life, although one can certainly come to the conclusion that his mother's deteriorating condition didn't help his mental state. Maybe, as one of his friends put it, he had simply "grown tired of living." Ronald Michael Luciano was buried at Calvary Cemetery in Johnson City, New York. His mother Josephine would follow him two years later.

DOUG AULT (1950–2004)

With all due respect to the NFL, NHL, and NBA, no other sport comes close to Major League Baseball when it comes to trivia. Such is the case with Douglas Reagan Ault, who is the answer to the following trivia question: "Who hit the first home run in Toronto Blue Jay history?" Born March 9, 1950, in Beaumont, Texas, Ault grew up in a financially challenged family that was hindered by the fact that his dad, Pete, who worked as a general contractor, was plagued by cardiomyopathy for many years, thus preventing him from gaining a steady income. (Pete Ault would pass away in 1967, at age 54, when Doug was just 16.)

Because of his father's illness, the job of family baseball coach and mentor fell to Doug's older sister Brenda. The left-handed throwing and right-handed hitting Ault spent many afternoons training with her at the local baseball field, where they would practice all facets of the game. Brenda would even attend his games and point out things that he needed to improve on.

Ault originally attended Panola College, a community college located in Carthage, Texas, where he starred on the baseball team. He was drafted by major league clubs on three separate occasions, the first time by the Pirates in 1969, the second time in the second round of the secondary phase in the 1970 Major League Baseball January draft by the Padres, and the final time by the Indians in the fourth round of the secondary phase in the 1970 Major League Baseball June draft. Each time he was drafted, he opted to stay in college. Transferring to Texas Tech in 1971, it was while playing with the Red Raiders that he became a star, achieving All-American status in 1972, the same year he was selected for the College Baseball All-America Team.

After his graduation in 1973, Ault signed with the Texas Rangers as an amateur free agent. Assigned to the Class A Gastonia Rangers of the Western Carolina League, he showed immediate promise, leading the circuit in homers, with 19. The next season, he moved up to the Double-A Pittsfield (Massachusetts) Rangers of the Eastern League. In 1975, he split the year between Pittsfield and the Spokane Indians of the Pacific Coast League. Playing for the Sacramento Solons of the Pacific Coast League in 1976, Ault had arguably his best minor league season, batting .313, with 25 homers and 83 RBI in 143 games. Texas rewarded him for his performance by calling him up when the rosters expanded on September 1st.

Doug made his major league debut on Thursday, September 9th, against the Minnesota Twins at Arlington Stadium. Texas manager Frank Lucchesi penciled Ault in as the designated hitter that night, placing him fifth in the lineup. In the bottom of the second inning, Ault came up against the Twins' veteran right-hander Dave Goltz and promptly struck out. He got his first major league hit when he singled in the fifth inning. Helped by Rod Carew's pinch-hit grand slam in the top of the seventh, Goltz went on to blank the Rangers, 6–0, giving up just three hits in nine innings of work. Ault would go on to appear in nine games for Texas, batting .300, with 6 hits and a walk in 21 plate appearances.

At season's end, Ault went back to work on an oil rig in the Gulf of Mexico, a job he had worked the prior few seasons to supplement his income. On November 5th, the Toronto Blue Jays selected him with the 32nd overall pick in the 1976 Major League Baseball expansion draft. The selection was made on the recommendation of soon-to-be Toronto manager Roy Hartsfield, who had known Doug since his days playing in the Pacific Coast League. The quiet, mild-mannered Ault was thrilled with having the opportunity to play every day in the majors, yet he remained steadfast in keeping a level head. His competition during spring training was former Padre slugger Nate Colbert and the well-traveled Ron Fairly, two veterans on the decline.

Named the starting first baseman by Hartsfield, Ault made his debut for the Jays in the first game in franchise history, April 7, 1977, at Exhibition Stadium. Toronto's opposition that day was the Chicago White Sox, a hard-hitting team managed by Hall of Famer Bob Lemon. The starter for the White Sox was veteran left-hander Ken Brett. The 44,000 hardy fans who braved the elements (the game was played in snowy, windy conditions) did not go home disappointed. With the Blue Jays trailing 2–0 in the bottom of the first inning, Ault hit a two-out homer to right field. With one swing, he became the first player in the baseball history to hit the first home run, drive in the first run, and score the first-ever run for a new team. In the bottom of the third, with his team trailing, 4–2, Ault hit another homer off of Brett, this time with a man on, to tie the score. The two homers tied a major league record for most home runs in a season-opening game, a record since broken by several players. The two home runs by Ault were also the first of his career. Doug added to his already historic day by walking in the sixth and smacking a RBI single to center in the eighth. On the strength of his performance, the Jays and starting pitcher Jerry Johnson went on to defeat the "Pale Hose," 9–5.

After starting out like a gangbuster, Ault finished the season with a .245 average, 11 homers, and 64 RBI in 129 games. His 64 RBI would remain a Jay rookie record until Eric Hinske drove in 84 in 2002. In November 1977, the Topps chewing gum company named him to their All-Rookie Team.

Feeling that the team needed more production at first base, Jay general manager Pat Gillick purchased John Mayberry from the Royals on April 4, 1978, just two games into the season. The move relegated Ault to a utility role, as he appeared in just 54 games that year. He spent the entire 1979 campaign with the Syracuse Chiefs of the International League and then split time between Syracuse and Toronto the following season, playing in just 64 games. His final year in the majors would be 1980, when he batted .194, with just 3 homers and 15 RBI. Ault made his final major league appearance on October 5th at Fenway Park in a 4–1 Toronto win. He pinch-hit for Jay designated hitter Al Woods in the fourth inning, staying in the game in that capacity and going 0-for-2, with a walk.

Ault continued his career in Japan the next season, playing with the Central League's Hanshin Tigers, where he batted .307, with 18 homers and 59 RBI in 102 games. He split the 1982 season between Syracuse and the Mexican League's Mexico City Tigres, after which he turned to managing. Finding work with his old organization, he became a highly regarded and well-liked manager, piloting the Single-A Kinston Blue Jays of the Carolina League in 1983 and 1984 before being promoted to lead his old team, the Syracuse Chiefs, in 1985. Ault's first year leading the Chiefs has often been described as a dream season, as he managed the team to its first-ever pennant and was named the International League's manager of the year. Returning to the Jay organization in 1988, he would spend six seasons managing in the low minors, where he became known for his rapport with young players. Future major leaguers whom he managed during this time included Mark Whiten, Ed Sprague, Mike Timlin, Carlos Delgado, Steve Karsay, and Alex Gonzalez. His last managerial job would be with the Thunder Bay Whiskey Jacks of the Northern League in 1995.

Ault had many personal setbacks during his lifetime. In 1990, he and his wife Julie divorced, although they remained close friends. Julie was often described by friends as Doug's personal confidant. Like many former athletes, Ault had a serious addiction to prescription pain medications, a condition that had begun years earlier when he began taking them to relieve chronic shoulder pain. It was because of his dependence that he and Toronto had a parting of the ways following the 1994 season. After he left managing, his life took on a roller coaster feel. Ault briefly worked for the Jays, setting up a team in Australia. While there, he entered into a relationship with a woman and fathered a daughter, Cidney. No matter how hard he tried, his addiction seemed to get the better of him.

Things came to a head in 2000, when he took a bus to Los Angeles to visit his older brother David. When he failed to arrive, his brother went looking for him. He found him, huddled up in an alley, under the influence and looking more like a resident of skid row than a former major league player. With the help of former major leaguer Sam McDowell, who worked for the Blue Jay employee assistance program, David was able to get his brother into a rehab program in Florida. After years of self-abuse, Ault was finally getting the treatment he so desperately needed. In 2001, after completing the program, the Blue Jays hired him to be part of their Winter Media Caravan as an alumnus, a job that he excelled at. Friends and family noticed how happy he was as he talked baseball with hundreds of fans, many of whom remembered his exploits 24 years earlier.

Along with his battle with addiction, Doug also suffered a series of financial setbacks and personal losses during the next few years. A second marriage in 2002, to a woman named Lynn Davidson, proved to be a disaster, both personally and financially. In July 2002, his sister Becky died from the effects of multiple sclerosis. Six months later, in January 2003, his other sister, Brenda, passed away from atrial fibrillation. In both cases, the emotionally fragile Ault chose not to show up to pay his condolences. In 2003, he was hired to sell cars for an auto dealership in Clearwater, Florida, a job that lasted about a year. In January 2004, his home in Tarpon Springs, Florida, was sold in a bankruptcy proceeding. The next month, Ault received the news that his ex-wife Julie had been diagnosed with an advanced case of myelodysplastic syndrome. Despite efforts to save her life, including aggressive chemotherapy, Julie passed away on June 29th, at the age of 49. When told of Julie's death by her brother, Ault went into shock, which eventually turned into perpetual grief from which he was never able to recover.

On December 22, 2004, around 3:00 p.m., Ault calmly walked down his driveway and sat in the front seat of his 1983 Porsche and shot himself in the head with a shotgun. While his death was not a complete shock, there were still many people who questioned why he took his own life. Some of his friends surmised that he could never come to grips with the mistakes and bad decisions he had made during the course of his life, while others felt that the loss of Julie had simply overwhelmed him. No matter the reasons, one fact remained: A kind, gentle, and caring man who just so happened to have played Major League Baseball was gone at the far too young age of 54. Ault was buried in Forest Lawn Memorial Park in Beaumont, Texas, in the Garden of Seasons, Block J, Lot 8, Space 6, just a short walk from the final resting place of his beloved Julie.

TERRY ENYART (1950–2007)

By all accounts, Terry Enyart was a great guy and teammate. His one problem came when he drank, which, in the end, led to his demise. Born October 10, 1950, in Ironton, Ohio, Enyart played baseball at Titusville High School in Titusville, Florida, and later with Chipola College in Marianna, Florida. A first -round pick in the 1969 amateur draft by the Phillies, he eventually landed in the Twin organization, where he pitched until his release before the start of the 1973 season. Signing with the Montreal Expos, he was playing with the Triple-A Memphis Blues of the International League when he was called up to the parent club in June 1974.

Enyart made his major league debut on June 17 in a 12–4 loss to the Cincinnati Reds at Riverfront Stadium. Entering the game in the fifth inning in relief of Chuck Taylor, who had relieved starter Steve Rogers the previous inning, Enyart had an inauspicious debut, as the Reds scored four runs on three hits and two walks. The Expos hurt their own cause by making two errors in the inning, one by Enyart on a pickoff play on Cesar Geronimo. Enyart's next and final appearance in the majors came a little less than a month later, on July 5th, when he pitched two-thirds of an inning in the second game of a doubleheader against the Dodgers at Jarry Park. He entered the game in the seventh inning and gave up one hit and two walks. Pulled with the bases loaded, his replacement, Tom Walker, gave up a two-run single to Ron Cey to finish up Enyart's game log. Sent back to Memphis soon thereafter, Enyart's major league record stood at 0–0, with a 16.20 ERA. He would bounce around the minors throughout the next eight seasons and never get another shot at the majors.

He retired from the game after pitching with the Reynosa Broncos of the Mexican League in 1982. Terry, who enjoyed all types of outdoor activities, including racing, motorcycling, fishing, and boating, eventually went to work as a diesel mechanic, a profession that he truly enjoyed.

On Thursday night, February 15, 2007, Enyart returned to his home, inebriated and "itching for a fight." He first started arguing with his son, whom he had a strained relationship with. He then began quarreling with his wife, striking her with a soda bottle. Then, for some inexplicable reason, he attempted to strangle the family dog. When his son tried to intervene, Enyart, who had a concealed carry permit, took out his pistol and shot him in the right hand. According to the sheriff's office, Enyart followed his family into the front yard of their home and, without warning, fatally shot himself in the head. After the shooting, many of Enyart's friends reflected on their loss. Almost all of them agreed that, when sober, he was helpful, agreeable, and fun to be around, the exact opposite of the person who, under the influence of alcohol, decided to end his life that night. Enyart, who was 57 years old, was cremated, and his ashes were given to his family.

MIKE FLANAGAN (1951–2011)

One of the greatest pitchers in Oriole history, New Hampshire native Mike Flanagan was a talented, self-effacing left-hander who won 167 games during his big-league career. Michael Kendall Flanagan was born into a baseball family on December 16, 1951, in Manchester, New Hampshire. His paternal grandfather, Edward Francis Flanagan (born September 3, 1881, died January 21, 1970) was an ambidextrous pitcher who once signed a contract with the Boston Braves and later became a well-known baseball barnstormer. "Grandfather Ed" would later have a career in law enforcement as an officer with the Manchester Police Department. Mike's father Edward played five years of minor league ball for the Red Sox and Tigers.

Flanny, as he was known to friends, was originally a 15th-round draft pick (346th overall) by the Houston Astros in the 1971 Major League Baseball Draft, but an injury to his pitching arm convinced him not to sign, and he instead attended the University of Massachusetts in Amherst, where he also played basketball. When the Orioles selected him in the seventh round (159th overall in the 1973 draft), Flanny decided the time was right to go pro. Progressing rapidly through the Oriole minor league system, he played with Miami, Asheville, and Rochester, before making his major league debut on September 5, 1975, in a 5–4 victory over the Yankees at Memorial Stadium. The game, the first of a twi-night doubleheader, saw him pitch one and two-thirds innings in relief of starter Wayne Garland. His first major league decision was a 3–2 loss to those same Yankees on September 28.

In 1976, Flanny appeared in 20 games with the Orioles, going 3–5 in 85 innings of work. Making the rotation out of spring training the next season, he went 15–10 in 36 starts, with a 3.64 ERA, while logging 235 innings of work. The 1977 campaign would be the first of four consecutive seasons in which he would pitch 230 innings or more. Flanagan was not the prototypical crafty lefty, as he had a good fastball, along with a hard sinker, slow curve, and an above average changeup, using all four pitches with equal effectiveness. His best season was 1979, when he accrued a record of 23–9, with a 3.08 ERA, leading the American League in wins and taking home the Cy Young Award. The Orioles won the American League East, beat the White Sox in the ALCS, and went on to face the Pirates in the World Series. Flanny went 1–1 in three games versus the Bucos, pitching a complete-game, 5–4 Game 1 victory and losing the fifth game, 7–1. He made a brief appearance as a reliever in the ninth inning of Game 7, which the Orioles lost, 4–1.

Flanny became so known for the nicknames he gave players that *Boston Globe* writer Peter Gammons included him in his Sunday column in a feature called the "Mike Flanagan Nickname of the Week." Mike dubbed reliever Don Stanhouse "Stan the Man Unusual" and "Full Pack," because each time he came into a game, he caused his manager, Earl Weaver, to smoke a full pack of cigarettes. He nicknamed John Castino "Clams" for Clams Casino. Brewer outfielder Sixto Lezcano was "Mordecai Six Toes" after Mordecai "Three-Finger" Brown. He nicknamed himself "Cy Young," Jim Palmer "Cy Old," Steve Stone "Cy Present," and Scott McGregor "Cy Future." Flanagan's humor and jokes were endless. After the Oriole mascot, a man in an Oriole suit, fell off the roof of the dugout, Flanny chirped, "Take two worms and call me in the morning." When the O's honored former manager Earl Weaver with a waist-high plaque on the wall of the Oriole dugout, Flanny quipped, "Oh, life size." Commenting about the Orioles in 1992, he dryly observed, "You know you're having a bad day when the fifth inning rolls around and they drag the warning track."

Flanagan continued his winning ways in 1980, going 16–13, although his ERA was up a full run, at 4.12. During the strike-shortened season of 1981, he went 9–6 in 20 appearances and had some late-season problems with tendonitis but was back to his usual workload in 1982, accruing 236 innings, with a 15–11 record and 3.97 ERA. A knee injury limited him to just 20 games in 1983, as he went 12–4 and compiled a tidy 3.30 ERA. Despite his abbreviated season, Flanny looked at 1983 as the most satisfying year of his career, as new Orioles manager Joe Altobelli led the team to a 98-win season, the American League pennant, and a 4 games to 1 win over the Phillies in the World Series. He experienced his last effective season for Baltimore in 1984, going 13–13, with a 3.53 ERA, after which a series of injuries, including recurring tendonitis and a torn Achilles tendon, limited his effectiveness.

On August 31, 1987, Flanny was traded to the Blue Jays for a player to be named later and Oswaldo Peraza. While he was saddened by the thought of leaving Baltimore, he was excited about playing with a talented Jay team that had yet to reach its full potential. Mike would spend the following three seasons with the Jays, going 26–27, with a 3.94 ERA, in 76 games. He started the fourth game of the 1989 ALCS for the Jays, a game that is remembered for the third-inning home run he gave up to Jose Canseco that landed in the upper deck at the SkyDome, 480 feet away.

Released by the Jays in early May 1990, Flanagan took the rest of the season off to contemplate his future. Invited by the Orioles on a minor league contract the next season, he made the club as a bull pen arm. On July 13th, Flanny once again became part of Oriole history when he pitched the seventh inning of a combined no-hitter against the Oakland Athletics. He also had the honor of pitching the ninth inning and recording the final two outs in the history of Memorial Stadium later that season. The inaugural season of Camden Yards, 1992, would turn out to be Flanny's final professional season, as he posted a 0–0 record, with an 8.05 ERA, in 42 games.

Two years later, Mike was elected to the Oriole Hall of Fame, the same year he started his broadcasting career as a television color analyst on HTS (Home Team Sports). Between the end of his baseball career and entrance into broadcasting, he served two stints as Oriole pitching coach, one in 1995, under Phil Regan, and the other in 1998, under Ray Miller. His longest run as a broadcaster was from 1999 to 2002, with Comcast SportsNet Mid-Atlantic. After the 2002 season, Flanagan was named coexecutive vice president of the Orioles, along with Jim Beattie, and after Beattie's dismissal in 2005, Flanny held that post by himself until the arrival of Andy MacPhail in 2007. He would remain in the Oriole front office until his contract expired at the end of the 2008 season. In 2010, he joined MASN (Mid-Atlantic Sports Network) as the secondary analyst, with his old buddy Jim Palmer. Flanny's return to the booth was applauded by Oriole fans everywhere, as he used his dry wit and humor to full effect.

Flanny was married twice. His first wife, Kathy (Walsh), whom he married in 1977, gained fame when she gave birth to one of the country's first test tube babies, Kerry Ellen Flanagan, in 1982. Kerry was the first "vitro" delivered without a Caesarean section. All told, Flanny and Kathy would have two daughters, the aforementioned Kerry, followed by Kathryn "Katie" Kendall Flanagan. His second marriage, to Alex Lynn Debes, brought him his third girl, Kendall.

On Wednesday, August 24, 2011, police in Sparks, Maryland, responded to a 911 call at the Flanagan home. Flanny's body was found along a trail behind the family residence, approximately 250 feet away. While authorities would not give details, initial reports said that he had taken his own life. The medical examiner would later rule he had used a 12-gauge shotgun on himself. The news of his death shocked the baseball community. No one except Alex had any clue how troubled he was. It was later revealed that he had suffered from depression and been seeing a therapist for more than 20 years. Unfortunately, he could never seem to shake the dark clouds that accompany the disease.

In the first interview after her husband's death, Alex sadly remembered how her husband "used to talk about shadows" and mention how "'Sometimes there's this shadow that comes into my life.'" According to Alex, "he wouldn't see anything good, just these shadows. . . . He would see the world in black and white, without color."

One of the numerous and terrible symptoms of depression is the feeling of worthlessness and self-doubt, which was what Flanny had felt for many years. Alex also revealed that Mike had a long-standing drinking problem. After his death, reports leaked out that he had been despondent about his inability to turn the Orioles into a contender during his time as vice president. It was also revealed that he had financial problems during the two years following his departure from the Baltimore front office. For Alex, the saddest part was that she was unable to help the man she called her "best friend."

Flanny, who was just 59 years of age, was survived by his three daughters, his ex-wife Kathy, and his wife Alex. His remains were cremated and given to his family. As a tribute, the Orioles wore a black circular patch with the name FLANNY embroidered in white on the right sleeve of their uniform tops for the remainder of the 2011 season.

HIDEKI IRABU (1969–2011)

Hideki Irabu always seemed to have a hard time assimilating into society. The product of an American GI father and Japanese mother, he was born in Hirara, Okinawa, on May 5, 1969. Irabu's mother Kazue married Ichiro Irabu, a restaurateur from Osaka. The elder Irabu moved his new family to Amagasaki, Hyōgo Prefecture, where, by all accounts, Hideki experienced an unhappy childhood, living in impoverished conditions. Worse yet was the extreme prejudice and bullying that he experienced because of his biracial heritage. He learned to fight early and often, with his solace coming when he stepped onto the baseball field.

Taking up pitching, Irabu realized that because of his size (he was bigger than the average Japanese youth), he could easily overpower most hitters with his fastball. He also found extreme pleasure in striking out opposing players who had been cruel to him in the past. By the time he reached high school, it had become clear that his future would be on the baseball diamond. At the age of 19, Irabu was drafted by the Lotte Orions (who later became the Chiba Lotte Marines) of Japan's Pacific League. During his tenure there, he led the circuit in ERA and strikeouts twice, while gaining a reputation for loathing the Japanese press, whom he regarded as lower than paparazzi.

In 1995, Irabu's manager, Bobby Valentine, compared him to Nolan Ryan, telling the press, "If he played in the U.S., he would do a lot to remove the fantasy that U.S. baseball is better than the Japanese version." When the international press picked up on Valentine's statement, they stuck Irabu with the unfair moniker of the "Japanese Nolan Ryan." Before the 1997 season, Irabu made it known that he wanted a chance to pitch in the American major league with the New York Yankees, even though he had not yet achieved the 10 years of service time needed to become a free agent. Infuriated by his insistence to play only for the Yankees, Chiba traded him to the San Diego Padres in January 1997.

On May 29, 1997, Irabu finally got his wish when Yankee general manager Bob Watson worked out a deal to acquire him. Signing a four-year, $12.8 million contract, he was sent to the minors for conditioning purposes. On July 10, 1997, Hideki made his major league debut against the Detroit Tigers before a raucous weeknight crowd of 51,901 at Yankee Stadium. His debut went splendidly, as he struck out nine Bengals in six and two-thirds innings of work for the win. Irabu would go on to have a mediocre 5–4 record in 1997, with an ERA of 7.09, certainly not "Ryanesque."

In 1997, Hideki also entered into an arranged marriage with a woman named Kyonsu Kanemitsu, an ethnic North Korean who came from a wealthy family and had been a teller at Chiba Bank. In the spring of 1998, he finally got the chance to meet his biological father, spending a week with him while at spring training camp in Tampa. Even though the two men had problems communicating, a bond, however small, was forged. Irabu experienced his best season in 1998, the year the Yankees won 114 games and their second World Series in three years. In 173 innings of work, he logged a record of 13–9, with a 4.06 ERA.

During spring training of 1999, Irabu made headlines of a different sort when he drew the ire of Yankee owner George Steinbrenner, who, after seeing him fail to cover first base on a ground ball, commented, "Irabu looks like a fat, pusy toad out there." Yankee radio announcer Michael Kay remembered the statement years later, saying, "None of the writers were sure about how to spell the word *pusy*. Was it spelled pusy or pussy? Everyone scrambled to double check the spelling so they wouldn't make an X-rated typo." Steinbrenner also refused to let Irabu accompany the team to Los Angeles but apologized two days later and allowed him to make the trip.

Spelling errors aside, the comment by "The Boss" deeply wounded Irabu, who was having a hard time adjusting to life in the United States. As in Japan, he was known as a good teammate and decent guy, but he was often depressed and melancholy. On the road, he would stay alone in his hotel room, only venturing out to have an occasional meal with a teammate. As he did in Japan, Irabu had an adversarial relationship with the press and even fans who booed him. Part of two championship teams, in 1998 and 1999, he appeared in just one postseason game in the 1999 ALCS against Boston.

Tired of his inconsistencies, the Yankees traded Irabu to the Expos, along with Jake Westbrook and a player to be named later, on December 22, 1999, in return for Ted Lilly and Christian Parker. Released in September 2001, after two injury-plagued seasons, he signed on to play with the Rangers three months later. In Texas, Irabu finally found his comfort level when manager Jerry Narron inserted him as the closer. He was leading the team with 16 saves when he made his final big-league appearance on July 12, 2002, in a 4–3 loss to the Twins at the Metrodome. Admitted to a Kansas City hospital three days later, he was found to have blood clots in his lungs. On advice from doctors, he was ordered to sit out the remainder of the season to receive the proper treatment. Released from Texas that November, he would pitch for the Hanshin Tigers the following season until a serious knee injury forced him to retire.

Well off financially, Irabu retired to Southern California, where he ran a successful restaurant chain with a Japanese American businessman. During a visit to Japan in 2008, he was arrested for assaulting the manager of an Osaka bar after consuming 20 mugs of beer.

Still feeling the need to play, Hideki made one last attempt at a comeback in 2009, when he toed the rubber in 10 games for the Long Beach Armada of the independent Golden Baseball League. In August of that year, he signed a contract to pitch for a Japanese semiprofessional team, the Kochi Fighting Dogs, but injuries kept him from appearing in a single game.

Moving to Rancho Palos Verdes, he became increasingly disenchanted with living in the United States due to his lack of friends and failure to master English. When he approached his wife with the idea of moving back to Japan permanently, Irabu was soundly rejected, as she wanted their children to be bicultural. In May 2010, he was arrested for drunk driving in Gardena, California, an incident that put a strain on his already fragile marriage. In early 2011, Kyonsu left him, taking their two young daughters with her. The estrangement from his family proved to be his undoing, for without them, all happiness seemed lost.

On Wednesday, July 27, 2011, at approximately 4:25 p.m., police received a call from a friend of Irabu's, Ichiro Sakashita. Police and EMT units quickly responded to a house located in the 2200 block of Via Velardo. When authorities entered the garage, they found Irabu dead, his life taken by his own hand. While the authorities did not immediately give an exact cause of death, TMZ reported that he had hung himself. An autopsy revealed that he had been inebriated at the time of his passing. Thus ended the life of one of baseball's greatest enigmas, who, despite his talent, struggled to find happiness and a place in the world. Hideki Irabu was just 42.

RYAN FREEL (1976–2012)

The next time you see a player run into a wall to make a great catch or a nasty collision at home plate, say a prayer and take a moment to re-member Ryan Freel. Ryan Paul Freel was born March 8, 1976, in Jacksonville, Florida, to Patrick and Norma Freel. He and his brother Patrick, who was two years older, were raised by their mother, who was Cuban American. It was not unusual for Norma, who was a teacher, to put in a full day at school and then work her own house cleaning service to make much-needed extra money. Norma would later find personal happiness when she met Clark Vargas, whom she eventually married.

Even as a young child, Ryan was like a little meteor, going full speed at whatever he did. Freel played shortstop at Englewood Senior High School in Jacksonville before switching to second base in college, where he played for both Lincoln Memorial University in Harrogate, Tennessee, and Tallahassee Community College. Picked in the 13th round of the 1994 amateur entry draft by the St. Louis Cardinals, he opted not to sign, choosing to play college ball. The following June, the Toronto Blue Jays chose him in the 10th round of the amateur draft. Freel signed his first professional contract on June 17th and was immediately assigned to the Class A St. Catharines Blue Jays of the New York-Penn League. He would play six seasons in the Jay minor league system before making his major league debut on April 4, 2001, in an 11–8 win over the Tampa Bay Devil Rays at Tropicana Field.

Freel, who had made the club out of spring training, replaced Homer Bush at second base in the bottom of the ninth. He appeared in nine games for Toronto, batting .273, with 3 RBI and 2 stolen bases, before being sent back to the minors. Granted free agency after the season, he ironically signed on with the team he made his major league debut against, the Devil Rays. Freel spent the entire 2002 season with Tampa's Triple-A affiliate, the Durham Bulls, where he hit .261, with 8 home runs and 48 RBI, as well as 37 steals. He signed on with the Cincinnati Reds that November. During his six seasons playing in the Queen City, the versatile Freel played all three outfield positions, plus second base and third base, with equal effectiveness, while his fearless, all-out style of play made him an immediate fan favorite. Well-liked by teammates, he gained a reputation as a high-energy, fun-loving person who enjoyed joking around. Extremely religious, he had a sweet disposition that shined brightly when he was with his wife and daughters. Known for never turning down an autograph request, he treated people with dignity and respect, no matter what walk of life they came from.

From a historical point of view, Freel's style of play can best be compared to that of Pistol Pete Reiser, the old Brooklyn Dodger outfielder who had his career cut short due to his habit of running into outfield walls. He helped develop the Reds Rookie Success League and also served as the Reds' players' ambassador to the league. Due to injuries, he had only three seasons where he appeared in 100 games or more, with a career-high 143 in 2004. During his time with Cincinnati, he batted .270, with 502 hits, 22 home runs, and 104 RBI, along with 134 stolen bases and 294 runs scored. His best year was 2004, when he hit .277, with 3 homers, 28 RBI, 37 stolen bases, and 74 runs scored in 143 games. He also started 10 games or better at five different positions, becoming the first Cincinnati player to achieve the feat in 12 years. Ryan also led the team in stolen bases three straight seasons from 2004 to 2007.

While it is estimated that Freel was the recipient of at least 10 concussions during his playing career, his stepfather, Clark Vargas, estimated that he may have suffered upward of 15 during his lifetime, the earliest one coming when he was only two. When considering the number of head injuries he suffered, it was a minor miracle that he was able to play as long as he did. During his time with the Reds, Ryan was diagnosed with adult attention deficit disorder, a condition he often joked about with his teammates and friends. In an August 2006 interview with the *Dayton Daily News*, he made headlines when he admitted to having conversations with an imaginary voice whom he called "Farney," remarking,

> He's a little guy who lives in my head who talks to me, and I talk to him. That little midget in my head said, "That was a great catch, Ryan." I said, "Hey, Farney, I don't know if that was you who really caught that ball, but that was pretty good if it was." Everybody thinks I talk to myself, so I tell 'em I'm talking to Farney.

Freel later said that Farney's name arose from a conversation with Red trainer Mark Mann: "He actually made a comment like, 'How are the voices in your head?' We'd play around, and finally this year he said, 'What's the guy's name?' I said, 'Let's call him Farney.' So now everybody's like, 'Run, Farney, run' or 'Let Farney hit today. You're not hitting very well.'" While it remains unclear whether Farney was a product of his concussion symptoms, his ex-wife Christie later admitted to the *Jacksonville Times* that he would often talk about "blacking out or seeing stars."

The most memorable of Freel's on-field mishaps took place on May 28, 2007, in a game against Pittsburgh at the Great American Ball Park. In the top of the third, Pirate backup catcher Humberto Cota hit a long drive to deep right-center. Freel, who was playing center field, collided with right fielder Norris Hopper as the two converged on the ball. Freel made the catch just before the collision. He took an elbow to the head and went down hard on the warning track, the impact actually knocking him out for a few seconds. Put on a stretcher with his head and neck immobilized, he was taken by ambulance to Good Samaritan Hospital, where a CT scan of his head and neck came back normal. Soon afterward, Ryan began experiencing symptoms related to a concussion, including severe headaches and dizziness. The symptoms continued while he was on rehab assignment with the Triple-A Louisville Bats a few weeks later.

In April 2005, Freel was arrested and charged with driving under the influence in Bellevue, Kentucky. Pleading guilty, he paid a $500 fine and had his license suspended for 90 days. Nine months later, in January 2006, he was arrested in Tampa for disorderly intoxication. While it is only speculation, Freel's alcohol problems pointed to self-medication. His hard style of play finally caught up with him in 2007, when he was limited to just 75 games. The next season, he appeared in

Grave of Ryan Freel. Courtesy of Thousandwinds.

only 45. In December 2008, he was traded to the Orioles in a deal that sent catcher Ramon Hernandez to Cincinnati. Bad luck followed him to Baltimore, where he was hit in the head by a pickoff throw in an early season game. Traded to the Cubs for Joey Gathright on May 8th, he was sold to Kansas City two months later but released on August 13th. Signing with the Texas Rangers two weeks later, he was assigned to the Oklahoma City Red Hawks of the Pacific Coast League, where he appeared in nine games, going 12-for-30 for a .400 average. Released that November, he signed with the Somerset Patriots of the Atlantic League in April 2010, but retired after appearing in just nine games.

With his playing career over and his marriage coming to an end, Ryan decided to move in the direction of coaching. He founded Big League Development Baseball, a travel baseball program that used coaches with ties to pro ball. In June 2012, he was named head baseball coach at St. Joseph Academy in St. Augustine, but he soon quit to concentrate on his business. In spite of the success he was experiencing with his coaching, those closest to him saw a noticeable change in his mental state during the last two years of his life. The combination of his postconcussion symptoms and his on-again, off-again drinking problem only served to exacerbate his various mental health issues.

On the night of December 22nd, Freel returned home after having dinner alone and, sometime thereafter, put a shotgun to his face and pulled the trigger. His body was found the next day by his mother and a friend who had dropped by to pick up two of his guns. (Freel was an avid hunter who owned several firearms.) Despite the fact that those closest to him knew how much he had been suffering both physically and mentally, his suicide came as a complete shock.

A short time after his death, Freel's family was contacted by the staff at the Boston University Center for the Study of Traumatic Encephalopathy, who were interested in studying Ryan's brain tissue. Hoping to find some answers, Norma, Clark, and Christie gladly accepted the offer. In December 2013, one year after his death, the findings of the postmortem examination revealed that he had been suffering from stage II CTE (chronic traumatic encephalopathy), a condition normally

Bench marker at the grave of Ryan Freel. Courtesy of Thousandwinds.

associated with football players. CTE is a degenerative condition and incurable disease that is associated with erratic behavior, including memory loss, confusion, impaired judgment, impulse control problems, aggression, and depression, along with progressive dementia. Even though Ryan's family will remain forever brokenhearted, the CTE diagnosis at least gave them some explanation for the erratic behavior that led to his death, as well as some closure. In his memory, the Reds established the "Ryan Freel Heart and Hustle Award," which is awarded annually to a player in each league.

Ryan Freel was buried at Oaklawn Cemetery in Jacksonville in Section N, inside a gated private area.

6

UNNATURAL CAUSES

The average person will be exposed to more than their share of dangerous situations during the course of their lifetime. The same holds true for baseball players. For more than 140 years, major leaguers have been falling by the wayside due to drownings, train crashes, slips and falls, auto accidents, and plane crashes, just to name a few. There is a great line from the movie *Full Metal Jacket* that states the obvious: "The dead only know one thing. It is better to be alive." No statement might ever ring truer. No one wants to leave their mortal coil any earlier than they have to. As it was with the following players, sometimes it's simply a case of luck, bad or otherwise, as to whether one assumes room temperature.

AL THAKE (1849–1872)

An outfielder in the first professional league, the National Association (1871–1875), Albert Thake played 18 games in left field for the 1872 Brooklyn Atlantics. Born September 21, 1849, in Wymondham, England, his family settled in Brooklyn, where he would eventually play amateur ball with two highly ranked teams, the Star Club and the Athletics. One of his teammates on the Athletics was Lip Pike, who would become professional baseball's first Jewish star.

On Sunday, September 1, 1872, Thake went fishing with a friend off Fort Hamilton in proximity to where the Verrazano-Narrows Bridge now stands. Seconds after he and his friend had caught a fish, a wave hit the boat, knocking Thake into the water. The *New York Post* reported that he became entangled in fishing nets and drowned, while the *New York Times* stated that he was swept away by the current. His body was found washed up on the shore of Bass Creek, located on the South Shore of Staten Island in Raritan Bay.

Thake was known as a man of "exceptional personal character" and was well-liked in and out of baseball. The game the following day between the Atlantics and Eckfords was postponed, with flags at both the Union Grounds and Capitoline Grounds flown at half-staff. Thake's funeral took place at his mother's residence on September 10th, with members of both the Eckfords and Atlantics in attendance. On October 23rd, a benefit exhibition game between the famous Cincinnati Red Stockings and "Old" Brooklyn Atlantics was played to raise funds to help Thake's mother with expenses. Some of the baseball luminaries that participated included George and Harry Wright, Al Spalding, Bob Ferguson (who arranged the event), Charlie Gould, George Zettlein, and Black Jack Burdock. Due to the inclement weather, they were only able to raise about $300.

One can only speculate on how good a ballplayer Thake would have become if he had lived longer. His .295 lifetime batting average suggests that he might have had a promising career ahead of him, a career cut short at age 22. Al Thake, professional baseball's first-ever fatality, is buried at Greenwood Cemetery in Brooklyn.

ED KNOUFF (1868–1900)

Ed Knouff pitched for three teams in parts of five seasons in the majors, all in the American Association. Knouff's name was often spelled Knauff in box scores and newspaper stories. Before his professional debut, he played for several teams in the Southern Association. He played in his first Major League game on Wednesday, July 1, 1885, against the New York Metropolitans, in a 12–11 loss. Knouff entered the contest in relief of A's pitcher Phenomenal Smith in the fifth inning, after the Philly pitcher walked off the field because he felt that the umpire was not giving him a square deal. (Smith had walked two Mets and then became incensed, leaving the field in a huff.) Quite a way to start a career!

Knouff played with Macon and Memphis in 1886. He was so good at Memphis that he struck out 16 men in a game against Charleston. Coveted by Charley Comiskey—then the captain of the St. Louis Browns—he joined the Old Roman team during the 1887 season. Ed had gone 9–6 in 15 games for St. Louis in 1887 and 1888, when he was released on July 21st. He immediately found work with the Cleveland Blues of the American Association, joining them after going on a brief holiday to refresh his spirits. The next year, he rejoined his old team, the Athletics, for three games, twirling to a 2–0 record. After his major league career, he managed the Pennsylvania State League's Lebanon Pretzel Eaters for a time and pitched for the Memphis Giants of the Southern Association.

Knouff retired from baseball to take a job with the Philadelphia Fire Department. In 1897, he was severely injured when he was hit by a falling beam in a house fire. The beam broke his back, permanently disabling him. Remaining bedridden for the rest of his life, the only thing that could be done for him was to make whatever time he had remaining as comfortable as possible. The last three years of his life were spent in the hospital, where he was often visited by friends and former teammates.

Knouff passed away on Friday, September 14, 1900, at German Hospital, located at 267 North 5th Street in Philadelphia. The official cause of death was uremia. Knouff, who left behind a grief-stricken wife and many friends to mourn his passing, was buried on the 18th at Holy Cross Cemetery in Yeadon, Pennsylvania, in Section 11, Range 4, Lot 41, Grave NHA.

JIM DUNCAN (1871–1901)

James William Duncan came from an area of Pennsylvania known for three things: iron, oil, and baseball. Born in Saltsburg, Pennsylvania, on July 1, 1871, he lived during a time when iron foundries, oil wells, and refineries were the main sources of employment for the local population. As a teenager, he took up the trade of boilermaker, as well as playing semipro ball in the Iron and Oil Association with both Franklin and the Oil City Club. Duncan later moved on to play minor league ball with such teams as Jamestown, Portland, Springfield, Rome, and Toronto. By the late 1890s, he was considered one of the top minor league catchers in the country.

Duncan got his big break in 1899, while playing with the Eastern League's Toronto Canucks, when Washington Senator manager Art Irwin inquired about him. Irwin was looking for a backup catcher to replace Aleck Smith, who was holding out for a better contract. When Irwin asked about the young Pennsylvanian, Canuck manager Wally Taylor enthusiastically recommended Jim, telling him, "That Duncan is one of the hardest-hitting backstops in the Eastern League and a reliable catcher." Duncan made his major league debut on July 18, 1899, in the second game of a doubleheader with Cleveland, starting at catcher. Washington won the game, 11–4.

His stay with the Senators was brief, as he appeared in just 15 games. On Wednesday, August 23, 1899, he was released, along with Frank Bonner, Charlie Atherton, and Bill Coughlin, in a purge of what one sportswriter called "DC's Dead Wood." Duncan signed a contract with the Cleveland Spiders before the end of the month and appeared in 31 games, batting just .229. He made what would be his last major league appearance on October 15th. Signing with the St, Louis Cardinals during the winter, he was released in April 1900, before ever playing a game for them. Duncan decided to retire after his release from St. Louis and went to work as a boiler inspector for the Philadelphia and Western Railway.

On Wednesday, October 16, 1901, Jim was out on a fishing excursion with two of his friends in Foxburg, Pennsylvania. The boat capsized, and all three men drowned. Eyewitnesses saw Duncan making a vain attempt to swim back to shore. His body was soon recovered and buried at Grove Hill Cemetery in Oil City, Pennsylvania, proving once and for all that the world doesn't run on Duncan.

ED DELAHANTY (1867–1903)

Near the end of his life, John McGraw, baseball's "Little Napoleon," was asked to compare the players of his era with the more modern players of the 1920s and 1930s. McGraw, who was never at a loss when it came to his opinions on the national game, said, "Ed Delahanty was as great a hitter as I have ever seen"—strong words from a man who saw both Delahanty and Babe Ruth at their physical peaks. One of the most prolific power hitters of his era, Delahanty batted .400 or better three times, while driving in 100 runs or more seven times. Nicknamed "Big Ed" by the press, he was usually referred to as Del by his teammates and friends.

The oldest of the five baseball-playing brothers from Cleveland, Ohio, Ed began his baseball career with the semipro Cleveland Shamrocks before making stops with Mansfield of the Ohio State League and Wheeling of the Tri-State League. It was while playing with the latter that he signed with the Philadelphia Quakers for the 1888 campaign. After two seasons as a part-time player, Del jumped to Cleveland of the ill-fated Players League, where he would appear in more than 100 games for the first time in his career. Returning to Philadelphia after the Players League closed its doors, he became the starting left fielder for the newly named Phillies. Due to his fondness for liquor and extra-curricular activities, Delahanty batted just .243 in 1891. After his dismal performance, manager Harry Wright advised him that he needed to take the game more seriously. Taking this advice to heart, Big Ed would come back to hit .306 the next season, leading the National League in triples, with 21.

Before the 1893 campaign, the National League instituted a rule change where the pitching distance was increased from 50 feet to the modern distance of 60 feet, six inches. With the ability to see the ball better, Del became one of the premier hitters of his generation, the first to bat over .400 three times. Along with Del, the Phillies featured some of the great hitters of the era, including home run king Sam Thompson, fleet-footed Billy Hamilton, catcher Jack Clements, third baseman Lave Cross, Elmer Flick, and Nap Lajoie. The Philadelphia teams of the 1890s might be the greatest never to win a pennant.

While Delahanty did take the game more seriously, it didn't prevent him from indulging in his many vices, which included alcohol, cards, and the racetrack. When inebriated, Del could display a rather bad temper, what some people today might call "beer muscle." Philadelphia pitcher Kid Carsey remembered Del as someone with an alcohol-fueled temper, stating, "Del was a good man as a whole, but when he took to

Ed Delahanty. Courtesy of the Library of Congress.

drink, he would go bad sometimes. I always tried to stay clear of him when he was riled."

Due to the penurious ways of team owner John Rogers, Del jumped his contract after the 1901 season and signed with the American League's Washington Senators. He batted a lusty .373 his first year in DC, while appearing in 123 games. Dissatisfied with his salary of $4,000, he once again decided to jump his contract prior to the 1903 season, signing a three-year deal with the New York Giants worth $8,000 per season. Del hoped that the new deal, which included a $4,000 advance, would help get him out of the financial constraints he was in, as he had squandered away much of his money on his usual improprieties of booze and gambling. Adding to his stress was the fact that his wife Norine had also fallen ill.

Before the start of the 1903 season, the National and American leagues signed a peace agreement in which both leagues agreed to honor one another's player contracts. On March 20th, it was officially announced by American League president Ban Johnson and National League president Harry Pulliam that Big Ed was to fulfill his contract with the Senators, and that he, along with the other contract jumpers, would first have to be released before signing with another club. Del was also ordered to pay back the $4,000 advance he had received from the Giants. Before he jumped his contract, Del was originally scheduled to make $4,500 with the Senators in 1903, of which $600 had already been advanced to him. Pulliam and Johnson's ruling put him in the red by $100, hardly chump change in those days. Desperate for money, Delahanty decided to hold out rather than report to spring training. A few days prior to the start of the season, he ended his holdout by agreeing to a two-year, $8,000 contract. As part of the deal, Washington paid off the $4,000 he owed the Giants by deducting $2,000 per year from his salary in 1903 and 1904. Essentially, Del would be playing for $2,000 a year.

Things were not good when he finally reported to spring training, for he was now estranged from his wife and daughter. The separation from his family led him to drink even more than usual. Del's self-medicating via alcohol drove him deeper into what was becoming an all-consuming depression. To make matters worse, he had come to spring training badly out of shape. In June, rumors swirled that he was to be traded, along with Scoops Carey, to the newly formed New York Highlanders for Jimmy Williams and John Ganzel, but the deal never came to fruition.

As June rolled on, Del became more and more unstable, showing clear signs of depressive behavior. Drinking binges became more common, and he began giving away many of his possessions, one of the clear signs of someone about to commit suicide. On June 25th, he played in his last major league game, a 4–0 loss to the Blues at Cleveland. The next day, he was given new hope when he read in the newspaper that President Pulliam had broken from the agreement and was allowing George Davis of the White Sox, another contract jumper, to join the Giants (a decision that would later be reversed by a court order). Seeing an opportunity for himself, he left the Senators and went on a celebratory drinking binge. Several more drinking episodes followed, even as he traveled with the team for their next series in Detroit. His behavior became so erratic that several of his family members, including his mother Bridget, rushed to Detroit to keep an eye on him.

On July 2nd, Del boarded a Michigan Central train destined for New York. News reports of the day state that he was planning on meeting Norine in the hopes that the two might come to a rapprochement. Others speculated that he was headed to New York in an attempt to plead his case to New York owner Andrew Freedman and manager John McGraw. The train's route would take it briefly into Canada before reentering the United States by way of Niagara Falls. As the locomotive plodded along, Delahanty did what he did best, taking on the booze. One conductor said that he saw him down at least five glasses of whiskey during the course of the trip. By the time the train reached Fort Erie, on the Canadian side, he was feeling no pain. He had also become quite nasty, wielding a straight razor in front of passengers. What brought about this behavior remains unclear. What is clear is that the conductor, John Cole, stopped the train at the Bridgeburg Station, on the Canadian side of the International Bridge, and with little fanfare, kicked the big fellow off. The fact that Delahanty should have been delivered into the hands of the local police made little difference to Cole, who apparently did not know that he was kicking off one of baseball's biggest stars.

As the train pulled away, Ed began making his way across the bridge to Buffalo. The night watchman, an elderly gentleman named Sam Kingston, tried to prevent him from crossing on foot, which, of course, was illegal. No match for the burly Irishman, Kingston was shoved down after a brief scuffle and watched helplessly as the big lug walked off into the darkness, never to be seen alive again. His body was found one week later, floating near the landing of the famed *Maid of the Mist*. Official investigations concluded that Delahanty fell off the bridge, which had opened to allow a boat to pass through. In his wobbly, drunken state, this seems like the most feasible explanation for his demise, even though his youngest brother, Frank, floated the idea that he may have met his end at the hands of a thug. Another scenario had Del jumping off the bridge, taking his own life. Frank, as well as the rest of the Delahanty brothers, dismissed the theory, stating that despite his problems, their brother had "too much to live for."

No one will ever know for sure what triggered Del's actions on that hot summer night. A century has passed, and there is still no definitive proof of what happened. Delahanty's mysterious death at the age of 35 has, to some extent, overshadowed his career, one that saw him achieve a .346 lifetime average, with 2,596 hits and 1,464 RBI. Elected to the National Baseball Hall of Fame in 1946, Ed Delahanty is buried in the family plot at Calvary Cemetery in Cleveland, Ohio, in Section 10, Lot 135-B, Grave 7.

JOE STEWART (1879–1913)

Joseph Lawrence Stewart appeared in two games for the 1904 Boston Beaneaters. Stewart, who went to Erskine College, was also known as "Ace." He made his debut on June 11, 1904, when he relieved Boston hurler Vic Willis in the fourth inning of a 19–1 loss. The game was basically lost before he even warmed up. By the time he got into the game, the Pirates were already leading, 8–1. Prior to his brief time in the majors, Stewart played for Indianapolis and St. Paul of the Western League. While with Indianapolis, he was a teammate of former major leaguer Marty Hogan. Afterward, Ace was drafted by the Boston Nationals but eventually fell out of favor with the organization, signing with the Niles, Ohio, independent club managed by Charles Crow. Crow found Stewart employment after his arm gave out, and he worked as a bartender and then ran a pool room. Stewart followed Crow to Youngstown, Ohio, where Crow also managed a team.

Stewart died on Sunday, February 9, 1913, after he fainted and fell out of a window he was attempting to open, suffering a crushed chest and massive trauma and hemorrhaging. Suffering from pleurisy at the time, he was simply trying to get some air when the accident happened. Newspaper accounts of the tragedy actually mention that he had only suffered a fractured femur and that the accident was not a factor in his death, stating that he had really died as a result of complications from various diseases. Joe Stewart, who was 33 years old and single, was buried in his hometown of Monroe, North Carolina.

BOB UNGLAUB (1880–1916)

Robert Alexander "Bob" Unglaub played Major League Baseball as an infielder for six seasons (1904 to 1905 and 1907 to 1910) with the New York Highlanders (Yankees), Boston Red Sox, and Washington Senators. An average player at best, he was continuously at odds with management regarding his salary.

Born in Baltimore on July 31, 1880, Unglaub grew up three blocks from Union Park, where the old Orioles played. He graduated from fan to batboy/mascot in a short period of time, all the while learning baseball secrets from the likes of John McGraw, Joe Kelley, Willie Keeler, Steve Brodie, and the rest of the legendary Orioles, often shagging flies in the outfield with the team. After graduating high school, he went to college at the University of Maryland, where he played ball and completed a degree in engineering.

Unglaub started his professional baseball career by playing with semipro teams on the Delmarva Peninsula. He played in many venues, with stops in such places as Meriden, Connecticut, and Worcester in the Eastern League. He was a jack-of-all-trades, usually filling in wherever he was needed. He jumped to Sacramento of the outlaw California State League in 1902, where he played first base and short. In 1903, Bob shifted to Milwaukee of the American Association. At the end of the 1903 campaign, his contract was purchased by the Boston Americans, and he split time with Boston and the New York Highlanders in 1904, playing in only 15 games. The next year, he appeared in 43 games and continued to make good with his performance, although he

Bob Unglaub, 1909, White Borders Baseball Card. Courtesy of the author.

was never a great hitter. He became increasingly dissatisfied with his salary.

The National Agreement between organized baseball clubs stated that a player would make more money with each step up in class. Unglaub felt that he was being unfairly treated, since he was actually making less money in the majors than in the minors. In 1906, he jumped to Williamsport, Pennsylvania, of the Tri-State League, which had recently become an outlaw league. In 1907, however, he was back in the majors, joining the Red Sox and becoming the starting first baseman, batting .254 for the season and setting career highs, with 13 triples, 62 runs, and 49 RBIs. He also took over the reins of the team, becoming the fourth Boston manager of the season (Chick Stahl, the team's first leader in 1907, had committed suicide during spring training). After posting a 9–20 record, Unglaub was replaced by Jim "Deacon" McGuire.

During this time, Unglaub began experiencing fielding problems, causing fans to turn on him. Tired of the constant booing, he asked for, and was granted, a trade to the Washington Senators, where he rejoined Joe Cantillon, his former minor league manager; however, Bob refused to show unless he was paid the same salary that he made in Boston, once again threatening to go "outlaw." Finally reporting to Washington, the reunion revived his career, and he batted .308 for the remainder of the season. In 1911, his contract was sold to the Lincoln Railsplitters of the Western League. Unglaub became player-manager, a position he held until the end of the season. He would continue to play in the minors with Baltimore of the International League, Minneapolis of the American Association, and Fargo-Moorhead of the Northern League, where, as player-manager, he would spend the final four seasons of his career.

During the off-season, Unglaub worked for the Pennsylvania Railroad in Baltimore in their repair shops. He was killed in a horrific shop accident on November 29, 1916, while supervising repair work on a locomotive in a railroad pit. He was only 35 years old. Originally interred in Baltimore's Loudon Park Cemetery, Bob Unglaub was reinterred in the Sunny Ridge Memorial Park in Crisfield, Maryland.

HERM MERRITT (1900–1927)

Herm Merritt's life and career in baseball were tragically cut short before they ever had a chance to begin. The son of Charles and Etta Merritt, Herman G. Merritt was born in Independence, Missouri, on November 12, 1900. Merritt, a shortstop by trade, had a memorable 20-game stint in the majors in 1921, for the Ty Cobb-led Detroit Tigers. From August 24th to October 2nd, Merritt batted a lusty .370, with a walk, a double, and two triples in 20 games. In the field, Merritt proved that he could be a fairly reliable fielder, although his 6 errors in 17 games at shortstop were a bit on the high side. Manager Cobb said of him, "The boy comes to play." The Tigers decided that he still needed a little seasoning and farmed him out to the Augusta Tourists of the South Atlantic League for 1922.

On April 23, 1922, Merritt was riding in a car with four of his Augusta teammates just outside of Greenville, South Carolina, when it flipped, causing injuries to everyone inside. Merritt was the most seriously injured, suffering a severely fractured spine. Not only did his baseball career come to an abrupt end, but physicians predicted that the resulting injury would prove fatal. Despite great pain and suffering, Merritt proved the experts wrong, as he was able to hang on for another five years. He finally succumbed to acute nephritis as a result of the spinal fracture on April 26, 1927, at his home at 1521 Wayne Avenue in Kansas City, in the 15th Ward. He left behind his wife, Nellie Irene. He was taken back to his birthplace for burial and laid to rest at Mount Washington Cemetery in Independence, Missouri, on May 28, 1927.

TOMMY DOWD (1869–1933)

The son of Jeremiah and Mary Dowd, "Buttermilk" Tommy Dowd attended Brown University, Georgetown University, and the College of the Holy Cross from 1888 to 1890. The ten-year major leaguer's greatest claim to fame was discovering future Hall Of Fame player Rabbit Maranville. Dowd's "Salad Days" were spent with the St. Louis Browns (Cardinals), whom he played with for the better part of six seasons. He also managed St. Louis for 63 games in 1896, and 29 games in 1897. On June 1, 1897, he was traded to the Phillies for Bill Hallman, Dick

Harley, and $300 cash. He was sent back to St. Louis later that fall in a trade that brought the Phillies Monte Cross, Klondike Douglass, and Red Donahue. St. Louis also received Jack Clements, Lave Cross, Brewery Jack Taylor, and $1000 cash in the deal.

Dowd's stay in St. Louis lasted just one year, as he was assigned to the Cleveland Spiders, who were called the Perfectos, on March 29, 1899. The Spiders and St. Louis were both owned by the Robison brothers, a sort of ownership dubbed "syndicate baseball." The Robisons decided to move the best Cleveland players to St. Louis, and in so doing, Dowd wound up playing for the worst team in major league history. The 1899 Spiders went a pitiful 20–134, finishing dead last in the National League. Buttermilk played 147 games in the outfield that year and batted a respectable .278.

In the spring of 1900, Dowd announced that he was sitting out the season to take an interest in a laundry business in his hometown of Holyoke. Some thought it a strange move, but with players' salaries being what they were at the time, slashed to near-record levels by National League owners, Dowd felt that it would behoove him to work for himself rather than accept a low bid from a major league club or a minor league deal. He would soon change his mind, however, as he signed on with the Chicago White Stockings of the American League (the American League was still considered a minor league in 1900), playing with the likes of Frank Isbell, Dick Padden, Dummy Hoy, Frank Shugart, and Steve Brodie. Dowd played both infield and outfield during that campaign, finishing the year with the Milwaukee Brewers. He batted .262 overall, finishing sixth in fielding amongst American League outfielders, with a .965 average in 68 games. The 1901 season would prove to be his swan song in the majors, as he signed on with the Boston Pilgrims. In 138 games, he batted .268, making his final big-league appearance on September 28th.

Tommy's baseball career did not end, however, as he would make stops in numerous minor league venues throughout the next few years, so many that he probably could have used a map and compass to help him navigate. Nonetheless, before his traveling odyssey began, he attempted to buy the New London Club of the Connecticut State League. After that fell through, he bought the Amsterdam-Johnstown-Gloversville club of the New York State League. Baltimore, Holyoke, Atlantic City, Nashua, New Orleans, Des Moines, Altoona, Hartford—

Dowd made stops in all these towns while continuing to inquire about buying and managing minor league clubs. It's a shame they didn't have frequent flyer miles back then, because Tommy could have used them. He even scouted for the Red Sox and found time to coach the Williams College baseball team. Ever the entrepreneur, he also opened a cigar business in Holyoke. In 1919, he went to Europe as a secretary for the Knights of Columbus, helping develop the 4th Division League.

Dowd was single and living at 317 Appaton Street in Holyoke when his body was found floating in the Connecticut River on Sunday, July 2, 1933. His remains were taken to a local mortuary, where they were identified two days later (July 4th) by his brother Jeremiah. The coroner ruled out foul play and declared that he died from an accidental drowning. Tommy Dowd was laid to rest in Calvary Cemetery in Holyoke, Massachusetts.

ADRIAN LYNCH (1897–1934)

Born February 9, 1897, in Laurens, Iowa, to James and Nora Ryan Lynch, Adrian Lynch spent the majority of his pro career pitching for minor league teams in the Midwest. Breaking in with the home state Waterloo, Iowa, club in 1917, the Washington Nationals purchased his contract that fall. Clarke Griffith once remarked to a reporter that Lynch was one of the best prospects "he had seen in quite some time." Lynch would bounce around the minors during the next few seasons in a valiant attempt to pitch his way to the big leagues. Because the Senator brain trust felt that he lacked the stamina to be a successful major league pitcher, he was never given a fair shot at making the club. No matter, as Lynch soldiered on, twirling for franchises in Atlanta, Jersey City, Wichita, and finally the Des Moines Boosters of the Western League. It was during his time with this organization that his contract was purchased by the St. Louis Browns in early August 1920.

Lynch's major league debut came on August 4th in a 7–2 loss against the Athletics at Sportsman's Park. He relieved "Brownie" starter Carl Weilman with one out in the sixth inning, allowing just one hit in 2.2 innings of work. He would go 2–0 during his brief five-game stay in "The Show," allowing 23 hits in 22.3 innings of work. Released to Des Moines for 1921, Adrian would remain in Iowa until August 29, 1922, when the Braves purchased his contract. He reported to the Braves a few days later but never saw the light of day, as he was relegated to the bench by manager Fred Mitchell. Lynch would be back with Des Moines the next season, staying there until his sale to the American Association's Minneapolis Millers in 1924. He also hurled for the Denver Bears and Lincoln Links of the Western League before retiring from the game after the 1927 season.

Lynch was living in Cedar Rapids, Iowa, and working as a roofing supply salesman for Certainteed Products Corporation of Omaha, Nebraska, when he was involved in an auto accident near Davenport, Iowa, on March 16, 1934. Newspaper accounts of the crash state that he drove his car into a ditch on U.S. Highway 61, just west of Davenport. His death certificate, on the other hand, states that he was involved in a head-on collision and that he died as a result of a fractured neck. He left behind his wife Leah and was buried at Glendale Cemetery in Des Moines on Block F, Lot 77, Grave 1 on March 17th. Adrian Lynch was only 37 years old.

JOHN WOODS (1898–1946)

The son of Judge John Hugh Gordon Woods and Margaret Peck Woods, John Fulton Woods was born in Princeton, West Virginia, on January 18, 1898. He embarked on his baseball career after his graduation from Wesleyan College in 1924. He joined Charleston, and the Red Sox purchased his contract in September 1924. He debuted on Tuesday, September 16, 1924, in an 8–4 loss to the White Sox. In his one inning of work, he gave up no hits but walked three. Bib Falk had four hits for Chicago and Earl Sheeley tripled with the bases loaded in the first inning to give the South Siders a lead they would not relinquish. In 1925, Woods played with both Spartanburg and Binghamton. His last professional stop was with Easton, Pennsylvania, in 1927.

Retiring soon afterward, John joined the Norfolk, Virginia, police department in 1929. Steadily promoted through the ranks during the next 17 years, he became chief of police in 1939. He was residing with his wife Elisabeth at 2701 Marlboro Avenue when he was killed in a terrible auto accident. On Friday, October, 4, 1946, his squad car smashed into the rear of a wrecker that was pulling another vehicle out of a ditch. The incident happened on the Cottage Toll Road (now Tidewater Drive). Woods died as a result of a fractured neck and crushed right-side chest. He was buried two days later at Forest Lawn Cemetery in Norfolk, Virginia, in Block 9, Lot 19, Space W.

BILL STEELE (1885–1949)

William Mitchell Steele, also known as "Big Bill," had a fairly unsuccessful and brief career as a pitcher with some dreadful Cardinal teams. He started off with minor league Altoona in 1909. Joining the Cardinals in 1910, he went 4–4 for a St. Louis club that went a disastrous 63–90. Cardinal manager Roger Bresnahan decided to clean house and dropped five pitchers the following season, with Steele surviving. Steele worked 287 innings and led the National League in losses, with an 18–19 record in 1911, but he had a respectable 3.73 ERA. The following year, he was hit hard, as he gave up 245 hits in 194 innings, his ERA ballooning to 4.69. Relegated to the bull pen shortly thereafter, he was used mostly in long relief and mop-up duty.

Big Bill was sold by St. Louis to the Brooklyn Robins in July 1914, where he appeared in the final eight games of his major league career. He played for minor league clubs in Newark and Syracuse in 1915, and was with Gettysburg in 1916, when he retired. Throughout his career, which spanned 129 league games, he accrued a 37–43 record, with 7 saves and a 4.02 era, in 676.2 innings pitched.

Steele, who worked at an A&P Store warehouse as a maintenance man, was killed when he was hit by a streetcar on the rainy night of October 19, 1949, in Clayton, Missouri. Taken by ambulance to St. Louis County Hospital, he was pronounced dead on arrival. His death certificate, which was filled out by the coroner on October 23rd, states that his death was due to "crushing chest and skull injuries, internal injuries, and shock." What is more interesting is the fact that the coroner also declared his death a homicide. Since the operator of the streetcar, Walter F. Hibler, declined to make a statement and sheriff's deputies were unable to find any other witnesses, the accident remained under investigation.

A *St. Louis Post-Dispatch* article from October 21st states:

STEELE-ST.LOUIS-NAT.

Bill Steele, 1912, Brown Backgrounds Baseball Card. Courtesy of the Library of Congress.

A verdict of homicide in the death of William M. Steele . . . was returned by a coroner's jury at Clayton yesterday. The jury recommended also that Walter F. Hibler, operator of the streetcar, be held for the grand jury. There were no witnesses to the accident, and Hibler . . . declined to testify on advice of counsel.

In the end, Steel's death would definitely make for a great episode of *Cold Case* or *Unsolved Mysteries*. Bill Steele is buried in Memorial Park Cemetery in St. Louis, Missouri, in Section 1, Lot 373.

MARSHALL RENFROE (1936–1970)

Marshall Daniel Renfroe honed his baseball skills on the sunny fields of Pensacola, Florida. The son of Graham and Elizabeth Renfroe, he played pro ball for three organizations but only appeared in the majors for one of them, the San Francisco Giants. In 1954, he played for Pulaski of the Appalachian League and Crestview of the Alabama-Florida League. Renfroe was sent to the Phillies in an unknown transaction before the 1955 campaign, playing with St. Petersburg of the Florida State League that season. Just prior to the 1956 season, he was obtained by the New York Yankees from St. Petersburg as part of a minor league working agreement. He also was with Quincy, Illinois, and McAlister, Oklahoma, that year. On October 16, 1958, the Bombers sold his contract to the San Francisco Giants.

Marshall made the Giant Opening Day roster but did not see any action and was dispatched to Phoenix of the Pacific Coast League on May 12th, where he compiled an 8–8 mark for the season. Recalled on September 5th, along with Andre Rogers, he made his only major league appearance on September 27, 1959, in the second game of a doubleheader against the St. Louis Cardinals. (The Giants lost the first game, 2–1, officially eliminating them from the 1959 pennant chase.) Renfroe lasted just two innings, giving up six runs on three hits and three walks in a 14–8 St. Louis victory, although he did manage to strike out three. Bob Gibson was the winning pitcher for the Cards. In March 1960, Marshall was sent to Tacoma of the Pacific Coast League, where he had a 5–12 mark for the year, with a 3.71 ERA. He was recalled by the Giants on October 2nd but did not appear in any games. Renfroe had a younger brother, Dalton, a catcher who played in the Washington Senator system.

After his baseball career ended, Marshall became a welder for Westinghouse. He was living at 3 San Carlos Street in Gulf Breeze, Florida, with his wife Peggy at the time of his death. On November 23, 1970, Renfroe was involved in a horrific accident on the Pensacola Bay Bridge, when the pickup truck he was in was rear-ended by a gasoline tanker. He had stopped to help a driver whose vehicle had stalled when the accident occurred. The resulting explosion caused his vehicle to explode, with the former major leaguer receiving second- and third-degree burns to 70 percent of his body. For the next 17 days, he clung to life at Sacred Heart Hospital in Pensacola. Pneumonia eventually set in, causing the respiratory arrest that led to his death on the afternoon of December 10th. Renfroe was only 34 years old. He was buried at Bayview Memorial Park in Pensacola two days later in Section 11, Lot 417, North 2nd.

ROGER MILLER (1954–1993)

A graduate of Uniontown Senior High in Pennsylvania, Roger Wesley Miller starred on the school's baseball team. During his senior year, he pitched to a 0.62 ERA and averaged an incredible 19 strikeouts per game. Drafted by the Milwaukee Brewers in the 15th round of the amateur draft on June 6, 1972, he was signed to his first professional contract by Bradley Kohler. Assigned to Newark of the New York–Penn League in 1972, in 13 games Miller had a 1–3 record, with a 5.49 ERA, although he struck out 43 batters in 41 innings. In 1973, he moved up to Danville of the Midwest League, bettering himself with an 8–4 record and a 3.42 ERA. He spent part of the 1974 season with Sacramento of the Pacific Coast League, where he went 11–5, with a 4.48 ERA, good enough for a September call-up to the parent club.

Miller's major league debut was a relief appearance in an 8–6 loss to Boston at Fenway Park. He would appear against the Red Sox again four days later, this time in Milwaukee, his last appearance in the major leagues. He would play three seasons in the Pacific Coast League before retiring after the 1977 campaign. Roger, who worked at a sawmill during the off-season, played in the Fayette County League after his professional career ended. Known as a great guy by teammates and opposing players alike, he never had a cross word to say about anyone and had a wonderful demeanor, even though he was a fierce competitor.

Miller was working as a welder for Commercial Stone Incorporated of Mill Run when he met his demise on the morning of April 26, 1993. As he was preparing to do some work on the bucket of a front-end loader, one of the acetylene tanks exploded, the blast sending out a giant shock wave that could be heard for miles. An unconscious Miller was found by a coworker a few moments later. Efforts by emergency workers to revive him proved fruitless, and he was pronounced dead on the scene by the Fayette County deputy coroner, with blunt force trauma being the official cause of death. Roger Miller, who was 38 years old, was survived by his wife, son, and daughter. He was laid to rest at Indian Creek Baptist Cemetery in Mill Run, Pennsylvania.

JIM MCKNIGHT (1936–1994)

The father of former major leaguer Jeff McKnight, James Arthur McKnight was a career minor leaguer, except for 63 games played with the Chicago Cubs. Also known as Jamie, he honed his skills playing American Legion ball in his hometown of Bee Branch, Arkansas, playing both infield and outfield. A standout basketball player at South Side High School, McKnight made the all-district team three times. Signed to a major league contract by Fred Hawn of the St. Louis Cardinals, he broke in with the Paducah Chiefs of the Kitty League in 1955. In 1956, he moved to Gainesville of the Florida State League. He had his breakout season with Ardmore, Oklahoma, of the Sooner State League, where he led the circuit in hitting with a .340 average in 1957.

It was on August 8th of that season that McKnight witnessed a rather interesting, if not dangerous, event on the field at Ponca City, Oklahoma, when his manager, J. C. Dunn, was shot in the ribs and right leg by an irate fan with a 38-caliber pistol. In 1959, he was named the Texas League All-Star second baseman, when he batted .333 for Tulsa. On June 15, 1960, McKnight was traded by St. Louis to the Cubs for Walt Moryn. He was called up from Houston on September 6th and made his debut on Thursday, September 22, in the second game of a doubleheader with the Pirates. After winning the first game, 3–2, in 11 innings, the Pirates took the second game, 6–1, McKnight pinch-hitting for pitcher Joe Schaffernoth in the fifth inning and flying out. Jim went 2–6, with 1 RBI, in his three appearances.

In 1961, the Cubs sent him back to Houston, where he batted .283 for the year. McKnight made the team during spring training of 1962, and appeared in 60 games that season, batting a disappointing .222. That winter the Cubs traded him to the Milwaukee Braves, reacquiring Ken Aspromonte in a deal that was brokered on December 3. McKnight would soldier on in the minor leagues for another nine seasons, playing in the International League and Pacific Coast League. His last stop in pro ball was as manager of the Single-A Decatur Commodores of the Midwest League in 1972. In the off-season, he worked as a pipe fitter, a profession he continued in full-time after his retirement. During his free time, he enjoyed playing golf, hunting, and spending time with his family.

On February 4, 1994, at approximately 5:40 p.m., McKnight was involved in a head-on collision while driving westbound on Highway 330, just outside of Choctaw, Arkansas. His Chevy S10 pickup truck veered into the oncoming lane as he was negotiating a curve, slamming into a GMC van carrying two women. The impact killed McKnight instantly. His pickup was so badly damaged that rescue workers had to use the Jaws of Life to extract his body. Jim McKnight was remembered as a great teammate, but, more importantly, as a wonderful husband and father to his wife Joy and six children. He was laid to rest in Blackwell Cemetery in Bee Branch, Arkansas.

MIKE DARR (1976–2002)

Michael Curtis Darr came from a baseball family. His father, Mike Darr Sr., was a right-handed pitcher who appeared in one game for the 1977 Toronto Blue Jays. Originally a second-round draft pick of the Detroit Tigers in the 1994 amateur draft, Darr was traded by the Tigers, along with Mike Skrmetta, to the San Diego Padres for Jody Reed on March 22, 1997. He would go on to play parts of three seasons with the Padres from 1999 to 2001. The Opening Day starting center fielder in 2001, Darr hit only two home runs that season, both of which were game-winners against the Mets and Giants. Great defensively, but lacking power, he was known for a great sense of humor and intensity on the playing field, as well as his love for the game. The 2001 season would be his best in the majors, as he batted .277 in 105 games. As the 2002 season approached, Darr was looked upon by Padre fans as one of the young cast of players who would help the team achieve success in the coming seasons.

On Friday morning, February 15, 2002, just a few scant hours before the Padres were to open spring training, Darr was involved in a high-speed rollover accident on a highway near Peoria, Arizona. He and childhood friend Duane Johnson were both thrown from the vehicle. (Neither man was wearing a seat belt; a third passenger, who was wearing his seat belt, survived.) Twenty-five-year-old Mike Darr, a young man with his entire life and career ahead of him, was killed almost instantly. He left behind his wife Natalie and two young children.

Mike Darr Jr. had a lifetime .273 batting average, with 5 home runs, 67 RBIs, and 148 hits in 188 games played. In his memory, the Padres wore a black circle patch embroidered with his number, 26, on the right sleeve of their uniforms during the 2002 season. He was buried at Pierce Brothers Crestlawn Memorial Park in Riverside, California, in the Garden of the Resurrection, Lot 43, Grave B.

Grave of Mike Darr. Courtesy of Bill Lee.

CORY LIDLE (1972–2006)

Baseball needs more personalities like Cory Lidle. A straight shooter who never pulled any punches, he was one of the first players to call out Barry Bonds when he was about to break Hank Aaron's home run record, stating,

> I don't want to see Barry Bonds break records. If he breaks them it will be a shame, because I think when all is said and done, the truth will come out. It hasn't yet, but I think if he was in front of a jury and there had to be a verdict, I think the verdict might be guilty. It's sad. I'm not a player hater. I like to see players get paid as much as they can. But without cheating.

Cory Fulton Lidle was born in Hollywood, California, on March 22, 1972, to Doug and Rebecca Lidle. As a youth, he and his twin brother Kevin were both heavily involved in West Covina baseball leagues, playing in the American Little League, Mustang Pony League, Mickey Mantle League, and West Babe Ruth League. Lidle attended South Hills High School in West Covina, where he was classmates with future Yankee teammates Jason Giambi and Aaron Small. During his senior year, Cory recorded a 12–2 record, with a 1.02 ERA and 100 strikeouts, with just 26 walks. He was named the All San Gabriel Valley Pitcher of the Year for 1990. Equally as special as his accolades and awards was the fact that twin brother Kevin was his batterymate. After high school, the two brothers' baseball careers took very different paths, as Cory was signed by the Minnesota Twins right out of high school, while Kevin went on to attend Mount San Antonio College in Walnut, California. Kevin would eventually be drafted by the Detroit Tigers in the 24th round of the June 1992 amateur draft and go on to have a 12-year minor league career.

Released by the Twins on April Fool's Day 1993, Cory signed on to play with the Pocatello Posse of the Pioneer League. It was while pitching for Pocatello that he was signed by the Milwaukee Brewers that September. Lidle pitched in one spring training game for the Brewers during the 1995 major league players' strike. His one-inning stint as a replacement player would later make him ineligible to join the Major League Baseball Players Union. Traded to the New York Mets for catcher Kelly Stinnett in January 1996, he would pitch for New York's minor league affiliates in Binghamton and Norfolk before making his major league debut on May 8, 1997, in a 4–2 loss to the Astros at the Astrodome. Lidle came into the game in the top of the seventh inning in relief of starter Rick Reed, giving up a two-out single to Jeff Bagwell.

The 1997 campaign turned out to be a great one for Lidle, who, on January 7th, married the love of his life, Melanie Varela. The couple would go on to have one son, Christopher, born in 2000. Used almost exclusively out of the bull pen, Lidle appeared in 54 games for the Mets, ending the year with a 7–2 record, compiling 2 saves and a 3.53 ERA. Drafted by the Arizona Diamondbacks in the 1997 expansion draft, he was selected off waivers by Tampa in October 1998. On January 8, 2001, Cory was sent to the Oakland Athletics as part of a three-team trade that included the Kansas City Royals. As it turned out, Oakland was the perfect venue and the Athletics the perfect team for him to show his wares. It was also in Oakland that he earned the nickname "Snacks" for his love of junk food, which he was often seen munching on in the bull pen.

Known as a great teammate and clubhouse man, Lidle could often be seen playing chess, pool, and, later on, poker with his teammates. He loved poker so much that he was looking forward to becoming a professional player after his retirement. Like many ballplayers, he also loved the game of golf, which he found both fun and challenging. Cory's best season was arguably 2001, when he went 13–6, with a 3.59 ERA (10th in the American League), helping the A's win the wild card. Another high point in his career occurred in 2002, when he gave up just one run during the month of August, which helped Oakland set a record for consecutive innings without allowing an earned run. Cory won all five of his starts that month as part of an A's team that won 20 straight games. Lidle would go on to pitch for the Blue Jays, Reds, and Phillies before being traded to the Yankees, along with Bobby Abreu, on July 30, 2006.

During a conference call with the media, Lidle criticized his former Philadelphia teammates, stating, "Unfortunately over the last few years I haven't had a clubhouse that expected to win with me. We would go to the field on the days I was pitching, and it was almost a coin flip as to knowing if the guys behind me were going to be there." The comments did not sit well with several of his former teammates, including Arthur Rhodes, who called Lidle a "scab" in the press in reference to his one-game stint as a replacement player.

The highlight of Cory's stay with the Bombers took place at Fenway Park on August 21st, when he threw six shutout innings, allowing just three hits, as the Yankees went on to win, 2–1, completing a five-game sweep that was later dubbed by some as the Boston Massacre 2. Lidle went 4–3 for the Yankees, with an overall record of 12–10 for the season. Although he never let it be known to the press, it was later learned that he had been taking antiinflammatory medication during the season to deal with an arm injury and that doctors had forced him to come off the meds due to possible dangerous side effects to his liver.

Lidle's final major league appearance came on October 7th, in the fourth game of the 2006 American League Division Series against the Detroit Tigers. Entering the game in the bottom of the third inning in relief of starter Jared Wright, he would pitch one and one-third innings, allowing 3 earned runs on 4 hits, as the Yankees lost the contest, 8–3, and the series, three games to one. After the game, Lidle spoke with a reporter regarding the Yankees' poor performance, stating, "We got matched up with a team that, I think, was a little more ready to play than we were." His remarks were immediately misconstrued by the press as being a jab at manager Joe Torre, which, of course, was not the case.

One of the hobbies that Lidle had taken up in the past year was flying, specifically prop aircraft. Said to be a "natural flyer" by his certified flight instructor, Tyler Stanger, Cory had just received his pilot's license on February 6th, and he purchased a four-seat Cirrus SR20 four months later. With the season over, his plan was to make the trip home to California in his plane with Stanger. The flight would take approximately 15 hours, with two planned stops in Tennessee and Arizona for rest. The night before his departure, the Lidles and Stangers went out for a night on the town, seeing a show and having dinner. Melanie had plans to fly home via commercial jet with their son Christopher.

The next day, October 11th, at approximately 2:29 p.m., Lidle's SR20 took off from the Teterboro Regional Airport in New Jersey. It remains uncertain who was piloting the plane. What is known, however, is that Lidle's plane headed south down the Hudson River, circled the Statue of Liberty, and headed north up the East River toward the Queensboro Bridge. It was around this time that radar lost track of the aircraft as it began to descend into a 180-degree turn. At approximately 2:42 p.m., an easterly gust of wind pushed the little plane off course and

Grave of Cory Lidle. Courtesy of Bill Lee.

into the north side of the Belaire Apartment complex, located at 524 East 72nd Street. Both Lidle and Stanger were killed instantly. Approximately 21 people were injured as a result of the crash, about half of which were firefighters. The National Transportation Safety Board would later blame the crash on pilot error and "inadequate pilot judgment," citing the fact that the plane didn't have enough space to make such a tight turn. At the time of the incident, Lidle had only logged 87.7 hours of flight time.

News of Lidle's death brought back terrible memories of when Yankee captain Thurman Munson had perished in a private jet crash 27 years earlier. Munson and Lidle's tragic deaths were actually connected through Kevin Lidle, who was a minor league teammate of Jeff Anderson. Anderson was the son of Jerry Anderson, who survived the crash that had killed Munson. Derek Jeter remembered Lidle as a good guy and great teammate, adding, "You're around your teammates pretty much more than you're around your family. The plane crash was a terrible tragedy, something that will never be forgotten." Barry Zito and Eric Chavez, two of Cory's former teammates with the Athletics, were so overcome with grief that they started breaking down in front of the press. As expected, his wife and family were shocked and brokenhearted. Yankee manager Joe Torre said in a statement, "This is a terrible shock. I was with Ron Guidry and Lee Mazzilli when I heard the news, and we were just stunned. Cory's time with the Yankees was short, but he was a good teammate and a great competitor. My heart goes out to his family."

Lidle left behind a legacy of charitable endeavors that ranged from charity golf and poker tournaments to sports and entertainment memorabilia auctions, one example being the Cory Lidle Celebrity Charity Poker Tournament, which benefited the Make-A-Wish Foundation. The Cory Lidle Foundation was established after his death to allow his spirit of charitable giving to continue. Cory Lidle was buried at Forest Lawn Memorial Park in Covina, California, in the Vale of Faith Section, Lot 9067, Space 3.

7

FINAL OUT

It's always a shock when a major league player, active or retired, passes away at a young age. It's a sad story that has been told time and again since the first professional players suited up almost 150 years ago. It would take a book the size of an encyclopedia to tell the stories of all the players who have passed before their time. Sadly, many of these figures have been largely forgotten. This chapter is a sampling of some of the players who made their "final out" a little too soon.

JIMMY HALLINAN (1849–1879)

Born in Ireland on May 27, 1849, Jimmy Hallinan played amateur baseball with the Aetna Club of Chicago in 1870, before turning pro with the Fort Wayne Kekiongas of the National Association in 1871, a stint that lasted all of five games. He was back playing amateur ball with the Aetnas the following season, continuing to do so for the next three seasons. The Aetnas, who were later renamed the Franklins, were mostly comprised of employees from the *Chicago Times*. In 1875, Jimmy was back playing pro, spending the campaign with the Keokuk Westerns and, after that club disbanded in June, the New York Mutuals.

With the formation of the National League in 1876, Hallinan stayed in New York to man shortstop for the Mutual Club. The 1877 season saw him play a handful of games with Cincinnati before moving to the Chicago White Stockings in mid-May. Hallinan sustained a severely ruptured index finger above the knuckle in a game against the Hartford team on June 21st. The injury kept him out of the lineup for more than a fortnight. Back with Chicago in 1878, Jimmy became dissatisfied when Chicago manager Cap Anson used him in only a utility role. Through July, he had only appeared in 13 games and was getting tired of warming the bench. On July 31, Hallinan asked for, and was given, his release by the White Stockings. He immediately found work with the Indianapolis Blues but lasted only three games and was out of the pro game during the entire 1879 season.

Jimmy Hallinan died from gastritis at his residence at 89 North LaSalle Street in Chicago on October 28, 1879. Only 30 years of age, he was laid to rest on October 30th at Calvary Cemetery in Evanston, Illinois, in Section K, Block 7, Lot 3. His grave remains unmarked.

DAVE FOUTZ (1856–1897)

Dave Foutz spent 13 seasons in the majors as a pitcher, infielder, and outfielder, a feat that is pretty amazing since he suffered from an asthmatic condition. His first six seasons were spent in the American Association with the St. Louis Browns, where he became a star pitcher. St. Louis owner Chris von der Ahe bought the entire Bay City, Michigan, team just to obtain Foutz's services. The adaptable fielder would go on to win 114 games in a four-year stretch that spanned 1884 to 1887, with a career high of 41 in 1886. In a game against the Cincinnati Reds on August 14, 1887, Foutz suffered a broken right thumb that essentially ended his career as a pitcher, since he was ineffective thereafter. He began a new phase when he was sold to the Brooklyn Grays in late November 1887. Showing his versatility, he would become one of the few players to appear in at least 250 games or more as a pitcher, outfielder, and first baseman.

A son of the Monumental City, Foutz always kept Baltimore near and dear to him, residing there in the off-season. He was nicknamed "Scissors" due to his skinny frame (six feet, two inches, and 161 pounds). A fan favorite, he also managed Brooklyn from 1893 to 1896, finishing up with a lifetime 264–257 record. Dave pitched to a lifetime 146–66 mark, and as a batter he notched a .278 lifetime average, with 749 RBI.

In 1897, at the age of 40, Dave Foutz died from an asthma attack at his home in Waverly, Maryland. His funeral was a sad and somber affair attended by former opposing players and teammates, including executives from the National League and the Brooklyn and St. Louis clubs. He is buried in Louden Park Cemetery in Baltimore next to his wife Minnie, who passed away a year later.

BILL STEARNS (1853–1898)

A lifelong native of Washington, DC, Bill Stearns was a pitcher and infielder who spent most of his career playing for teams based in his hometown for the National Association. Despite the fact that he was only 12 years old at the end of the Civil War, he served in the Union Army during the conflict in some capacity, most likely as a drummer or in the medical corps, hence his membership in the Grand Army of the Republic, a fraternal order composed exclusively of Union veterans of that war. Stearns logged a miserable 12–64 record in 83 games during his five years in the National Association, his best year coming in 1873, for the Washington Blue Legs, when he logged a 7–25 record.

Stearns was working in Washington, DC, as a clerk when the Spanish-American War broke out in 1898. Enlisting in the U.S. Army, he was assigned to Company H of the 1st DC Infantry, part of the Engineer Corps, a provisional engineering unit. Shipped to Puerto Rico, he eventually contracted malaria. In his weakened condition, he was only able to perform the "lightest of duties" and, after spending just three weeks there, was sent back to his home in the District of Columbia to rehabilitate. Arriving home on September 16th, Bill's condition was described by friends as "weakened and frail." He gamely battled the disease throughout the fall and early winter, but with the rudimentary medical treatments of the time, his condition continued to deteriorate. Stearns succumbed to his malady at his home at 326th 4th Street, NW on December 30, 1898. His official cause of death was malarial poisoning with uremic convulsions and cardiac insufficiency.

With his death, Bill Stearns became the only former major league player to become a casualty of the Spanish-American War and one of 2,061 nonbattlefield casualties suffered in the war. He was laid to rest

Grave of Bill Stearns. Courtesy of Dr. Fred Worth.

with full military honors in Arlington National Cemetery on December 31, in Grave 13931.

FATTY BRIODY (1858–1903)

With his thinning hair, round face, and portly physique, Charles Frank "Fatty" Briody bore a striking resemblance to silent film actor Roscoe "Fatty" Arbuckle. Of course, in this day and age of political correctness, Briody would probably be hung with a new nickname. Fearless and stouthearted, the five-foot, eight-and-a-half-inch Irishman was also given the nickname "Alderman" because of his leadership qualities. As far as his birth name was concerned, Briody preferred being called by his middle name, Frank, rather than his first name, Charles.

Born in Lansingburgh, New York, on August 13, 1858, Briody moved with his family to Wisconsin as a young child but eventually returned to the Lansingburg area to play semipro and minor league ball. Primarily a catcher, he was also considered nimble enough to play first, second, or third base, as well as the outfield when needed. His first professional assignment was with the Troy Haymakers of the League Alliance in 1877, after which he would spend two of the following three seasons playing semipro ball.

Alderman made his debut with a one-day contract appearance for the hometown Troy Trojans on June 16, 1880, at the age of 22, in a 9–5 loss to the Cleveland Blues. After the game, he went back to playing semipro and later minor league ball with the New York Metropolitans, Washington Nationals, and Albany of the Eastern Championship Association. Briody would return to the majors in 1882, when he signed on to play with the Cleveland Blues of the National League. One only has to look at his lifetime statistics to realize that he was not known for his hitting, as he batted a paltry .228. In 1,186 at bats and 323 major league games, he had 271 hits, with 4 home runs and 105 RBI.

The 1884 season would be a pivotal one for the national game, as it was the first and only year during which the Union Association, an "outlaw" major league that promised better player salaries than those offered by National League and American Association clubs, was in operation. Briody, along with Cleveland teammates Jim McCormick and Jack Glasscock, signed contracts on August 8th to play with the Cincinnati Outlaw Reds for the remainder of the season. Suspended by National League president Nick Young, he would be reinstated the following April on the condition that he pay a $1,000 fine. Briody would go on to play four more seasons in the majors, with St. Louis and Kansas

City, of the National Association and American Association, and the National League's Detroit Wolverines.

With his career over, Fatty would eventually settle in Chicago, where he would became a committeeman for the Seventeenth Ward and later open his own independent trucking business. He died on the morning of June 22, 1903, as a result of dilation of the heart caused by nephritis and lung edema. Fatty Briody, who was only 44 years old, was buried in St. Johns Cemetery in Lansingburgh, next to his wife Margaret.

BILL HOGG (1881–1909)

Nicknamed "Buffalo Bill," William Johnston Hogg was a right-handed pitcher for the New York Highlanders from 1905 to 1908. Born in Port Huron, Michigan, he moved to Pueblo, Colorado, with his family while still a young boy. He started his professional career in 1902, with the Class B Seattle Clamdiggers of the Pacific Northwest League. Throughout the next three seasons, he would pitch for various teams in the Great Northwest, including the Spokane Indians and Seattle Chinooks of the Pacific National League and the Seattle Siwashes and Portland Browns of the Pacific Coast League.

It was from Spokane that Hogg was drafted by the Highlanders in the 1904 Rule 5 Draft on September 1, 1904. He made his major league debut on April 25, 1905, in a 6–5 win over the Washington Senators. Normally the Highlanders' third or fourth starter, he was known for bouts of wildness and occasional aggressiveness. He once hit Cleveland Nap third baseman Bill Bradley with a pitch, fracturing his arm, after which he was quoted saying, "That big Frenchman (Nap Lajoie) is next on my list."

The 1908 campaign would be a major disappointment for Buffalo Bill, both physically and professionally. Hampered by ill health and a host of injuries, he recorded a 9–16 record, after which his contract was sold to the Louisville Colonels of the American Association, where he would pitch to a 17–14 record in 1909. With his career again on the upswing, Hogg joined a team of minor and major leaguers for an off-season barnstorming trip of southern cities. As the team was getting ready to play a series of games in New Orleans, his health took a turn for the worse. He passed away from acute fever complicated by nephritis on December 8, 1909, at the age of 28.

During the span of his four-season major league career, Bill Hogg pitched in 116 games, accruing a lifetime record of 37–50 in 730 innings of work. He was buried at Lutheran All Faiths Cemetery in Middle Village, Queens, New York, in the Hogg family plot, Lot 4769.

EDDIE QUICK (1881–1913)

Born Edwin S. Stillwell in Baltimore, Maryland, Eddie Quick was a one-hit wonder with the 1903 New York Highlanders. He was selected by the Greater New Yorks from Salt Lake City of the Pacific Coast League in the Rule 5 Draft in September 1903. He made his debut and only major league appearance against the Detroit Tigers on September 28th. The *New York Times* notes that Quick was part of "Griffith's Pony Battery" that day. He didn't last long, pitching only two innings and giving up five hits and five runs (only two of them earned). He was relieved by Elmer Bliss, another pitcher making his debut and only big-league appearance. Bliss came on to save the day by allowing only one run and four hits in the next seven innings, as New York won, 7–6.

In January 1904, the Highlanders traded Quick, along with Jack Zalusky, to Toledo of the American Association for catcher Red Kleinow. The deal proved to be a good one, as Kleinow went on to become one of the better defensive catchers in the American League, while Quick was relegated to Class A ball for the remainder of his minor league career, which ended in 1909. It was while playing with the semi-pro Rocky Ford, Colorado, club in June 1913, that "Fast Eddie" caught a cold. The cold turned into pneumonia, which eventually took his life on June 19th, at the age of 31. At the request of his mother, who lived in Baltimore, Quick was buried on June 20th in Block 61, Lot 88, Section S½ of Fairmount Cemetery in Denver, next to his brother John, who had died the year before.

ALECK SMITH (1871–1919)

One of the few Jewish ballplayers in action at the turn of the century, native New Yorker Alexander Benjamin Smith was also known by the moniker "Broadway Aleck." Although primarily a catcher, he was talented enough to fill in at any infield position, and also in the outfield, when needed. Never much of a power hitter, the gregarious and bighearted Smith had only one lifetime homer in the big leagues, although he managed to bat .300 or better three times and was known for being a fairly decent defensive catcher. Signing with the Brooklyn Bridegrooms in 1897, he stayed with that club until 1899, when he was assigned to the Baltimore Orioles on March 11th. The Orioles and Brooklyn (now known as the Superbas) were owned by the same group of men. There had been talk as early as January of Smith's possible departure to the Monumental City, as Oriole manager Ned Hanlon had coveted the husky Brooklyn catcher for some time.

Smith's first stay in Baltimore was short-lived, as he was traded back to the Superbas on April 4, 1899, for Pat Crisham and George Magoon. After batting just .188 in 17 games, he was once again traded on July 14th, in a package deal with first baseman Dan McGann, to the Washington Senators for catcher Deacon McGuire. When Broadway Aleck finally reported to the Senators, he immediately requested that he be dealt to another team, as the Washington club, which was floundering near the bottom of the standings, was not to his liking. Washington president Earl Wagner eventually granted the request, selling Smith's contract to the Orioles on August 5, 1899. Smith started the 1902 season with Providence of the Eastern League before his contract was purchased by the American League's Baltimore Orioles. In 1905, he signed with Wilmington of the outlaw Tri-State League as player-manager.

After his baseball career came to a close, Smith was often seen as a guest of his friend John McGraw at the Polo Grounds, as well as at the famous Tod Sloan's billiard parlor in New York. In addition, he frequented the racetracks. Aleck Smith died at his home, located at 2465 Broadway in Manhattan, as a result of acute myocarditis on July 9, 1919, at the age of 47 (some newspapers list him as being 46). He left behind his wife Adelaide and countless friends in baseball. He was buried in

Grave of Broadway Aleck Smith. Courtesy of the author.

Woodlawn Cemetery in the Bronx in the Honey Suckle Section, Range 8, Grave 103, in an unmarked grave.

ART WEAVER (1879–1917)

A good fielding, no-hit catcher who could also play first base, Art Weaver was nicknamed "Six O' Clock" by fans because he was so thin that he looked like the hands of a clock at six. Weaver, who was called "Buck" by friends, played for four teams during the span of four seasons in the majors. Arthur Coggshall Weaver was born on April 7, 1879, to John and Belle Weaver in Wichita, Kansas. He joined the St. Louis Cardinals from the Cedar Rapids Club in 1902. In the minors, Weaver was known for being an "exceptionally brilliant thrower and good sticker," batting .271 lifetime in nine seasons. His time in the major leagues was different, however, as his lifetime .183 average suggests. Weaver split the

1903 season with the Cardinals and Pirates, being sold to Pittsburgh on June 3, 1903.

Buck was back in the minors the next two seasons before saddling up with the St. Louis Browns for 28 games in 1905. The Chicago White Sox purchased his contract from the Western Association's Wichita Jobbers in 1907, and it was with that club that he played the final 15 games of his Major League Baseball career. Weaver, who would often pitch batting practice on his days off, later played with the Denver Bears of the Western Association, followed by Salt Lake City, Great Falls, and Boise of the Union Association, before retiring after the 1914 campaign.

In 1915, he was badly burned in an industrial fire at the Mountain Motor Fuel Company. It was thought that the burns caused extreme complications to the asthmatic condition that had forced his retirement from baseball. On March 14, 1917, Weaver entered St. Joseph's Hospital in Denver, Colorado, suffering from peritonitis due to a ruptured appendix. After an emergency appendectomy, he clung to life for another nine days, finally succumbing to the peritonitis on the evening of March 23rd. For some odd reason, many newspapers report that his cause of death was due to his asthmatic condition. Art Weaver, who was 37 at the time of his passing, was survived by his wife Louise and a daughter. He was buried in Block 33, Lot 154, Section SW1/4 at Fairmount Cemetery in Denver on March 25th.

FRED HOUSE (1890–1923)

The son of Joseph and Carolyn Dailey House, Willard "Fred" House was born October 3, 1890, in Cabool, Missouri. He was selected by the Detroit Tigers from the Kewanee Boilermakers of the Central Association in the Rule 5 Draft on September 16, 1912. He appeared in 19 games for Detroit during the 1913 season, making his debut on April 22nd against the Chicago White Sox. House lost the game, 3–2, a loss that was marked by the absence of one Tyrus Raymond Cobb, who was sitting out the contest due to a contract dispute. His presence surely would have been welcomed, especially by House, who pitched quite well, giving up just six hits in seven innings. His only big mistake was giving up a home run to Shano Collins in the first inning, a shot into the left field bleachers. The Tigers rallied for two runs in the top of the ninth inning but fell short. House's lone major league win came on April 12th, 8–7 over the Red Sox. He pitched to a 5.20 ERA in 53.7 innings during his time in the majors. He would not get another start in the "Bigs," as Detroit assigned him to Providence of the International League on January 3, 1914, ending his major league career.

House was living at 533 Crescent Street in the Mount Washington section of Kansas City, Missouri, and working as a station engineer when he died from acute heart dilation complicated by an appendectomy at St. Luke's Hospital in Kansas City on November 16, 1923. He was buried at Mount Washington Cemetery in Independence, Missouri, on November 19th, in the Garden of Eternal Love, Lot 624.

EDDIE PLANK (1875–1926)

Often overlooked by members of baseball's advanced statistical community, Edward Stewart Plank was one of the winningest pitchers in major league history and—until Warren Spahn broke his record—the winningest left-hander in baseball history. The fourth of seven children of David Luther and Martha McCreary Plank, he was born on the family farm, located just outside of Gettysburg, Pennsylvania, on August 31, 1875. Eddie was a bit of a rarity, as he didn't actually take up the game until he was 17. From that point onward, he played for various town teams (amateur teams, as they are called in modern-day baseball). Almost from the time he took to the mound, Plank had a habit of throwing a baseball against his family's barn door. It was while doing this repetitive exercise that Eddie found himself being scolded by his father for denting the door and, according to father David, shattering it several times. Plank's natural pitching motion of throwing across his body led him to develop his signature pitch, the "cross-fire," which cut across the plate at an angle disconcerting to batters, especially left-handed ones.

At the age of 22, Plank enrolled in Gettysburg Academy, a preparatory school under the patronage of Gettysburg College. While he never attended class there, he did pitch for the Gettysburg College baseball team, which was coached by former major league pitcher Frank Foreman. Eddie signed a contract to play with the Richmond Colts of the Virginia State League in 1900, but the team folded before he could set foot on the mound. The following May, on a tip from Foreman, Philadelphia Athletic owner Connie Mack invited Plank to join his team. He made his major league debut on May 13th, in a 14–5 loss at Baltimore. He would go on to have a fine rookie campaign, pitching to a 17–13 mark, with a 3.13 ERA in 32 starts, 28 of which were complete games. Not bad for a 25-year-old rookie.

The 1902 campaign would be the first of eight 20-win seasons for the lefty, as he logged a 20–15 record, with a 3.30 ERA. The Athletics won the American League pennant, and Mack was quick to point out the contributions made by his sophomore southpaw, as Plank was second in wins, behind only the eccentric Rube Waddell, who led the pace with 24 tallies. Because he never led the American League in victories, ERA, or strikeouts during his career, the naturally quiet and unassuming Eddie was usually second banana to other pitchers on the Athletics—originally the wild and crazy Rube Waddell, followed by Chief Bender, whom Eddie always referred to as Albert.

Eddie Plank, Philadelphia Athletics. Courtesy of the Library of Congress.

Almost from the start, Plank gained a reputation for his workman-like ethic and reliability. Other pitchers might have been more glamorous, especially in the eyes of the press, but Plank was the workhorse, a consistent winner year after year. One dilemma that Plank had to deal with was Mack's tendency to overuse him, often resulting in a sore arm. He might also have been the most unlucky pitcher in the history of World Series play. In four World Series, he logged but a 2–5 record, but with a sparkling 1.32 ERA in 54 innings of toil. The reason for such a record was because he usually found himself going head-to-head with the great Christy Mathewson. Plank never complained about his match-ups with "Big Six," since it was Mr. Mack who told him when and where to toe the rubber. Opposing players throughout the American League had high praise for the hurler. Babe Ruth considered Plank to be the toughest pitcher he ever faced, while Ty Cobb ranked him as the great-est left-handed pitcher of the prewar era and named him to his all-time team.

By the time his career ended, with the St. Louis Browns in 1917, Eddie had accrued a 326–193 won–loss record, with a remarkable 2.34 ERA, 69 shutouts (fifth all-time), and 412 complete games. A serious, self-contained man, he was deliberate on the mound, often talking to the baseball before he threw it, but there was a method to his madness, as his constant fidgeting made opposing batters anxious. Respected and loved by his teammates, especially fellow pitchers Chief Bender and Jack Coombs and second baseman Eddie Collins, Plank was extremely fond of little Louie Van Zelst, the hunchback Athletic mascot/batboy.

Unlike many players of his era, Eddie was extremely generous to rookie pitchers, offering kindly critiques and imparting advice. As solid a family man as you could ever find, he was unswervingly loyal to his relatives, especially his wife and son, Eddie Jr. While he had no prob-lem pitching inside to opposing hitters, he was never known to be malicious and certainly not a headhunter. After his retirement, Plank pitched in the Bethlehem Steel League and later opened a Buick deal-ership in Gettysburg. Connie Mack regarded Eddie as the greatest left-handed pitcher baseball has ever known. Mack once commented, "Bender was the money pitcher, Coombs the brilliant strikeout hurler, and [Plank] was not as spectacular as Waddell, but he was a pitcher who combined a rare knowledge of his opponent's weakness and had marve-lous control."

On Monday morning, February 22, 1926, Eddie's wife Anna arose to find her husband lying in bed, paralyzed from a stroke. When the family physician arrived, he found that Plank was paralyzed on the left side and his speech garbled. After deliberating with the family, both the doctor and Anna decided that it would be best to treat Eddie at home rather than try to move him to a hospital. After some minor improvement, Plank soon lost his ability to speak and began drifting in and out of consciousness. Maintaining the vigil at his bedside were Anna, Eddie Jr., and two of his three brothers. By the afternoon of the 24th, his condition had deteriorated to a point where all hope of recovery had been abandoned. At 2:49, as the late winter sun began to set on his beloved Gettysburg, Eddie Plank passed away. The news of his death quickly spread. One of the first to receive the news was Mr. Mack, who had been monitoring the crisis from his home in Philadelphia. Perhaps the most frustrating thing about the southpaw's passing was that he had shown no signs of ill health.

On the morning of February 26, 1926, Plank's wake was held at the family residence, located at 343 Carlisle Street, with the funeral taking place at the First Presbyterian Church of Gettysburg. What could possibly be considered the greatest tribute given to Plank was delivered by the Rev. W. C. Space, who said, "Eddie contended lawfully in the great game of life, and so death is his coronation. He was true to his manhood, true to his parents, true to his wife and home, true to his God and church. What better could be spoken of any man?" Eddie Plank was laid to rest on February 28th in Evergreen Cemetery in Gettysburg in Section X, Lot 219, Grave 1. His beloved wife joined him in eternal rest in 1955.

SPENCER HEATH (1893–1930)

Spencer Paul Heath was widely known in Chicago as a semipro ballplayer, playing in the famous Chicago City League with such teams as Garden City, the Gunthers, and the Ciceros. Enlisting in the U.S. Navy during World War I, he trained as an electrician and served at the Great Lakes Naval Station, where he played on the baseball team. In 1919, after his discharge, Heath pitched for Winnipeg, from whom he was signed to a contract by the White Sox in August of that year. With the

Sox in spring training of 1920, the 26-year-old "rookie" showed good enough form to make the Opening Day roster, which was no mean task, since the majority of the Sox pitchers where holdovers from the previous pennant-winning season.

Making his major league debut on May 4th against the St. Louis Browns, Heath relieved Dickie Kerr in what can only be described as a 12–4 debacle. In four games, all in relief, Spencer gave up 19 hits and 12 earned runs, with a very untidy 15.43 lifetime ERA. Released by Chicago in mid-July, he went back to playing semipro ball, eventually taking a job with the Chicago Police Department.

Spencer Heath died on January 25, 1930, at Edgewater Hospital in Chicago, from double lobar pneumonia and influenza complicated by a cerebral hemorrhage. Heath, who was only 35 and single, was survived by his mother Agatha and laid to rest in St. Boniface Cemetery in Chicago, next to his father, Spencer Sr., on January 29th.

LES COX (1904–1934)

Unlike many players who failed to have a successful major league career and had little to fall back on, Texan Les Cox served himself well by preparing for a life outside of baseball before he ever stepped on a big-league field. Born August 14, 1904, in Junction, Texas, Leslie Warren Cox pitched just two games for the 1926 Chicago White Sox. Deciding to get his education first, he attended the University of Texas at Austin and, upon graduation in 1926, joined the Palestine Pals of the Texas League. It was from that club that the White Sox purchased his contract on August 4th.

Called up in September after the minor league season ended, Cox made his major league debut against the Philadelphia Athletics on September 11th. Coming into the game in the fourth inning in relief of starter Jim Joe Edwards, he held the fort until a seventh-inning error by Ray Morehart opened the floodgates. Philly went on to win, 11–5. Sam Gray inked the win, while Cox went home the loser. Cox got into just two games for Chicago, recording a 0–1 record, with a 5.40 ERA.

Rather than quit his dream of becoming a full-time major league pitcher, he continued to pitch in the minors, hoping for another shot. He was invited to spring training the following two years but was sent to the minors for seasoning each time. Cox was called up by Chicago on two separate occasions, in 1927 and 1928, but much to his disappointment, he did not make any appearances. The closest he came to getting into another game was when he was asked to warm up in the bull pen. He would continue to pitch in the minors until 1931, when he finally quit to take a job as a school teacher.

Les Cox died as a result of appendicitis and general peritonitis at St. John's Hospital in Stephenville, Texas, on October 14, 1934, at the age of 29. He was survived by his wife Pauline and a five-year-old son. He was buried at West End Cemetery in Stephenville.

TURKEY GROSS (1896–1936)

Mesquite, Texas, native Ewell "Turkey" Gross started his pro career playing infield for the Paris, Texas, club in 1915. He moved on to McAlister and Joplin in 1916 and 1917, before taking time off for service in World War I. He returned to the Lone Star State in 1919, to play with San Antonio and was with that club when his contract was sold to the New York Giants on September 12, 1920. There was quite a bit of talk about Gross's chances of making the Giant roster during spring training of 1921, but New York manager John McGraw decided to return him to San Antonio. He stayed there until December 3, 1924, when he was traded to the Boston Red Sox for Danny Clark.

Gross made his major league debut on April 14, 1925, against the Philadelphia A's. The starting shortstop that day, he saw his team blow a 6–0 lead and eventually lose the game in the tenth inning, 9–8. Although he played well in the field, Turkey's .094 batting average sealed his fate. He was released to the Minneapolis Millers of the American Association on April 30, with Minneapolis sending him to the Dallas Steers later in the season. He played with the Steers until 1927 (he was manager of the team in the latter half of the '27 season). He spent the final season of his pro career with the Paris, Texas, team in 1928. Gross then retired to become a highly successful pharmacist in his hometown of Mesquite.

In mid-December 1935, he started to experience bladder and kidney problems and was admitted to St. Paul Hospital in Dallas just before Christmas. He died there at 11:05 p.m. on January 11, 1936, from pyelonephritis (a kidney infection) and toxemia at the age of 39. Turkey Gross was laid to rest at Mesquite Cemetery on January 12th.

AL YEARGIN (1901–1937)

In 1922, 19-year-old South Carolina native James Almond "Al" Yeargin was pitching in his first year of professional ball for the Greenville Spinners of the South Atlantic League when his contract was purchased by the Boston Braves on July 24th. On the day of his call up to the parent club, September 1st, he won his farewell game for the Spinners, 10–3, over Spartanburg. Making his major league debut against the New York Giants on October 1st, Yeargin pitched well, giving up only five hits, one of them being a homer to Mahlon Higbee in a 3–0 loss. Sent back to Greenville for 1923, he was back with the Braves for 1924, pitching to a miserable 1–11 record in 32 games. Yeargin was sent to Seattle of the Pacific Coast League in 1925 and Greenville (again) in 1926, and he was sold to Atlanta in mid-1928. Near the end of the season, he was back with Greenville, staying there until 1930, when he was released. His last pro stop was with the Augusta Tourists, after which he retired.

After his baseball career ended, Yeargin became a successful farmer. Suffering from ulcers, he entered Greenville General Hospital in early May 1937. His stay there lasted just two days, as he died on May 6, 1937, as a result of general peritonitis due to a ruptured duodenal ulcer. Yeargin, who was 37, was buried at Cross Roads Baptist Cemetery in Greer, South Carolina.

JIM CURRY (1886–1938)

What James L. "Jim" Curry lacked in physical stature, he more than made up with his pugnacity, grit, and determination, and while he was typical of the many ballplayers whose names are listed in baseball encyclopedias and other baseball resources, his is a story that is, in many ways, atypical of the thousands of cup-of-coffee players who have graced major league fields since the inception of the professional game.

Curry learned his baseball acumen on the sandlots of his native Camden, New Jersey, and he was a career minor leaguer except for a brief ten-game, three-team stay in the majors. He never got the chance to make the type of name for himself that he felt he always deserved. A scout once wrote of Curry, "Could use a few extra pounds, a little too short, tough as nails, short fuse." Had he possessed those few extra pounds and inches, he surely would have been looked upon differently by major league executives and given a fair shot at sticking with a major league club.

Jim made his major league debut with the Philadelphia Athletics on October 2, 1909, in the first game of a doubleheader with the Washington Senators. Replacing Eddie Collins at second base in the top of the eighth inning in a 5–5 tie, it was in the bottom half of the stanza that he found himself facing the legendary Walter Johnson in his first major league at bat. Newspaper accounts of the day state that, "Curry was unafraid of Johnson's high, hard one" and "showed good form," as he smacked one of Johnson's curveballs for a two-base hit. He would later score the winning run in the A's 6–5 victory. It was a memorable debut for the plucky second baseman. Curry made his debut on the same date that Washington first baseman Jiggs Donahue made his final major league appearance. After the season, when asked what it was like to finally play in the big leagues, Jim told a local newspaper, "I only wish I could've gotten into the second game. That really would've been something."

With Collins firmly entrenched as the team's second baseman and the up-and-coming Stuffy McInnis waiting in the wings, there was little chance that Curry could stick with the Athletics the following season. Farmed out to Reading of the Tri-State League, he would make it back to the majors two years later, making a four-game appearance with the New York Highlanders. It was with the Highlanders that Curry solidified his reputation as a tempestuous player.

The story goes that one day after practice, Curry came into the clubhouse, only to find his street clothes tied in knots and soaked in water. Livid, he yelled out, "Who did that? Did you do it?" to Highlander pitcher Jack Warhop, who had been riding him hard since he first arrived. From that point onward, eyewitness accounts vary. According to Highlander manager Hal Chase, Warhop boldly stepped forward, admitted to the handiwork, and started hurling expletives Curry's way.

Shortstop John Knight recalled that Warhop "didn't have a chance to say much of anything." The "official story," as related by Curry to his hometown *Camden Courier Post*, went as follows: "After Jim made his accusations clear, Warhop boldly stepped forward and defiantly proclaimed, 'I did it and what are you going to do about it?' Before you could say Stanley Ketchel, our Jimmy threw a roundhouse right that landed square on Jack's chin for the one-punch knockout." The altercation convinced New York management that Curry's temper was too out of control for them to take a chance on him. Chase noted, "The kid is no swell head and has a lot of vinegar in him." Curry's nemesis, Warhop, who was known by the nickname "Crab" due to his grinding and surly disposition, would eventually gain unwanted fame when he gave up Babe Ruth's first career home run in 1915.

Sent back down to Reading, Jim would continue to play a fearless, belligerent style of baseball, never backing down and always willing to mix it up when called out. He managed to make it back to "The Show" one last time, appearing in five games with the 1918 Detroit Tigers. Curry batted .250, with 5 hits in 20 at bats, and was again sent back to the minors. Resigned to the fact that he would most likely never make it back to the majors, he continued to play minor league ball until 1928, after which he played local semipro ball for several years.

By the time he reached his mid-40s, he had come to the realization that his body could no longer stand the rigors of playing the game he loved, even at a semiprofessional level. In the spring of 1932, Curry joined the Haddonfield, New Jersey, police department. It was the type of job that Jim and his friends felt would be perfect for him. A man of temperate tastes and values who neither smoked nor drank, he felt that working as a police officer would keep his temper from getting the best of him. Lou Schaub, owner of the semipro Camden club that Curry had once played for, remarked, "Jimmy has gone from the crack of the bat to cracking heads with his nightstick."

Curry's career as a police officer would last but five years. A habitual chewer of tobacco, he was diagnosed with cerebral arteriosclerosis (hardening of the arteries in the brain) and forced into early retirement in May 1937. Showing a game face, he vowed to beat his affliction, telling friends and colleagues that, if given the chance, he would "look death straight in the eyes and spit in its face." It was a grand gesture indeed. Just fifteen months later, he was dead, stricken by a cerebral embolism at Camden County General Hospital. In the end, not even his moxie and fiery temper could save him. Curry, who was 52 (his death certificate lists his age as 45), left behind a wife and an 11-year-old daughter. He was laid to rest two days later at Lakeview Memorial Park in Cinnaminson, New Jersey, in Section 5A, Lot 82, Grave 2. His grave remains unmarked.

HACK SIMMONS (1885–1942)

A Brooklyn native, George Washington "Hack" Simmons was born on January 29, 1885. A versatile player who could play the outfield and all four infield positions, he broke into organized baseball with the Eastern League's Montreal Royals in 1906. In 1907, he jumped his contract to play with the Dayton Veterans of the Central League but was ordered back to Montreal by the National Commission. Before he could play another game for Montreal, he was sold to the New Haven Blues of the Connecticut State League. The New York Giants purchased his contract on August 14, 1908, for $1,500, but he never appeared in any games for them, as he was optioned to the Rochester Bronchos of the Eastern League instead. Simmons would finally get a shot at the majors when he was drafted by the Detroit Tigers in the September 1909 Rule 5 Draft. Pinch-hitting for Tiger pitcher Ed Willett, he made his major league debut the following April 15th in a 6–2, ten-inning loss to the Cleveland Naps. Detroit sent him back to Rochester again in the middle of the season, after he saw action in just 42 games.

With his purchase by the New York Highlanders in 1912, Hack joined one of the worst teams in that franchise's storied history. Led by manager Harry Wolverton, New York would go on to lose 102 games. Simmons wasn't much help to the Highlander cause, as he batted a meek .239 in 110 games, bad enough to have him sent back to Rochester at the end of the campaign. The 1913 season would be a memorable one for him, as he led the International League in batting, at .339, and fielded at a .932 clip at second base. In 1914, Simmons signed on with the Federal League's Baltimore Terrapins, batting .270, with 38 RBI in 114 games. After one more year in Baltimore, he returned to the minors for good, playing with Rochester in 1916. He finished up his career with a 15-game stint for the Kansas City Blues in 1917.

With baseball supposedly out of his blood, Simmons went to work for the Brooklyn-Manhattan Transit Authority Corporation as a general inspector, a job he would keep for the remainder of his life. In 1933, at age 48, he made a surprise, one-game appearance for the Jersey City Skeeters of the International League, although records fail to indicate what he did during the contest.

Simmons was living at 646 Argyle Road in Brooklyn, New York, at the time of his death, which occurred on April 26, 1942, while visiting his son's home on Long Island. He was involved in an automobile accident in early 1942, from which he never fully recovered. According to Johns Hopkins University's official records, Hack Simmons died as a result of arteriosclerotic heart disease and was buried at Evergreen Cemetery in Brooklyn, New York.

WALTER JOHNSON (1887–1946)

Walter Perry Johnson possessed a blinding fastball and wonderful curve, and pound for pound, he may have been the greatest pitcher of all time. But if you take a closer look at what made up certain aspects of this man—his heart and soul, his life in general—then, and only then, can you truly come to understand what Johnson was all about. Everyone knows about his records, his 417 wins and 110 shutouts while playing for the lowly Senators. During a time when Christy Mathewson was the "king of pitchers" and a national hero to millions, Johnson was toiling in Washington, DC, for a second division team. His blinding speed notwithstanding, people loved him for much more than his pitching ability. Unlike his friend Mathewson, who often shied away from the public, Walter was always courteous with fans and never tried to dodge them when asked for autographs. In an era in baseball when rowdy play and conduct was the standard, Johnson's character, attitude, and values shone brightly.

Born in Humboldt, Kansas, on November 6, 1887, his family later moved to California, where a young Walter discovered his fastball. In 1907, while playing with the semipro Weiser Kids of the Idaho State League, 19-year-old Johnson was discovered and signed by Washington Senator catcher Cliff Blankenship, who, at the time, was injured and on a western scouting trip for Senator manager Pongo Joe Cantillon. After seeing him pitch, Blankenship hurriedly wrote the following letter to Cantillon:

> You better come out here and get this pitcher. He throws a ball so fast nobody can see it, and he strikes out everybody. His control is so good that the catcher just holds up his glove and shuts his eyes, then picks the ball, which comes to him looking like a little white bullet, out of the pocket. He's a big, 19-year-old fellow like I told you before, and if you don't hurry up someone will sign him, and he will be the best pitcher that ever lived. He throws faster than Addie Joss or Amos Rusie ever did, and his control is better than Christy Mathewson's. He knows where he's throwing because if he didn't, there would be dead bodies strewn all over Idaho.

Detroit had actually been informed about Johnson first, but the tight-fisted Frank Navin decided against sending scouts to have a look at him.

Johnson never liked to pitch inside for fear that he might injure or even kill someone. He also rarely had problems with umpires. Tommy

Walter Johnson, Washington Senators. Courtesy of the Library of Congress.

Connelly called him the "easiest pitcher I ever had to call balls and strikes for. Just a wonderful man." He was nicknamed the "Big Train" because of the speed of his fastball, as well as "Barney," for Barney Oldfield, the legendary mile-a-minute auto racer that the famous Olds-mobile brand of cars would later be named after. Walter also acquired the nicknames "Sir Walter" and the "White Knight" because of his chivalric attitude.

Possessing a wholly admirable character, he might have had the nicest disposition of any pitcher in history. Like Mathewson, he never blamed teammates for their mistakes and was the "soul of virtue' in the eyes of many. Johnson had many friends both inside and outside of baseball. When Mathewson died from tuberculosis during the 1925 World Series, before Johnson was scheduled to pitch, Walter broke down and cried. It was said that he secretly dedicated the game to his old friend. In addition, Johnson was loved and revered by his buddy Ty Cobb, who would frequently visit the Johnson house. The two great friends would pal around whenever they got the chance. A man of conservative roots, thoughtful and modest, with a mild disposition, Johnson's values, which were once described as Lincolnesque, person-ified a generation of people throughout the United States.

After his playing career was over, Big Train tried his hand at manag-ing. He headed Newark for one season, followed by his old club, the Senators, from 1929 to 1932, before moving on to Cleveland from 1933 to 1935. Even though he had a respectable .551 winning percentage, he was considered too easygoing. Johnson went on to become a play-by-play broadcaster and was a natural with his laid-back style and friendly delivery. It should also be noted that with all of his fame and fortune, the vices of success never touched him. He was a devoted husband and family man. His wife Hazel died in 1930, leaving him with five chil-dren—three boys and two girls.

Johnson died from a brain tumor on Tuesday, December 10, 1946, at the young age of 59. Upon hearing the news of his old friend's passing, Ty Cobb cried. The Big Train was gone. He left behind a legacy of excellence and countless pitching records. More importantly, he left behind a legacy of virtue and goodness that will probably never be seen again in American sports. Walter Johnson was buried in Section M of Rockville Cemetery in Rockville, Maryland, next to his beloved wife Hazel.

VERN BICKFORD (1920–1960)

Quiet and gentlemanly off the mound, right-handed pitcher Vernon Edgell Bickford was an aggressive, hard-as-nails competitor when he stepped between the lines. He spent the majority of his major league career with the Boston Braves, joining them for their pennant-winning season of 1948, his rookie year. A three-sport prep star, he began his pro career in 1939. Bickford never pitched for a minor league team above Class A during the first six years of his career. After service in the U.S. Army in World War II, he pitched the 1946 season for the Class B Jackson club of the Southeastern League, where he went 10–13. Just before the 1947 season, he was placed on the roster of Indianapolis of the American Association, a minor league affiliate of the Boston Braves. When Indianapolis president Frank McKinney acquired a controlling interest in the Pittsburgh Pirates just prior to the '47 season, he allowed Brave owner Lou Perini to pick up the contract of several players as compensation. The first player Perini chose was Bickford.

Sent to the Milwaukee Brewers of the American Association, Vern churned out a 9–5 campaign. He made the Braves out of spring training in 1948, but was not expected to stick with the parent club. After several so-so outings out of the bull pen, Brave manager Billy Southworth started him in place of a sick Red Barrett against the Pirates on May 19th. Bickford did not disappoint, as he turned his season around with a five-hitter. He went 11–5, with a 3.27 ERA, helping the Braves to their first pennant since 1914. He also appeared in the World Series against Cleveland, starting Game 3 against Gene Bearden. Bickford was a hard-luck loser, giving up 4 hits and just 1 run, while walking 5 in 3.3 innings pitched. He was relieved by Billy Voiselle in the 4th. The Braves lost the game, 2–0, and eventually the World Series, 4–2.

Bickford became a mainstay of the Brave rotation during the next several seasons, culminating with a 19–14 season in 1950. It was on August 11th of that year that he pitched a 7–0 no-hitter against Carl Erskine and the Brooklyn Dodgers. Bickford had one more decent season, after which arm troubles began to plague him. On February 10, 1954, he was traded to the Baltimore Orioles for Charlie White and $10,000 cash. He was released on May 17th, after posting an 0–1 record. He retired from baseball soon thereafter due to a pinched nerve and bone chips in his elbow. Vern attempted a comeback with the

International League's Richmond Virginians in 1955, but the venture proved to be unsuccessful.

After his career, Bickford worked as a car salesman, carpenter, and traveling salesman. Diagnosed with stomach cancer in July 1959, he battled the disease gamely. In March 1960, he entered McGuire VA Hospital in Richmond, Virginia. By this time, the cancer had metastasized, and he began to lose weight rapidly. Bickford remained upbeat despite his condition and was making plans to reenter pro ball as a coach as late as the week before his death, telling United Press International, "The doctors tell me I'll walk again, and that's just what I intend to do. I believe that because of my experience I could get a coaching job. At least, I could teach my three boys something about pitching." Vern Bickford died on May 6, 1960, at the age of 39, leaving behind his wife Jean and their three sons, Michael, Kenny, and Vern Jr. He was buried at Mount Zion Baptist Church Cemetery in New Canton, Virginia.

DON SAVAGE (1919–1961)

Born in Bloomfield, New Jersey, Donald Anthony Savage was a third baseman for the New York Yankees in 1944 and 1945. The second of three sons of Vincent and Millie Savage, he was born on March 5, 1919. He attended Bloomfield High School, where he starred as a halfback on the Bengal football team and at shortstop for the baseball team. It was on the gridiron during his sophomore year that he experienced the first of several knee injuries that would hamper him during his baseball career. One of his closest friends and teammates in both school and on the baseball diamond was future Yankee pitcher Hank Borowy. The two remained good friends until the end of Savage's life. After graduation from high school, Savage attended Rutgers University but left after only a year, when New York Yankee super scout Paul Krichell offered him a contract.

Don's first pro assignment was with the Butler Yankees of the Pennsylvania State Association in 1938. He then made stops with Easton of the Class D Eastern Shore League, Akron of the Mid-Atlantic League, and Norfolk of the Piedmont League. While playing with Norfolk, Savage met the girl who would become the love of his life, Marie Vizzini.

The two were married on March 1, 1941. Their union would bring them two sons, Donald Jr. (born 1942, died 1969) and Michael (born 1947).

For someone so young, Savage was well-traveled, as he played for the Augusta Tigers of the competitive Sally League (South Atlantic League) in 1941, where he hit a solid .292. While with Augusta, he had the chance to play with future Yankees Bill Bevens, Joe Page, and Ralph Houk. Diagnosed with diabetes in the off-season, Don would be forced to give himself insulin injections every morning for the rest of his life. Following the advice of doctors, he took the 1942 season off to rest and recuperate, as he had been drastically weakened by the disease.

Classified 4-F, Savage continued with his baseball career in 1943, playing with the famous Yankee farm team the Newark Bears. The Bears' primary shortstop in 1943, he batted .258, with 16 homers and 74 RBI in 144 games. With World War II putting a strain on manpower, he made the Yankee roster in the spring of 1944. Even though Savage's primary position was shortstop, Yankee manager Joe McCarthy elected to go with a platoon of Mike Milosevich and the aging Frankie Crosetti instead. With Snuffy Stirnweiss already penciled in at second base, the only other choices McCarthy had were to play Savage in the outfield or at third base. Don's own preference was third base, since he knew his bad knee would most likely hamper him when it came to chasing fly balls, particularly in Yankee Stadium's cavernous "Death Valley." McCarthy finally decided to place Savage at the "hot corner," where he would replace Billy Johnson, who was serving in the army.

Savage made his major league debut on April 18, 1944, in a 3–0 win over the Red Sox at Fenway Park. Savage would go 0-for-3 and be one of two Yankees to ground into double plays, the other being his old friend Hank Borowy, who was also the winning pitcher that day, scattering just 5 hits in 9 innings of work. Despite experiencing several nagging injuries, including two to his already gimpy knee, Savage would continue as the starting Yankee third baseman until mid-season, when he was finally replaced by Oscar Grimes. Don appeared in 71 games, batting .264, with 4 home runs and 24 RBI. His role diminished in 1945, as he appeared in only 34 games, batting .224. With the war now over and most of the Yankee players returning home, he had little chance of making the team in 1946. With his major league career coming to an end, Savage's lifetime stats stood at .256, with 4 home runs and 27 RBI in 105 games. Sent back to Newark, knee problems again became a factor, and he was able to appear in just 66 games. Retiring after the season, he attempted a comeback in 1949, as player-manager of the St. Jean (Quebec) Braves of the independent Provincial League, and then retired for good. Savage would continue to live in Bloomfield after the closing of his baseball career, where he worked for the Boylis Company, as well as for the Otis Elevator Company of New York.

On Christmas night 1961, Don Savage passed away at Mountainside Hospital in Montclair, New Jersey, with his family by his side. The cause of death was diabetic nephropathy (diabetes-induced kidney disease), which he had been battling for more than a year. He was buried at Mount Olivet Cemetery in his hometown of Bloomfield, in the St. Joseph Section, Path 5, Half Part of 10, in Grave 3. His final resting place is a baseball throw away from where longtime friend Hank Borowy was laid to rest in 2004.

GIL HODGES (1924–1972)

Quiet, strong-willed, good-natured, and a man of his convictions, Gil Hodges was loved by his teammates and beloved by Brooklyn fans. The memory of this wonderful ballplayer and, most importantly, wonderful man still lingers in the borough of Brooklyn more than 40 years after his death. His story coincided with that of a group of people who lived near Ebbets Field.

Born April 4, 1924, in Princeton, Indiana, Hodges was only 19 when he came up for a one-game appearance at third base near the end of the '43 season. The unimpressive first game included two strikeouts and a walk. Gil then joined the U.S. Marines, serving in the Pacific. The Marines, no doubt, helped mold his already incredible resolve and will to succeed.

Returning in 1947 as a catcher, Hodges was stuck on the depth chart behind Bruce Edwards and future star Roy Campanella, necessitating a move to first base, a position Gil would make his home for the next 16 seasons. Manager Leo Durocher remembered, "With my catching set, I put a first baseman's glove on our other rookie catcher, Gil Hodges, and told him to have some fun. Three days later, I looked up and, wow, I was looking at the best first baseman I'd seen since Dolf Camilli."

Gil was a model of consistency, collecting 100 RBI or more in seven straight seasons. He was a dead-pull hitter, perfect for the band box known as Ebbets Field. He was so well-liked and respected that it was claimed he was the only Dodger to never have been booed at the Polo Grounds. When he went hitless during the World Series, priests said mass for him in hopes that it would break his slump.

Hodges reminded many people of the great Lou Gehrig, because he was quiet, big and strong, and a gentle person. His character and personality commanded respect. He was loved and respected by friend and foe alike; as a manager, his players would do just about anything for him.

Gil, who was referred to as "The Quiet Man" on occasion, was given the moniker "Miracle Worker" after he piloted the '69 Mets to the world championship. He managed them for two more seasons before dying from a heart attack on April 2, 1972, in West Palm Beach, Florida, after finishing a round of golf during spring training. The baseball world, and New York, in particular, mourned a beloved hero, a man from Indiana whom they had made their own.

The Mets retired Hodges's number 14, and, in 2002, fans voted him the Mets' all-time manager. Although he is still not a member of the National Baseball Hall of Fame, to the many who ate and slept Dodger

Grave of Gil Hodges. Courtesy of the author.

baseball, he remains one of the most beloved players Brooklyn has ever known. Gil Hodges was buried in Holy Cross Cemetery in Brooklyn in St. Cathrine Section, Range B, Plot 191/193.

CARL MORTON (1944–1983)

Born to Clyde and Merle Morton in Kansas City, Missouri, but raised in West Tulsa, Oklahoma, Carl Wendle Morton had many ups and downs during his brief baseball career. Originally signed by the Milwaukee Braves as an amateur free agent in 1964, the six-foot, 200-pound Morton began his career as an outfielder, but it was not until the Brave organization converted him to the mound that he found success on the diamond. Drafted by the expansion Montreal Expos on October 14, 1968, as the 45th pick in the expansion draft, he made his major league debut on April 11, 1969. In eight games, Morton went 0–3, with a 4.60 ERA. His breakout year and best season came in 1970, as he compiled an 18–11 record, with a 3.60 ERA, good enough to garner National League Rookie of the Year honors.

After two subpar seasons, in which he went a combined 17–31, Morton was traded back to the Braves in a deal for pitcher Pat Jarvis. He rebounded nicely in Atlanta, stringing together three winning seasons for extremely mediocre Brave teams. After winning only four games in 1976, he was traded to the Texas Rangers as part of a five-player swap for Jeff Burroughs that also saw the Rangers receive $250,000 cash. Carl would never play a game for Texas, as he was given his pink slip the following April. He finished the season playing for the Phillies' minor league affiliate in the American Association. He attended spring training with the Pirates in 1978, but retired when he was not offered a contract.

On April 12, 1983, Morton collapsed in the driveway of his parents' home in Tulsa from a massive heart attack just moments after he and his son had finished jogging. Rushed to a local hospital, he passed away an hour later. With his untimely death at the age of 39, he became the first former member of the Expos to pass away. Carl Morton was buried in Memorial Park Cemetery in Tulsa, Oklahoma, in Section 14, Lot 942, Space 4. He was survived by his parents, wife Karen, son Brent, and stepdaughter Lori.

CRAIG KUSICK (1948–2006)

A native of Milwaukee, Craig Kusick was signed by the Minnesota Twins as an amateur free agent out of the University of Wisconsin, La Crosse, in June 1970. A first baseman by trade who could also play the outfield, he was considered to be slow of foot due to his six-foot, three-inch, 225-pound frame, although he could occasionally hit for power.

Spending the majority of his career with the Twins, Kusick's best season came in 1977, when he batted .254, with 12 homers and 45 RBI in just 268 at bats. On August 27, 1975, in a game against the Milwaukee Brewers, he tied a major league record when he was hit by a pitch three times. The game was eventually won by Minnesota, 1–0, in 11 innings. On July 25, 1979, Craig was sold to the Toronto Blue Jays, appearing in 48 games for them. Released by Toronto after the season, he signed with the San Diego Padres but never appeared in a game in a Padre uniform, instead playing for their minor league affiliate, the Hawaii Islanders of the Pacific Coast League, in 1980 and 1981. Kusick also spent time with the Evansville Triplets of the American Association before retiring for good. During the course of his seven-year major league career, he maintained a .235 average, with 46 homers and 171 RBI in 497 games.

Kusick turned to coaching after his baseball career ended, eventually taking a job as a physical education teacher and baseball coach at Rosemount High School in Rosemount, Minnesota, a suburb of Minneapolis. A highly respected and well-liked in his 13 years there, he coached Fighting Irish teams to the state tournament seven times. Craig left Rosemount High in 2004, to take care of his wife Sara Beth, who was battling ovarian cancer. In December, he was diagnosed with myelodysplastic syndrome (MDS), a condition that can eventually lead to leukemia. Kusick didn't let this double whammy affect him, as he continued to take care of his Sara Beth until her death the following December.

Deciding on a new course of action to fight his disease, he began taking an experimental drug for MDS. Unfortunately, complications set in. On Sunday, September 24, 2006, Kusick was hospitalized with a high fever. By this time he was battling leukemia as well. The former major leaguer hung on for four days, passing away on Thursday, the 26th, just three days shy of his 58th birthday. Kusick was remembered fondly by former teammates, and especially the students and players he taught, as more than just a terrific coach and teacher, but as a person who generally cared about the welfare of others. He was buried next to his wife in Saint Germain Cemetery in Saint Germain, Wisconsin.

JOE KENNEDY (1979–2007)

Nicknamed "The Patriarch" by baseball writers and announcers in reference to Joseph P. Kennedy, head of the famous Kennedy political family, Joseph Darley Kennedy was a six-foot, four-inch, 237-pound left-handed pitcher who played for five teams during his seven-year big-league career. An eighth-round selection by the Tampa Bay Devil Rays in the 1998 amateur draft out of Grossmont College, Kennedy's pitching arsenal included a two-seam and four-seam fastball, slider, slow curve, and changeup, all thrown from a three-quarter sidearm slot.

Called up to join the Ray rotation in early June 2001, Joe made his major league debut on June 6th in a 6–2 win over the Toronto Blue Jays at the SkyDome. He went five innings, allowing five hits and two earned runs, walking four, and striking out five to earn the win. Kennedy would log a 7–8 record, with a 4.44 ERA in 20 starts, during his rookie season—not all that bad considering that the D-Rays finished the year with a horrendous 62–100 record, a mark that tied the Pirates for the worst in Major League Baseball. Cocky and self-assured, he thrived on competition, never backing down from a challenge. Described as an awesome teammate with a great sense of humor, Kennedy was funny, outgoing, and popular amongst his peers. The next year, the hurler went 8–11, with a 4.53 ERA in 30 appearances, all of which were starts. The 2003 campaign saw him take a step back, with a 3–12 record and 6.13 ERA, as well as a demotion to the bull pen.

That December, Kennedy was sent to the Rockies as part of a three-team trade with the Blue Jays that saw Tampa Bay receive pitcher Mark Hendrickson. On January 31, 2004, Joe married the love of his life, a vivacious, dimpled blonde named Jami Dawn. The two first started dating in early 2003, while she was attending the University of South Florida.

In his season and a half with the "Rox," Kennedy went a combined 13–15, with a 4.64 ERA in 43 games and 254.1 innings of work. On the personal side, he and Jami absolutely loved the area, eventually making it their permanent home. On July 13, 2005, Kennedy was traded again, this time to the Oakland Athletics, along with Jay Witasick, for Eric Byrnes and Omar Quintanilla. Used as both a starter and reliever by A's manager Ken Macha, Joe went 4–5, with a 4.45 ERA in 19 games. The 2006 season saw him finally find his comfort level, as he pitched entirely out of the bull pen, going 4–1, with a tidy 2.31 ERA in 39 games, despite the fact that he missed half the season with shoulder problems. In the American League Championship Series against the Tigers, he threw 3.2 scoreless innings of relief, striking out 2, walking 2, and allowing just 2 hits while facing 16 Bengal batters. In the off-season, Joe and Jami celebrated the birth of their first child, a son named Kaige, born on November 17th.

In spring training of 2007, Joe earned a spot as Oakland's fifth starter but was sent back to the bull pen in July after accruing a 2–7 record. Falling out of favor with management, he was eventually placed on waivers and picked up by the Diamondbacks on August 4th. Given his unconditional release 18 days later, after making just three relief appearances, he eventually signed with the Toronto Blue Jays, with whom he would play for the remainder of the season and, as it turned out, the rest of his career. On September 29th, Kennedy would ironically make his last major league appearance against the team he started out with, the Devil Rays.

A free agent after the season, Toronto management made it known that they were extremely interested in having him back. Whether he would have accepted an offer from the Blue Jays or tested the free agent market remains a matter of conjecture. What is known is that he was looking forward to both his professional career and his life as a husband and father. Indeed, he had much to be thankful for, especially since Jami was expecting their second child the following summer.

In November, the Kennedys traveled to Florida to spend Thanksgiving with Jami's family and also so that Joe could be best man in the wedding of Derek Anderson, one of his former minor league teammates in the Ray organization. They would be staying at Jami's parents' home, located in Brandon, a suburb east of Tampa. In the early morning hours of Friday, November 23rd, at approximately 1:15 a.m., Joe woke up not feeling well. As he headed to the bathroom, he suddenly collapsed and fell backward. Taken to Brandon Hospital by Hillsborough County Fire Rescue, he was pronounced dead on arrival. While

Kennedy's family had a history of heart disease, it was almost unfathomable that someone as young as Joe could succumb to such a malady. The news of his sudden passing shocked the baseball community, since he was more than just a journeyman pitcher, as some stories in the press portrayed him, for if you knew him as a person, you quickly came to realize he was much more than your "average Joe."

Private services for Kennedy were held at Rockland Community Church in Golden, Colorado, where he was fondly remembered by family, friends, and teammates as a great husband, father, teammate, and friend. In January 2008, the Hillsborough County medical examiner's office released their findings, stating that his death was attributed to hypertensive cardiovascular disease and myxoid valvular disease, with degeneration of the mitral valve.

That June, Jami gave birth to a beautiful baby girl she named Joie, as a namesake for Joe. With the help of friends and family, she picked up the pieces as best she could and continued to raise her children, unsure of what the future would bring. While she never expected to find happiness so soon, she began dating the best man from her and Joe's wedding, former major league pitcher Nick Bierbrodt.

Bierbrodt, who was also one of the pallbearers at Joe's funeral, eventually proposed to Jami. The two were married in a wonderful ceremony at the Westin Riverfront Resort and Spa, located on Beaver Creek Mountain in Colorado, on November 12, 2011. Before the ceremony, Bierbrodt and his dad shared a toast to Joe, using a flask that Kennedy gave him for being his best man. One would have to think that at that moment, Joe Kennedy was looking down, smiling, and nodding with approval.

DAVE SMITH (1955–2008)

David Stanley Smith might have been the quintessential Southern California "surfer dude." Born January 21, 1955, in Richmond, California, he attended Poway High School, where he played on the baseball team. In high school, his priorities were surfing, girls, and baseball, usually in that order. Known for being a wild child as a teenager, he wore his hair long, drove a beat-up blue van, guzzled beer with his buddies, and, of course, hit the beach as much as possible. Recruited by San Diego State baseball coach Jim Dietz during his senior year at Poway, Smith would continue to walk to the beat of his own drum when he got to college, often putting him at odds with Dietz, who was a straight-laced, follow the rules type of guy.

Things changed dramatically for Smitty after his sophomore year, when he met the girl who would eventually become his wife, a brown-haired beauty named Mia Boardman. The two met at a San Diego State frat party and hit it off immediately. They dated for six years before finally tying the knot. Almost from the start, Mia's influence on Dave was noticeable, as he calmed down and started to take life a little more seriously. The one thing Mia couldn't do, however, was change his quirky way of looking at life. Before their first child, Kellen, was born, Dave and Mia were supposed to take Lamaze classes. The problem was that Smitty missed all of them. To make up for it, he took a crash course from one of the nurses on how to help with the delivery. When they were through, the nurse asked him if he had any questions. He replied, "Yeah, when I bring her to the emergency room, will there be valet parking there?"

The other voice of reason in Smitty's life turned out to be Coach Dietz, who had battled with him since he first set foot on San Diego State's baseball field. "Yeah, I think he finally got through to me," Smith told the *Los Angeles Times*. "And the fact that I could make a living throwing a baseball. I'd never thought of that real seriously before." On the suggestion of Dietz, Smith also played two summers in an Alaskan All-Star league, where he raised his level of play, throwing against the likes of future major league pitchers Floyd Bannister and Scott Sanderson. Knowing that he could compete at a higher level gave him even more confidence.

Smitty played for Coach Dietz and the Aztecs from 1974 to 1976. After Astro scout Bob Cluck expressed interest in him, he was chosen in the eighth round of the June 1976 amateur draft. Signed to a contract by Cluck, Smith was immediately assigned to the Covington Astros, Houston's Rookie League team located in Covington, Virginia. Years later, Dave would remember how he had bragged to Mia about going straight to the majors when he signed his first pro contract. As it turned out, Covington was a long way from the majors, let alone the beach where he grew up.

After four seasons in the minors, Smitty made his major league debut on April 11, 1980, in a 10–6 win over the Los Angeles Dodgers at the Astrodome. Coming into the game in the eighth inning, his team down, 6–5, he struck out catcher Steve Yeager. After loading the bases on a single and two walks, he ended the inning by inducing a Reggie Smith foul out pop-up, followed by a Steve Garvey ground out. The "Stros" rallied for five runs in the bottom of the stanza, as they won going away. Frankie LaCorte came in to earn the save, while Smitty earned the win.

Smitty would go on to become an integral part of a veteran Houston bull pen that included the aforementioned LaCorte, closer Joe Sambito, Joaquin Andujar, and Randy Niemann. He had a good rookie campaign, logging a 7–5 record in 57 games, with a stingy 1.92 ERA and 10 saves in 102.2 innings of work. He also made three appearances in the National League Championship Series (NLCS) against the Phillies, getting the win in the third game.

While Smitty got along great with his teammates, he was especially close with his fellow relievers. In a September 20, 1986, interview in the *Los Angeles Times*, he told reporter Tom Friend, "My locker was between Joaquin Andujar and Frank LaCorte, a couple characters. Andujar? He was like he is now. Nuts. He's a good man. He's just completely off the wall. LaCorte? One time he burned his uniform. He got hit pretty good, came inside, and set his uniform on fire."

Smith's pitching repertoire included a fastball, curveball, forkball, and his bread-and-butter pitch, the changeup. His changeup became so effective that opposing batters couldn't hit it even if they knew it was coming. Known for being a wonderful and giving teammate, he treated both rookies and veterans with respect and, unlike many pro athletes, never acted like he was better than the average fan. During his time in the majors, he was known for being one of the biggest tippers, and as his tenure with the Astros lengthened, he took his role as a club leader more and more seriously.

One of his closest friends in baseball was Padre infielder and fellow surfing enthusiast Tim Flannery. "I saw him a couple of times [during the 1981 strike] when I was surfing," Smith remembered in a 1989 interview. "It was weird. We didn't go out together. We just ran into each other in the ocean. Not literally though. He's goofy-footed, so he likes to take off to the left. I keep my left foot forward, so I like to go right." Former Astro pitcher and Smith protégé Charlie Kerfeld told the *Houston Chronicle* how Smith mentored him on how to treat people: "He said treat everybody right because the same people you see on the way up are going to be the same people that you'll see on the way down."

Smitty became one of the National League's better relievers during the 1980s, achieving six straight seasons of at least 23 saves between 1985 and 1990, with a career high of 33 in 1986, the year the Astros won their second National League Western Division title. In the subsequent NLCS against the Eastern Division champion New York Mets, Smith gave up a game-winning home run to Lenny Dykstra in game three. Even in defeat, he showed true professionalism and class, answering questions from the press and taking full responsibility for the loss. Some Astro fans blamed Smith for the series loss, but truth be told, the team never would have gotten to the playoffs without his great regular season, as he led the club in saves, with 33.

A member of three Astro playoff teams, in 1980, 1981, and 1986, Dave would pitch for Houston until 1990, after which he became a free agent. The Chicago Cubs, in need of a reliable closer to solidify their bull pen, signed him to a two-year deal that included a $1 million signing bonus and a club option for a third year. The move to the "friendly confines" of Wrigley Field didn't work out for either Smitty or the Cubbies, as numerous injuries hindered his performance, including one to his right knee that required arthroscopic surgery in July. There were also whispers that his late-night lifestyle had finally caught up with him. After two underachieving seasons on the North Side, the Cubs finally decided to part ways with him. Smith signed a minor league contract with them the following January but never played in the majors again.

After his playing career ended, Smitty went to work for the Padres as a minor league instructor and coach, and spent two and a half seasons as the Friars' pitching coach, a position he held from 1999 until midway through the 2001 season. He missed the first month of the 2001 season while seeking treatment for alcoholism and then left the coaching staff for good in June to spend more time with his family. He was also one of the directors at the San Diego School of Baseball, a position he held for nearly 30 years.

During his 13-year career, Smith accrued a 53–53 record and 2.67 ERA, with 216 saves in 609 major league games. He was named to the National League All-Star team in 1986 and 1990, and holds the Astro team record for games pitched, with 586. In addition, he is second in career saves behind Billy Wagner, with 199.

On December 17, 2008, Smith died from a heart attack at his Carmel Valley, California, home at the age of 53. He was survived by his second wife, Alix, and three children, Kellen (26) and Cameron (21) from his marriage to Mia, and Dakota Maggie (1). With his passing, Smitty became the third member of the 1980 Astro team to pass away, joining Joe Niekro, who died from a brain aneurysm in 2006, and Vern Ruhle, who died of cancer in 2007. His remains were cremated and scattered into the Pacific Ocean during a paddle-out ceremony held by his good buddy Flannery and a few of his other surfing comrades. As Tim told the Associated Press, "That was what he asked for. That is what surfers do."

CHARLIE LEA (1956–2011)

Born in Orleans, France, and raised in Memphis, Tennessee, Charles William Lea was a pitcher for seven seasons, primarily with the Montreal Expos. A ninth-round pick by Montreal in the 1978 amateur draft out of the University of Memphis, he made his major league debut on June 12, 1980, as the starting and winning pitcher in a 9–1 win over the San Diego Padres. The six-foot, four-inch right-hander would go on to start 19 games that season, finishing with a 7–5 record and 3.72 ERA. Lea would make baseball history the following season, when, on May 10, 1981, he threw a 4–0 no-hitter against the San Francisco Giants in the second game of a doubleheader at Olympic Stadium in Montreal. In so doing, he became the first French-born player to throw a no-no. Becoming a member of the Montreal rotation the following year, his best seasons were 1983, when he accrued a 16–12 record and 3.12 ERA, and 1984, when he went 15–10, with a 2.89 ERA.

Injuries slowly began taking their toll on Lea, as he missed both the 1985 and 1986 campaigns due to injuries to his pitching shoulder. After appearing in just one game in 1987, he signed a free agent contract with the Minnesota Twins on February 4, 1988. The 1988 season would prove to be his final one in the majors, as he pitched to a 7–7 record, with a 4.85 ERA in 23 games. Granted free agency at season's end, he retired from baseball, eventually becoming a radio analyst with the minor league Memphis Redbirds.

During his career, Charlie Lea accrued a 62–48 record, with a 3.54 ERA in 152 games. On November 11, 2011, he was found dead in his home in Collierville, Tennessee, from a heart attack. He was laid to rest at Memorial Park Cemetery in Memphis, Tennessee.

CONCLUSION

The players included in this book are a diversified group whose careers spanned from the beginnings of professional baseball to today's modern game. Baseball, in my opinion, embodies a never-ending tradition that will continue as long as the game is played. For each player who leaves the game, there are new, fresh, and exciting personalities ready to replace him.

For a baseball writer/historian/necrologist such as myself, this is a wonderful time. The growth of the Internet, "new media," and advanced metrics throughout the past decade has brought about new and exciting ways for the average fan to research their favorite player or delve into the past to explore the life of some forgotten hero who played his last inning decades ago. As for yours truly, I will continue on with my baseball research and, hopefully, continue to write and put forth more interesting work for the public to enjoy.

As I once told a good friend of mine, retired baseball scout Robin Gunn, the game of baseball and baseball research go hand in hand. Baseball has always been a significant part of my life, and researching and writing about it is what I will continue to do.

BIBLIOGRAPHY

In addition to the sources cited in the text, I used death certificates, obituaries, and articles from player files located at the National Baseball Hall of Fame's A. Bartlett Giamatti Research Center, in Cooperstown, New York, as well as an interview with Wesley Fricks, national Ty Cobb historian.

ONLINE SOURCES

Ancestry.com:http://www.ancestry.com
The Baseball Necrology—Live:http://www.thebbnlive.com
Baseball-Reference.com:http://www.baseball-reference.com
Brooklyn Daily Eagle:http://eagle.brooklynpubliclibrary.org
California Digital Newspaper Collection: http://cdnc.ucr.edu/cgi-bin/cdnc
TheDeadballEra.com: Where Every Player Is Safe At Home:http://www.thedeadballera.com
FamilySearch.org:https://familysearch.org/
Library of Congress:http://www.loc.gov/library/libarch-digital.html
New York City Department of Health and Mental Hygiene:http://www.nyc.gov/html/doh/html/home/home.shtml
New York State Historical Newspaper Pages:http://www.fultonhistory.com/Fulton.html
Retrosheet.org:http://www.retrosheet.org
Society for American Baseball Research:http://sabr.org
Sporting Life:http://library.la84.org/SportsLibrary/SportingLife
Sporting News Archives:http://www.sportingnews.com/

BOOKS

Appel, Marty. *Munson: The Life and Death of a Yankee Captain*. New York: Doubleday, 2009.

Appel, Marty. *Thurman Munson: An Autobiography with Marty Appel, Memorial Edition*. New York: Coward, McCann & Geoghegan, 1979.

Bak, Richard. *Ty Cobb: His Tumultuous Life and Times*. Dallas, TX: Taylor Publishing Company, 1994.

Bjarkman, Peter C. *Encyclopedia of Major League Baseball: American League/Team Histories*, 9th ed. New York: Carroll & Graf Publishers, 1992.

Charlton, James. *The Baseball Chronology: The Complete History of the Most Important Events in the Game of Baseball*. New York: Macmillan, 1991.

Gutman, Dan. *Baseball Babylon: From the Black Sox to Pete Rose, the Real Stories Behind the Scandals That Rocked the Game*. New York: Penguin, 1992.

Hageman, William, and Warren Wilbert. *New York Yankees: Seasons of Glory, with a Salute to the 1998 New York Yankees*. New York: Jonathan David Publishers, 1999.

Hickok, John. *A Who's Who of Sports Champions, Their Stories and Records: The 2,200 Most Important Figures in North American Sports*. New York: Houghton Mifflin, 1995.

Honig, Donald. *The New York Yankees: An Illustrated History*, rev. ed. New York: Crown, 1987.

Johnson, Lloyd, and Brenda Ward. *Who's Who in Baseball History*. New York: Barnes and Noble, 1994.

Lee, Bill. *The Baseball Necrology: The Post-Baseball Lives and Deaths of Over 7,600 Major League Players and Others*. Jefferson, NC: McFarland, 2003.

Lowery, Phillip J. *Green Cathedrals: The Ultimate Celebration of All 273 Major League and Negro League Ballparks Past and Present*. Boston: Addison-Wesley, 1992.

Reidenbaugh, Joe, and Joe Hoppel. *Baseball's Hall of Fame: Cooperstown—Where the Legends Live Forever*. New York: Crescent Books, 1997.

Ritter, Lawrence S. *The Glory of Their Times: The Story of the Early Days of Baseball Told by the Men Who Played It*. New York: Macmillan, 1966.

Ritter, Lawrence S. *The Story of Baseball*, 3rd ed. New York: William Morrow and Company, 1999.

Robinson, Ray. *Iron Horse: Lou Gehrig in His Time*. New York: Harper Perennial, 1991.

Russo, Frank, and Gene Racz. *Bury My Heart at Cooperstown: Salacious, Sad, and Surreal Deaths in the History of Baseball*. Chicago: Triumph, 2006.

Skipper, James. *Baseball Nicknames: A Dictionary of Origins and Meanings*. Jefferson, NC: McFarland, 2012.

Sullivan, George, and John Powers. *The Yankees: An Illustrated History*. Philadelphia, PA: Temple University Press, 1997.

Thorn, John. *The Armchair Book of Baseball*. New York: Collier, 1985.

Thorn, John, Peter Palmer, Michael Gershman, David Pietrusza, Matthew Silverman, and Sean Lahman. *The Official Encyclopedia of Major League Baseball: Total Baseball*, 6th ed. New York: Total Sports, 1999.

Tullius, John. *I'd Rather Be a Yankee: For the First Time, the Men Behind the Legend Tell the Complete Story of Baseball's Greatest Team in Their Own Words*. New York: Jove Books, 1986.

Various. *The Baseball Encyclopedia: The Complete and Definitive Record of Major League Baseball*, 10th ed. New York: Simon and Schuster, 1996.

INDEX

ABOUT THE AUTHOR

A resident of East Brunswick, New Jersey, Frank Russo is a nationally known baseball researcher and baseball necrologist who has been researching deceased major leaguers for more than 45 years. He is owner/webmaster of thedeadballera.com, the first website dedicated to deceased major league players and personalities. A rabid New York Yankees fan, he is also a fan of the New York Giants and the New York Islanders, although he hopes you won't hold that against him. A member of the Society for American Baseball Research (SABR), he is also a former radio announcer and blogger for Mike Silva's nybaseballdigest.com, where he covered the Yankees. Russo's friends in the media include Mike Vaccaro and Kevin Kernan of the *New York Post*, Bill Madden of the *Daily News*, and Kevin Burkhardt of Fox Sports.